Public Procurement Dictionary of Terms

The Comprehensive Reference for Public Purchasing Terms and Concepts

Andrea Black

REVISED APRIL 2012

NIGP: The Institute for Public Procurement
151 Spring Street, Herndon, VA 20170
800.367.6447 • Fax: 703.736.9639 • nigp.org

Public Procurement **Dictionary** of **Terms**

Information in this book is accurate as of the time of publication and consistent with generally accepted public purchasing principles. However, as research and practice advance, standards may change. For this reason, it is recommended that readers evaluate the applicability of any recommendation in light of particular situations and changing standards.

National Institute of Governmental Purchasing, Inc. (NIGP)
151 Spring Street, Herndon, VA 20170
703-736-8900 • 800-367-6447 • 703-736-9639
education@nigp.org

This book is available at a special discount when ordered in bulk quantities. For information, contact NIGP at 800-367-6447. A complete catalog of titles is available on the NIGP website at www.nigp.org.

ISBN number 1-932315-13-6
ISBN number 978-1-932315-13-4

This book set in Berkeley Oldstyle

Design & production by Vizual, Inc. – www.vizual.com.

Printed & bound by HBP.

Preface

As the procurement profession continues to evolve as a critical component of the work of government, the need for a clear, concise and comprehensive reference for public purchasing terms and concepts becomes more essential. To this end, the National Institute of Governmental Purchasing (NIGP) offers this edition of one of its most popular publications, Public Procurement Dictionary of Terms. Although intended for use by the practitioner, the Dictionary is an easy reference for clarity of terms and a lexicon for all stakeholders invested in the work of government; be they in related fields or ancillary services.

Containing more than 2300 entries, this compilation of terms, acronyms and definitions articulates terms that have unique meanings relevant to purchasing activities. These definitions are intended to be informational only and should not be construed as legal.

With a commitment to excellence and a desire to develop, support and promote the public procurement profession, this dictionary offers a reliable source of information. May it serve you well.

Rick Grimm, CPPO, CPPB
NIGP Chief Executive Officer

Acknowledgments

This publication represents the culmination of countless volunteer hours. This volunteered generosity of time and effort has resulted in this living document designed as an effective resource for all procurement professionals. The National Institute of Governmental Purchasing (NIGP) is extremely appreciative of its members and the profession they serve. As the profession continues to change, new terms and definitions will need to be added to ensure its completeness.

The National Institute of Governmental Purchasing accepts full responsibility for the selection of terms for inclusion, as well as for the even more difficult task of rejection. The definitions themselves were, whenever possible, drawn from the most authoritative sources available (as indicated by the information in parentheses at the end of a definition) and supplemented by the experience of the editorial committee. The list of references and sources cited represent a relatively small segment of the available body of literature in the field of procurement.

If a word has not been included, or a more concise and relevant definition may apply, please submit these suggestions to the Editorial Board via dictionary@nigp.org. The Dictionary Task Force will review submissions on a semi-annual basis. In this manner, the dictionary will truly reflect the language of the profession while documenting relevant terms and phrases.

A

AAA: *See American Arbitration Association.*

A+B Bidding: A cost-plus-time bidding procedure that selects the low bidder based on a monetary combination of the contract bid items (A) and the time (B) needed to complete the project or a critical portion of the project. It is used to motivate the contractor to minimize the overall time on high priority and high usage projects. This encourages contractors to finish early by (1) offering bonuses for early completion and (2) assessing fines for late completion. *(www.ic.usu.edu/ic_over/a+b/a+b.php?heading=1)*

A & E: *See Architectural and Engineering.*

A/E (Architect or Engineer) Professional Services: Services that require performance by a registered architect or engineer. Professional services of an architectural or engineering nature that are associated with research, planning, development, design construction, alteration or repair of real property.

ABA: *See American Bar Association.*

ABA Model Procurement Code for State and Local Government (U.S. Law): Developed by the American Bar Association (ABA) and adopted in 1979, it is a collection of statutory principles and policies that provides guidance to public policy managers who wish to responsibly manage public procurement. State and larger local governments have individually codified it into procurement law and policy to effectively guide their procurement organizations. The code was updated in 2000 and contained enhancements in the following areas: Electronic Commerce, Cooperative Purchasing, Flexibility in Purchasing Methods and Processes for Delivery of Infrastructure Facilities and Services. *Also called Model Procurement Code.*

ABA Model Procurement Ordinance for Local Governments (U.S. Law): A code similar to the ABA Model Procurement Code, but intended for use by small local jurisdictions.

ABC: CANADIAN Aboriginal Businesses Canada, a division of Industry Canada. *(Summit Magazine on-line)*

ABC Inventory Classification: A means in which to categorize inventory that is applicable to any size business, regardless of industry. (e.g. government, manufacturing, services etc.) ABC classification allows for a review of the inventory based on the business' approach to the management or review of its inventory. For some agencies, the ABC of categories is based on the dollar value of the items. "A" in this application would be the top 10% of the inventory items and would account for approximately 70% of the annual inventory dollar volume. "B" would be the next 20% and would account for approximately 20% of the annual dollars in the inventory and "C" the remaining 70% of the annual inventory items with 10% of the overal monetary value of the annual inventory. The use of the terms "A", "B", and "C" may also be used to classify the need for accurate inventory records (tolerance) for various items, (very accurate, moderate accuracy), how often cycle counts are needed (weekly, monthly, or quarterly), or even to note who may be responsible for the inventory itself (i.e.: "A" is controlled by fleet, "B" is by purchasing and "C" by parks and recreation). Further, "A" may denote the items in the inventory that have the longest lead times (i.e.: JIT extended lead times), how the items are purchased (term contract, spot buy) or levels of safety stock required (highest turn-over, slow movers). Location of specific items in the inventory may also be denoted by the ABC Classification system. *(Janson, 1987)*

ABL (Approved Brands List): *See Approved Products List (APL); Qualified Products List (QPL); Acceptable Products List (APL).*

Absolute Advantage: The ability of a country to produce a specific good with fewer resources per unit of output than other countries. The ability to produce something with fewer resources than other producers would use to produce the same thing. A monopoly that exists when a country is the only source of an item, the only producer of an item, or the most efficient producer of an item. *Also see Comparative Advantage.* *(Schiller, 2000)*

ACAN: CANADIAN *See Advanced Contract Award Notice.*

Accelerator: The ratio between investment expenditures and the change in gross domestic product. This is based on the notion that business investment depends on the rate of growth of aggregate output. If the economy is expanding, then the business sector invests in more capital goods to produce the extra output needed. (www.amosweb.com)

Accept:
1. To receive as approved, adequate, or satisfactory.
2. To receive willingly with the intent of retaining.

Accept with Consideration of Non-conforming Goods: Terminology that describes the process that occurs after non-conforming goods have been rejected by the buyer. The vendor offers a discount or other incentive to encourage the buyer to accept the non-conforming goods and when the buyer then accepts them, it is done with consideration of non-conforming goods. Example: Buyer contracts for black color garbage bags and the vendor ships clear garbage bags in error. Buyer notifies vendor of the nonconforming goods and the vendor offers to reduce the price of this shipment in order to entice the buyer to keep and use the non-conforming goods.

Accept without Consideration of Non-conforming Goods: Terminology used to describe the process that occurs when a supplier ships non-conforming goods and the buyer accepts them knowingly or unknowingly. Example: Buyer contracts for 3 mil plastic garbage bags but the supplier mistakenly ships 2 mil gauge thickness bags instead. When the buyer accepts, knowingly or unknowingly, the non-conforming goods and uses them, it is done without any further consideration from the supplier to offset the lower quality of the plastic garbage bags that was sent to the buyer.

Acceptable Products List (APL): A pre-approved list of commodities/products, usually grouped by manufacturer, which have proven to be in conformance with developed specifications and standards. The list may result from performance testing of the product or as a result of field testing or laboratory analysis. *Also see Qualified Products List (QPL) and Approved Brands List (ABL).*

Acceptable Quality Level (AQL): The specified minimum performance that must be achieved by a product or service to assure the buyer that the goods or services will perform as per the specifications or stipulations contained within the statement of work. The maximum allowable number of defects or defective units. A predetermined quality level which has been deemed as being acceptable; generally used in the manufacturing of material items. Example: AQL of 1% defective rate is acceptable for this item. *Also see Acceptance Sampling.*

Acceptance:
1. Indication that an offeree is bound by the terms of the offer.
2. An indication by one party of a willingness to act in accordance with the contract or offer.
3. The assumption of a legal obligation by a party to a contract to the terms and conditions of that contract.
4. The act of receiving by an authorized representative with the intention of retaining.

Acceptance of Offer: The agreement of the vendor to deliver the goods ordered for the price offered.

Acceptance of Order: The agreement of the purchaser to an offer submitted by a vendor.

Acceptance Sampling (Acceptance Testing): A quality control technique used to evaluate the overall condition of a given lot by physically inspecting only a portion or sample of the lot. *Also see Acceptable Quality Level (AQL).*

Access to Information Office: CANADIAN A facility within Canadian governments for information regarding contract awards.

Access to Information Program (ATIP): CANADIAN Mandated by the Access to Information Act and the Privacy Act, this program gives any person in Canada the right to access information held in government records, subject to certain exceptions and limitations. (www.summitconnects.com/Tool_Kit/glossary)

Accessorial Transportation Charges: The costs that a carrier may charge in addition to the actual freight transportation charge such as: Inside delivery, interim storage, and redelivery charges. (ISM, 2000)

Account: A list or enumeration of monetary transactions between parties to a contract showing purchases, payments, and credits for goods or services.

Accountable: The concept that a person is obliged to give a reckoning or explanation for one's actions; responsible. *Also see Accountability.*

Accountability: The principle that employees who accept an assignment and the authority to carry it out are answerable to a superior or a higher authority for the outcome. *(Business, 2002)*

Accountable Advance: *CANADIAN* The advance of funds provided for a specific purpose and chargeable to a specific appropriation.

Accountable Item: *CANADIAN* Any item of equipment separately accounted for upon acquisition, removal, transfer, sale, demolition, abandonment, or write-off.

Accounting Cycle: The four-step procedure of an accounting system: examining source documents, recording transactions in an accounting journal, posting recorded transactions, and preparing financial statements. *(Business, 2002)*

Accounting Equation: Assets equal liabilities plus owners' equity. *(Schiller, 2000)*

Accounts Payable:

1. Financial obligations that arise as a result of making credit purchases.
2. An accounting function that is responsible for making payment to contractors and suppliers for charges incurred.
3. Liability accounts which indicate the charges owed on open accounts.

Accounts Receivable Turnover: A financial ratio calculated by dividing net sales by accounts receivable. *(Schiller, 2000)*

Accounts Receivables: Amounts that are due and payable to a firm as a result of sales to its customers. An accounting function that is responsible for the collection and deposit of payments received on open customer accounts for goods and services sold.

Accredited Purchasing Practitioner (A.P.P.): A certification given to qualified individuals by the Institute of Supply Management (ISM). *(www.ism.ws)*

Accrual Basis Accounting: An accounting system that encumbers or sets aside funds for a specified future expenditure. Using this system, transactions are recognized at the time they are incurred, as opposed to when cash is received or spent. This method of accounting is the most commonly used, especially among governmental entities. All agencies in the United States and Canada require an encumbrance and a receipt before payment can be authorized by demanding procedural separation between the ordering of goods and services; encumbrance of funds; and authorization of payment. *Also see Cash Basis Accounting.*

Acid Test Ratio: A financial ratio calculated by subtracting the value of inventory from the current asset amount and dividing by current liabilities. *(Schiller, 2000)*

Acknowledgement: A written or electronic communication sent by the supplier to the buyer that indicates that the supplier has accepted the order (purchase order). It may be a form of acceptance and may create a bilateral contract. It may also be a form of counter-offer from the seller to the buyer. *Also see Battle of the Forms.*

ACORD (Association of Cooperative Operations Research and Development): A non-profit association whose mission is to facilitate the development and use of standards for the insurance and reinsurance industry. ACORD is the focal point for providing standard insurance forms that meet all regulatory requirements for the U.S. property and casualty/surety market. *(ACORD Corporation, 1988)*

Acquisition:

1. As defined under FAR 2.101 Acquiring by contract, with appropriated funds, supplies or services (including construction) by and for the use of the Federal Government, through purchase or lease, whether the supplies or services already exist or must be created, developed, demonstrated, and evaluated.
2. The process of obtaining supplies, services, or construction through purchase, lease, or grants.

A

Acquisition Cost: The total sum of all actual and administrative costs incurred by the buyer in the process of acquiring goods and services. Total acquisition cost may include indirect labor and overhead costs. The costs associated with generating and processing an order including administrative costs is also included. The price level, or value of the supplies or services, to be purchased under a contract. *Also see Carrying Cost.*

Acquisition Fee: CANADIAN The amount billed to cover the cost of initiating a contract.

Acquisition Price: The amount paid to a vendor or contractor for the goods or services obtained.

Act of God: An unforeseen occurrence beyond human control, caused by nature, such as a tornado or hurricane. Not attributable to the negligence of the contractor. *Also see Force Majeure.* May be cause for contract termination and usually appears in the general conditions or boilerplate section of the solicitation. *(Harney, 1998)*

Actual Authority: The specific right to perform acts and make decisions or prescribe rules governing the conduct of others as given to an agent by a principal. *Also see Apparent Authority. (Garner, 2004)*

Actual Cost: All direct and indirect costs incurred for services, supplies, or construction, as distinguished from estimated or forecasted costs.

Actual Damages: Real damages to compensate for loss or injuries that have actually occured. This is in contrast to "nominal" damages (a small amount paid where there is no real loss) or "punitive" damages (intended to punish the party who must pay damages). When damages, which have been suffered by someone as a result of another's wrongdoing, can be precisely measured, they are called actual damages. Examples of actual damages are: loss of income because of an injury; medical expenses; costs of repairing damaged property; and specific business losses occurring because of a breach of a contract.

ADA: *See American with Disabilities Act.*

Ad Hoc Committee: A committee created for a specific purpose that is in place for a short period of time. They are now being replaced by cross-functional teams in a less formalized setting. *(Business, 2002)*

Addendum/Addenda: A written change, addition, alteration, correction or revision to a bid, proposal or contract document. Addendum/Addenda may be issued following a pre-bid/pre-proposal conference or as a result of a specification or work scope change to the solicitation. *(Harney, 1998)*

Adhesion Contracts: Contracts where the buyer is in no position to bargain effectively with the seller. In this context, the seller presents a "take it or leave it" contract for the purchase of goods with the intent to take advantage of the buyer's lack of knowledge and sophistication in order to get the buyer to enter into a patently unfair contract.

Adjectival Ratings: A notational scoring system in which adjectives are used to describe the quality of an offeror's proposal. Proposals may be rated using such terms as Outstanding, Highly Acceptable, Excellent, Good, Fair, and Poor. *(Nash, Schooner, O'Brien, 1998)*

Adjustment: CANADIAN The amount of variation permitted by an adjustment clause in the contract generally permitting a change upward or downward in the price or obligation in case certain events transpire.

Administered Price: A price determined by the deliberate price policy of a vendor rather than by competitive forces of the market place. *Also see List Price.*

Administrative Change: A unilateral change to a contract in writing, that does not affect the substantive rights of the parties, such as a change in the address to which an invoice is mailed.

Administrative Law: Rules, regulations, and executive orders promulgated by governmental administrative or regulatory agencies. Generally enacted to make statutes and ordinances more specific. Has the force and effect of law.

A

Administrative Remedies (exhaustion of): The completion of the process of direct appeal to a governmental body as defined by the governmental bodies' administrative regulations. When all procedures for review of the appeal by public officials have been followed and the relief sought by the appealing party still has not been obtained to that party's satisfaction, administrative remedies are considered to be exhausted. The appealing party may seek legal action through the courts. *(Garner, 2004)*

ADP: *See Automated Data Processing.*

ADR: *See Alternative Dispute Resolution.*

Ad Valorem: According to value. Customs duty (rate) that is generally charged on the value of goods irrespective of weight or other material considerations. Generally expressed as a percentage of the value of the goods as indicated on an invoice or bill of materials. *(ISM, 2000)*

Ad Valorem Duty: A customs duty or tax based on the value of the goods under consideration rather than on the quantity of the goods.

Advance Acquisition: The acquisition of items which require long lead times, or are required in extraordinary quantities, in advance of the fiscal year in which the product, service, or construction is required.

Advance Payments: Agreed upon payments between buyer and seller made prior to the actual receipt and delivery of the contracted goods and services. Payments may be for a stated amount or for a percentage of the purchase price. Sometimes referred to as cash in advance. *Also see Partial Payment and Progress Payment.*

Advanced Contract Award Notice (ACAN): CANADIAN A notice of intent to solicit a bid and negotiate with a single firm. Other suppliers are not invited to bid on these requirements but can forward letters of intent indicating their interest before the closing date. Notice of bidding requests will then be solicited from letters of interest that have been received. *(Summit Magazine, On-Line)*

Advertise: To make a public announcement or legal notice of a forthcoming solicitation with the aim of increasing the response and enlarging the field of competition; often required by law or policy.

Advertising: The act of preparing and distributing advertisements which call attention to a contemplated public purchase or sale.

Advice of Shipment: CANADIAN A notice sent to a purchaser advising that a shipment has been released.

AFC: *See Average Fixed Cost.*

Affidavit:
1. A written statement of facts provided by one party which may be made under oath before a person of authority. An affidavit may be required as part of a bid or request for proposal solicitation.
2. A written declaration made under oath before an authorized official.

Affiliate:
1. A branch or unit of a larger organization.
2. A company effectively controlled by another or associated with others under common ownership or control.

Affirmative Action:
1. A requirement contained within Federal law (Equal Opportunity Act of 1972) that requires organizations to achieve a work force that reflects the composition of the community. A plan designed to increase the number of minority employees at all levels within an organization.
2. A process of taking special or unusual steps to assure that businesses owned by specified minorities and/or women will have equal access to the purchasing process and will obtain an appropriate share of awards. *(Business, 2002)*

AG: CANADIAN *See Auditor General of Canada.*

Agency:
1. A legal relationship that exists between two parties by which one (the agent) is authorized to perform or transact specified business activities for the other (the principal).
2. An administrative or organizational division of a government.

A

Agent: A person authorized by a superior, i.e. principal, to act for him or her. In public procurement, this designation is usually incorporated into statute and ordinance. Empowered to act for another. *Also see Principal, Buyer and Law of Agency.* (NASPO, 2001)

Aggrandizement: To extend the scope of one's influence beyond what is normal or ethically acceptable. Personal gain obtained through an agreement established and intended to be on behalf of taxpayers that is unacceptable and taints the behavior of public professionals acting as stewards of the public trust.

Aggregate: To gather or collect quantities of a specific item (product or service) in order to achieve savings by leveraging economies of scale. An enabler of the economic theory that the larger the quantity the smaller the unit price. (Schiller, 2000)

Aggregate Award: A contract award made to the lowest responsive, responsible bidder based on the total price for all items. While this allows the public entity to enter into a contract with a single supplier, this method does not provide the best available pricing and may be overly restrictive, unless multiple bidders are able to supply all of the items contained in the solicitation document.

Aggregate Supply: The total quantity of output producers are willing and able to supply at alternative price levels in a given time period. (Schiller, 2000)

Aggregator: A technology reference to a website that contains product catalogs from many suppliers in one place as a convenience to supply management organizations. (Jansen, 2002)

Aggrieved Bidder/Proposer: The bidder/proposer who is adversely affected because they would be eligible to be awarded the public contract in the event that the protest or dispute was successful.

Agreement: An understanding, usually in writing, between two or more competent parties, under which one party agrees to certain performance as defined in the agreement and the second party agrees to compensation for the performance rendered in accordance with the conditions of the agreement. Agreements and contracts are sometimes used synonymously. Generally agreements are approved by an attorney "as to form" and legal sufficiency prior to execution. *Also see As To Form.* (Harney, 1992)

Agreement Type: CANADIAN Refers to the agreement under which the opportunity is governed, such as the Agreement on Internal Trade (AIT), North American Free Trade Agreement (NAFTA), etc. (Summit Magazine, On-Line)

AIA: *See American Institute of Architects.*

Air Freight:
1. Freight transported by air.
2. The amount charged for air transportation.

Air Freight Forwarder: As described in FAR 47.401: An indirect air carrier that is responsible for the transportation of property, from the point of receipt to the point of destination, and utilizes for the whole or any part of such transportation the services of a direct air carrier or its agent, or of another air freight forwarder.

Air Waybill: Documentary proof of the contract of carriage between the shipper and the carrier. It serves as a receipt of goods for shipment and is required for Customs clearance. This proof was issued by the airlines following the International Air Transportation Association (IATA) standard form. (Business, 2002)

Alien Corporation: A corporation chartered by a foreign government and conducting business in the United States. (Business, 2002)

Allocable Costs: Costs that are specifically related to the contract. (Harney, 1992) A cost that can be assigned or charged as an item of cost to one or more cost objectives, in accordance with the terms of the contract and applicable laws and regulations.

Allocation: The act of reserving inventory items in stock for later issue to a given using agency.

Allocation of Cost: To assign or charge an item of cost to one or more cost objectives, either as a direct cost or as a share of an indirect cost pool, based on the relative benefits received or other equitable relationship.

All-Or-Nothing Bid (All or None): A bid submitted for a number of different items, services, etc. in which the bidder states it will not accept a partial award, but will accept only an award for all the items, services, etc., included in the Invitation for Bids. Because the bidder has qualified their bid, their bid response may be deemed as non-responsive.

Allot: To divide an appropriation into amounts which may be encumbered or expended during an allotment period.

Allowable Costs: Costs that are recognized by law, regulation, or the contract. *(Harney, 1992)*
A cost that is reasonable.

Alpha: A word referring to the first of two pre-release phases of a commercial hardware or software product. The early version of the product is tested at the developer's site and is then improved accordingly. The release prior to the beta test or beta version. *(Jansen, 2002)*

Alphanumeric: A set of characters that contains both letters (alpha) and numbers (numeric). These characters may include punctuation and symbols found on a standard keyboard. Generally assigned to identify a specific item such as a model number. *(Jansen, 2002)*

Alternate Bid (Response):
1. A substitute bid.
2. A bid submitted with an intentional substantive variation to a basic provision, specification, term, or condition of the solicitation. *Also see Alternative (Alternate) Bid/Proposal.*

Alternate Service Delivery (ASD): CANADIAN An agency's process of looking at new ways of delivering some of its services, frequently by contracting to suppliers for services that were previously provided in-house. *(Summit Magazine, On-Line)*

Alternative (Alternate) Bid/Proposal: A response to a bid or proposal that does not meet the exact requirements of the specification or scope of work but offers an alternative for consideration. A bid/proposal submitted with an intentional substantive variation to a basic provision, specification, term or condition of the solicitation. This alternative, in the opinion of the bidder/proposer, achieves the same end result. Alternative bids and proposals may render the bid/proposal as non-responsive. *Also see Alternate Bid (Response).*

Alternative Dispute Resolution (ADR): A process or procedure used voluntarily between parties to resolve issues in controversy without the need to resort to litigation. ADR may include but are not limited to mediation, fact-finding and arbitration. *Also see Litigation.*

Alternative Project Delivery Method (APDM): A collective term to refer to the use of non-traditional contracting methods. The contractor may participate in or advise on the design or may be entirely responsible for the design; the contractor's selection is based on qualifications or best value. Traditional contracting methods may include Design-bid-build or design-build where alternative methods may include Construction Management or an Alliance/Relationship Contracting.

Ambiguity: Contract language that is capable of being understood to have more than one meaning. Such language is generally subject to more than one interpretation.

Amendment:
1. An agreed addition to, deletion from, correction or modification of a document or contract.
2. To revise or change an existing document; a formal revision, improvement or correction. *Also see Authorized Deviation, Change Order and Contract Modification.*

Amendment Previous Value: CANADIAN Value of a document as last amended.

Amendment Status: CANADIAN Identifies the number and description of amendments issued to a bid solicitation or contract document, and gives a description of the previous wording.

American Arbitration Association (AAA): A not-for-profit organization that provides resources for Alternative Dispute Resolution (ADR). Arbitration and mediation are being widely used to settle contractual disputes instead of litigation.

American Bar Association (ABA): With more than 400,000 members, the ABA provides law school accreditation, continuing legal education,

legal information, programs to assist lawyers and judges in their work and initiatives to improve the legal system for the public. *(www.abanet.org)*

American Institute of Architects (AIA): A national professional society founded in 1857 whose members are licensed architects, graduate architects or retired architects. AIA promotes design excellence and fosters professionalism and accountability through professional development programs and achievement awards. *(www.aia.org)*

American National Standards Institute (ANSI): Coordinates the development and use of voluntary consensus standards in the United States and represents the needs and views of U.S. stakeholders in standardization forums around the globe. The Institute oversees the creation, promulgation and use of thousands of norms and guidelines that directly impact businesses in nearly every sector. ANSI is also actively engaged in accrediting programs that assess conformance to standards. *(www.ansi.org, 2006)*

American Production and Inventory Control Society (APICS): A professional society whose mission is to improve and advance the field of production and inventory control. *Also known as The Association for Operations Management.* *(www.apics.org)*

American Society for Testing and Materials (ASTM): A not-for-profit institution that develops specifications, standards, test methods and other product testing data. *(www.astm.org)*

Americans with Disabilities Act (ADA): Federal legislation passed in 1990 that requires organizations with at least 25 employees to make reasonable accommodations for qualified workers and applicants with disabilities and to avoid discriminating against them. Compliance includes removing physical workplace barriers. *(Business, 2002)*

Amortization: To provide for the gradual reduction in the cost value. An accounting procedure that gradually reduces the cost value of limited life or intangible assets through periodic charges to income. *(Business, 2002)*

Analytical Skills: An individual's ability to identify relevant issues, recognize their importance, understand the relationship between them, and perceive the underlying causes of a situation. These skills are crucial in making most procurement decisions. *(Miller, 2006)*

Ancillary Services: Commercial type support services required by a government such as custodial, landscape maintenance, and refuse collection, etc.

ANSI: *See American National Standards Institute.*

Anticipatory Repudiation: Statements or acts of a contractor before an actual Breach of Contract that indicate that the contractor does not intend or is unable to complete, or continue to perform under the contract. *(Black's Law Dictionary, 93)*

Anti-trust Laws: State and federal laws enacted to ensure free, fair and open competition by prohibiting monopolies or conspiracies in restraint of trade in interstate and foreign commerce. The Sherman and Clayton Acts are examples of Federal Antitrust Laws. *(Miller, 2006)*

Anti-trust Legislation: Laws that attempt to prevent or eliminate monopolies or oligopolies and to prevent noncompetitive practices.

Antitrust Violations: Violations of federal or state laws that regulate trusts, cartels, or business monopolies by limiting or prohibiting non-competitive business practices. Violations of antitrust laws include such practices as price fixing, bid rigging, identical bidding and market division. *(Garner, 2004)*

APC: *See Average Propensity to Consume.*

APDM: *See Alternative Project Delivery Method.*

APICS: *See American Production and Inventory Control Society.*

APL (Approved/Acceptable Products List): *See Acceptable Products List. Also see Qualified Products List (QPL) and Approved Brands List (ABL).*

Apparent Agency (a.k.a. "estoppel agency"): An agency relationship whereby the principal's conduct implies that an agent has authority to

act on the principal's behalf and thereby the Principal becomes bound to and responsible for what the agent signed or did. *(Garner, 2004)*

Apparent Authority: Occurs when a principal allows or permits a person to function in a capacity that creates the illusion that the person is an authorized agent of the principal. *Also see Actual Authority.* *(Garner, 2004)*

Apparent Low Bidder: After conducting a price analysis from quotes/bids received, the buyer initially identifies the low bidder strictly based on the lowest price received before determining whether the bid is from a responsive and responsible bidder.

Appeal: An objection to a process, procedure or an award. An appeal may be taken to the proper authority responsible for receiving appeals by filing a Notice of Appeal within the required time period. This notice must be in writing, signed by a person of authority, (the contractor, an officer, if the contractor is a corporation, or its attorney) and should identify the contract by number, the final decision which is being appealed, and the agency issuing that final decision. Although express mail services are sufficient if you are certain that the Notice will be delivered within the specified timeframe, it is safer to send the Notice by registered mail which provides irrefutable proof of mailing within the specified time. *Also see Appeal Process and Appeal Rights.*

Appeal Process: The appeal process varies among different public agencies but the goal of the agency should remain constant – fair and equitable treatment of the parties. *Also see Appeal and Appeal Rights.*

Appeal Rights: The legal right to challenge the agency and to ask for a decision to be reviewed and changed. *Also see Appeal and Appeal Process.*

Appellate Court: A court that hears cases appealed from lower courts. *(Garner, 2004)*

Appropriation: CANADIAN Any authority of Parliament to pay money out of the Consolidated Revenue Fund.

Appropriation: Legislative authorization to expend public funds for a specific purpose. Funds that have been set aside for a specific purpose. *(Schiller, 2000)*

Approval Date: CANADIAN The date on which a procurement document was approved by the appropriate authority.

Approved Equal: *See Equal.*

Approved Products List: A list of vendors or products that have been evaluated and have been determined to be capable of satisfactory performance for a specific application. *Also see Qualified Products List (QPL), Acceptable Products List (APL), and Approved Source List. Also known as Approved Brands List (ABL).*

Approved Source List: CANADIAN A list of suppliers that can supply specific goods and services and are approved on the basis of the suitability of their facilities and capabilities.

AQL: *See Acceptable Quality Level.*

Arbitrage: The purchase of securities in one market for immediate resale in another financial market in order to profit from a price discrepancy. Used frequently in international currency transactions to profit from currency fluctuations. Aberrations in financial markets used to make a profit. *(Business, 2002)*

Arbitrary and Capricious: Actions by whim or caprice, with irrational disregard of facts or circumstances. May be the basis for courts to overrule or remand an administrative decision or ministerial action by a purchaser. A public official's improper use of discretionary powers to the detriment of the public good.

Arbitration:

1. A process by which a dispute between parties is presented to one or more disinterested parties (arbitrators or neutrals) for a decision whose decision the contending parties agree to accept with no further appeal process also known as binding arbitration.
2. The resolution of a conflict between parties by a party removed from the dispute.
3. A form of Alternative Dispute Resolution.

A

Architect: An individual, partnership, or corporation that performs professional architectural services for the agency as an independent contractor. A registered architect is an individual that is trained in the planning, design and oversight of the construction of buildings. To practice architecture means to offer or render services in connection with the design and construction of a building, or group of buildings and the space within the site surrounding the buildings that have as their principal purpose human occupancy or use. Architects are required to have Errors and Omissions Insurance.

Architectural and Engineering (A & E) Services: Professional services within the scope of the practice of architecture and professional engineering, as defined by the jurisdiction, usually involving research, design, development, construction, alteration, or repair of real property.

Archival Quality: A characteristic of paper and paper products that enables the paper to retain a specified percentage of its original physical and appearance properties for an extended period of time under specified controlled conditions. *(Business, 2002)*

Articles of Partnership: Legal documents that set forth the basic agreement between partners. *(Garner, 2004)*

As Is: A contract term describing products offered without guarantee or warranty. All risk is assumed by the purchaser without recourse to the seller.

As To Form: Documents and agreements that are approved by an attorney for legal sufficiency prior to their execution while not commenting on the business merits of their contents. *Also see Agreement.*

Asset:
1. An amount recorded on a contractor's balance sheet representing the value of property owned by or debts owed to the contractor. Assets may be cash, near-cash, or non-monetary.
2. The economic resources of a business. *(Schiller, 2000)*

Assignment: Legal transfer of a claim, right, interest or property.

Assignment of Payment: An authorization from a supplier that allows for their accounts receivable to be paid to a third party. Payments made to a supplier's creditor.

ASTM: *See American Society of Testing and Materials.*

ATC: *See Average Total Cost.*

Atomic Digital Clock Time: The atomic digital clock is located in Fort Collins Colorado and it is the master clock in the United States that provides the precise time as the basis for all other clock systems and for official bid openings. The telephone number to hear your local accurate local time is 1-303-499-7111.

Attach: To take legal possession.

Attorney Work Product Privilege: An exemption under the Freedom of Information Act, which protects documents prepared by an agency's attorney which reveal the theory of a case or proposed litigation from release. *(Nash & Rawicz, 1997)*

Auction: A public sale in which property or items of merchandise are sold to the highest bidder. Many governments will auction off government property and may contract with a private auctioneering firm to handle the complete transaction including advertising, the sale and collection of funds, etc. *(Miller, 2006)*

Auctioning: An unethical practice that can occur during negotiations on competitive sealed proposals if the negotiating team discloses information from one offeror's proposal to other proposers, who then change their offer so that it matches or is better than the first proposal evaluated. *(Harney, 1992)*

Audit: A detailed review and examination of records, documents and the business processes with the confirmation by outside experts of a situation or condition concluding with a detailed report of findings. A formal examination or veri-

fication of financial accounts or other business operations. Examples include financial, compliance and management audits.

Auditor General of Canada (AG): *CANADIAN* Audits government operations and provides the information that helps Parliament to hold the government accountable for its stewardship of public funds. *(Summit Magazine, On-Line)*

Authority: The right to perform certain acts or prescribe rules governing the conduct of others. *(Nash, Rawicz, 1997)*

Authorization to Release: Permission to release requested goods to the using agency against existing supply agreements.

Authorized Deviation: A change or deviation specifically allowed by the contracting authority. *Also see Amendment, Change Order and Contract Modification.*

Automated Data Processing (ADP): Input, storage, and manipulation of information using computer systems, and the discipline which deals with related methods and techniques. *Also called Electronic Data Processing.*

Automatic Stabilizer: Federal expenditure or revenue item that automatically responds counter cyclically to changes in national income, like unemployment benefits or income taxes. *(Bureau of Economic Analysis)*

Average: A number that is calculated to summarize a group of numbers. The most commonly used average is the mean - the sum of the numbers divided by however many numbers there are in the group. The median is the middle value in a group of numbers ranked in order of size. The mode is the number that occurs most often in a group of numbers. *(Bishop, 2004)*

Average Fixed Cost (AFC): Total fixed cost divided by the quantity produced in a given time period. *(Schiller, 2000)*

Average Propensity to Consume (APC): Total consumption in a given period divided by total disposable income. *(Schiller, 2000)*

Average Total Cost (ATC): Total cost divided by the quantity produced in a given time period. *(Schiller, 2000)*

Award:
1. *CANADIAN* The notification to a bidder or tenderer of acceptance of a bid or tender which brings the contract into existence
2. *US* The acceptance of a bid or proposal; the presentation of a purchase agreement or contract to a bidder or offeror.

Award by Group: A contract award that can be made to multiple suppliers based on the lowest total price for all items within a specific group. The public entity may group items by classification, commodity code, category, or geographic zone in its best interest. This method allows the public entity to target a logical grouping of bid items to a supplier for contract management purposes. *Also known as Class Award.*

Award Item by Item: A contract award that may be made to multiple suppliers because each item is awarded typically on the basis of the lowest unit price when being utilized in the bid process. This method offers the best pricing to the public entity but requires significant contract administration if multiple suppliers are selected for award. *Also referred to as Line Item Award.*

Award Protest: A formal complaint made against the methods employed or decisions made by a procurement authority in the process leading to the award of a contract. *Also see Bid Protest and Protest.*

Award Value: *CANADIAN* The monetary amount of the contract, in Canadian dollars, when awarded.

B

B2B (Business to Business): Web/Internet based business relationships and applications. An eCommerce business capability which implies that businesses conduct sales and marketing via the internet to other businesses; similar to B2C (Business to Consumer) eCommerce sales. *(Jansen, 2002)*

Back-Door Buying or Selling:
1. Unofficial, irregular, devious buying or selling, usually resulting from undue efforts to induce preference for a particular vendor with the intent of limiting competition; unauthorized actions.
2. A direct marketing/sales effort to induce preference on the part of the program manager or requestor for a particular product, service or seller with the intent to constrain competition.
3. Evasive actions taken by the seller to circumvent the Purchasing Department and agency rules and regulations trying to influence or sell directly to the agency's internal user/customer department.

Back Order:
1. The portion of a purchase order that a vendor does not deliver at the scheduled time and has re-entered for shipment at a later date.
2. Items ordered but not shipped due to insufficient inventory or some other reason. *Also see Partial Shipment/Delivery.*

BAFO: *See Best and Final Offer.*

Balance of Payments: A summary record of a country's international economic transactions in a given period of time. The difference between the flow of money into and out of a country. *(Schiller, 2000)*

Balance of Trade: The part of a nation's balance of payments that deals with imports and exports. *(Schiller, 2000)*

Balance Sheet: A financial summary of the dollar amounts of a firm's assets, liabilities, and owner's equity accounts at the end of an accounting period. *(Business, 2002)*

Balanced Budget: When total public sector spending equals total government income during the same period from taxes and charges for public services. *(Bishop, 2004)*

Baldrige National Quality Award: Named after former Commerce Secretary, Malcolm Baldrige, it honors those companies that have achieved national excellence in quality improvement. It is similar to the Deming Prize, awarded in Japan. The mission of the program is to enhance the competitiveness, quality, and productivity of U.S. organizations for the benefit of all residents. For more information: www.baldrige.nist.gov.

Bank/Banker's Acceptance: A draft or bill of exchange drawn on a bank and acknowledged as valid by that bank.

Bank Reserves: Assets held by a bank to fulfill its deposit obligations. *(Schiller, 2000)*

Bankruptcy: A legal procedure designed both to protect an individual or business that cannot meet its financial obligations and to protect the creditors involved. *Also see Voluntary bankruptcy.* *(Schiller, 2000)*

Bar Code: A pattern of parallel bars and spaces which may represent numbers and other characters that are read by a hand held device or other computer hardware. May be used to track inventory and other items in transit. *Also known as a UPC (Universal Product Code) label to identify specific products.*

Bargaining: In a competitive negotiation, discussion, persuasion, alteration of initial assumptions and positions, and give and take with respect to price, schedule, technical requirements, or contract terms.

Bargaining Unit: A specific group of employees represented by a union. A group of employees who collectively negotiate with management for wage and benefit enhancements. *(Business, 2002)*

Barriers To Entry: A variety of obstacles that make it difficult or impossible for would-be producers to enter a particular market, such as patents or copyrights. *(Schiller, 2000)*

Barter: A medium of exchange which does not use currency. Trading or exchanging goods and services by means of exchange other than money. A form of counter-trade used in international business.

Basis of Payment: CANADIAN The payment terms in a contract which specify the conditions under which payment will be made for receipt of goods or performance of services.

Basis Point: One one-hundredth of a percentage point. Small movements in the interest rate or the exchange rate is often described in terms of basis points. If a bond yield moves from 5.25% to 5.45%, it has risen by 20 basis points. *(Bishop, 2004)*

Basket: The combination of goods and services included in the computation of an index. *(ISM, 2000)*

Battle of the Forms: A colloquial reference to various forms that are exchanged between buyer and seller in an attempt to have their document prevail in the event of a disagreement between the contracting parties. *Also see Acknowledgement.*

BDP: *See Benefits Driven Procurement.*

Bear Market: A market in which average stock prices are declining. Market indicators for a bear market trend downward. *Also see Bull Market. (Schiller, 2000)*

Benchmark: A point of reference used in measuring an organization or a business unit's performance. *(Business, 2002)*

Benchmarking: The act of measuring a process, service, or product against the characteristics of the recognized leaders in the given area of review. A study, review, or process whereby a procurement organization identifies world-class organizations with which to compare its practices, policies and performance outcomes. An organization's performance is judged against selected criteria from other organizations deemed "best in class".

Benefit: The gain received from voluntary exchange. *(Schiller, 2000)*

Benefits: Non-financial forms of compensation provided to employees, such as health benefits, life insurance, pension benefits, paid holidays and vacation, etc. *(Business, 2002)*

Benefits Driven Procurement (BDP): CANADIAN An approach to procurement that stresses a focus on results and on the benefits that government and suppliers gain from the procurement. The supplier is asked to deliver certain agreed upon results rather than follow specific specifications. *(Summit Magazine, On-Line)*

Best and Final Offer (BAFO): In a competitive negotiation, the final proposal submitted after negotiations are completed that contains the proposer's most favorable terms for price, services and products to be delivered. Sometimes referred to as BAFO and utilized during the Request for Proposal method of procurement.

Best in Class: A standard of excellence given to an organization or business unit that demonstrates verifiable performance in a particular category or business area. Benchmarking may be one method of measuring and determining best in class designation.

Best Interest: A term which grants the chief procurement officer the discretion to take the most advantageous action on behalf of the entity they represent usually in the absence of law or regulation. *Also see Discretion. (NASPO, 2001)*

Best Practice: A business process, activity or operation that is considered outstanding, innovative or exceptionally creative by a recognized peer group. It may be considered as a leading-edge activity that has been successfully adopted or implemented and has brought efficiency and effectiveness to an organization. It may result in improved productivity, quality, reduced costs and increased customer service. *(Business, 2002)*

Best Value:

1. An assessment of the return which can be achieved based on the total life cycle cost of the item; may include an analysis of the functionality of the item; can use cost/benefit analysis to define the best combinations of quality, services, time, and cost considerations over the useful life of the acquired item.

B

2. A procurement method that emphasizes value over price. The best value might not be the lowest cost. Generally achieved through the Request for Proposal (RFP) method.

Beta: The very early testing stage of a commercial software or hardware application. Comes after the Alpha phase and is tested "in the field" by potential customers. *(Jansen, 2002)*

Bid: CANADIAN A tender, proposal or quotation submitted in response to a solicitation from a contracting authority. *Also see Tender and Solicitation.*

Bid: (noun) The response submitted by a bidder to an invitation for bids (IFB) or to a multi-step bid. Sometimes the complete bid document may be referred to as "the bid". The response to a request for proposal (RFP) is called a proposal or offer. *Also see Tender and Solicitation.*

Bid: (verb) To submit a bid response. By submitting a bid response, one person (the vendor/contractor) gives the buyer the legal power to create a contract with the responding seller in accordance with the bid response. *Also see Tender and Solicitation.*

Bid Analysis: A comprehensive review of all bids/offers received as a result of a competitive process usually for the purpose of comparing strengths and weaknesses of the bids received based on the requirements and criteria set forth in the invitation for bids. *Also see Bid Evaluation and Bid Tabulation.*

Bid Bond: An insurance agreement, accompanied by a monetary commitment, by which a third party (the surety) accepts liability and guarantees that the bidder will not withdraw the bid. The bidder will furnish bonds in the required amount and if the contract is awarded to the bonded bidder, the bidder will accept the contract as bid, or else the surety will pay a specific amount.

Bid Deposit: A sum of money, a check, or other acceptable cash alternative such as an irrevocable letter of credit or the contractor's pledge against owned property or against personal assets deposited with the buyer by a bidder as a guarantee that the bidder will enter into a contract if awarded. May also be in the form of a bond issued by a surety and deposited with a procurement activity guaranteeing the bidder will not withdraw the bid for a specified period of time, will furnish bonds as required, and will accept a contract if awarded, or forfeit the deposit.

Bidder: One who submits a response to an invitation for bid (IFB). *Also see Offeror.*

Bidders Conference: A meeting to discuss with potential bidders, technical, operational and performance specifications, and/or the full extent of financial, security and other contractual obligations related to a bid solicitation before the bid closes. *Also see Pre-Bid/Pre-Proposal Conference and Pre-Solicitation Conference.*

Bidders List: A listing of names and addresses of vendors from whom bids, proposals or quotations can be solicited. The list is generally retained in a retrievable data base. *Also see Source List.*

Bid Documentation: A file containing all of the information and records relating to the bid, which may include all of the original bids received, specifications, insurance requirements, addenda, bonds, correspondence and all other relevant data that may be subject to audit and further review.

Bid Evaluation: *See Bid Analysis and Bid Tabulation.*

Bid File: A file containing the individual bids from all vendors solicited by the Invitation for Bids (IFB).

Bid Guarantee: *See Bid Bond, Bid Deposit.*

Bid Identification Number: CANADIAN An alpha numeric code unique to the bid solicitation.

Bid Opening: The official process in which sealed bids are opened, usually in the presence of one or more witnesses, at the time and place specified in the invitation for bid. The amount of each bid is recorded and bids are made available for public inspection. It may be open to the public.

Bid Preference: Procurement laws mandating that bid prices for a preferred class of bidders be given special consideration when comparing their bid prices with those of other bidders not in the preferred class, i.e., local vendors may be given a bid preference over out-of-state vendors. *Also see Buy Local and Local Preference.*

Bid Protest: A formal complaint made against the methods employed or decisions made by a procurement authority in the process leading to the award of a contract. *Also see Award Protest, Protest and Dispute.*

Bid Rigging: The agreement among potential competitors to manipulate the competitive bidding process, for example, by agreeing not to bid, to bid a specific price, to rotate bidding, or to give kickbacks to purchasers.

Bid Sample: A sample to be furnished by a bidder to show the characteristics of a product offered in a bid. Bid samples are used only to determine the responsiveness of the bid. *(Nash, Schooner, O'Brien, 1998)*

Bid Security: A bond or deposit which guarantees that the bidder/offeror, if awarded the contract, will accept the contract as bid.

Bid Set: *CANADIAN* A package of data which identifies the article to be purchased, the quantity and delivery, and which includes designs, specifications, quality requirements and general conditions which govern the contract resulting from acceptance of a bid. *(Summit Magazine, On-Line)*

Bid Tabulation: A public document listing all vendors who received a copy of the Invitation for Bid (IFB), with a list of all items in the IFB, and showing unit prices for each item for each bidder. It may also include total prices, delivery terms and conditions, whether each bidder has met the requirements for licenses, bonds, evidence of insurance, or other information deemed appropriate by the contracting officer. Solicited vendors not responding to the IFB are shown as "no bid." *Also see Bid Analysis and Bid Evaluation.*

Bilateral Modification (of a contract): Requires the written approval of both parties to a contract in signatory form. Bilateral modification is often related to some alteration of one or more substantive terms of the contract. *Also see Unilateral Modification.*

Bilateral Monopoly: A market with only one buyer and one seller. *(Schiller, 2000)*

Bill: *See Invoice.*

Bill of Entry: A written account of goods entered at customs, whether they are to be imported or are intended for export.

Bill of Exchange: A document drawn by the seller on the buyer, instructing the buyer to pay the amount of the purchase under specified circumstances. *(ISM, 2000)*

Bill of Lading: A hauler or carrier's contract which may also act as the receipt of goods transported and delivered to the consignee. Examples of various bills of lading: Clear/Clear; Ocean; Order; Short-Form; Straight; and Through.

Bill of Materials (BOM): A list specifying the quantity and the specification, description or character of various materials and parts required to manufacture, produce or assemble a certain quantity of a finished product. A critical element of an automated Material Requirement Planning (MRP) system.

Bill of Sale: A written statement transferring ownership of something from seller to buyer.

Bin Tag: A tag attached to a storage bin on which a perpetual inventory is recorded.

Binding Arbitration: Specific to ADR, it involves the presentation of a dispute to an impartial or neutral individual or panel for issuance of a binding decision. The parties usually have the ability to decide who the individuals are that serve as arbitrators. *Also see Arbitration.*

Biodegradable: Capable of undergoing biodegradation whereby most paper products are converted by microorganisms into basic elements, such as water and carbon dioxide. *(ISM, 2000)*

B

Blanket Bond: A type of bond used to insure a bidder's performance on two or more contracts instead of issuing separate bonds for each contract. The amount and form of the blanket bond shall be established by the contracting entities.

Blanket Order:
1. An agreement to purchase a given quantity of specific goods over a specified period of time, usually one year.
2. The contract generally establishes prices, terms, conditions, and the period covered, although no quantities are specified; shipments are to be made when and as required by the purchaser which in certain cases may be the end user. *Also see Demand contract, Price agreement, Schedule contract, and Systems contract.*

Blanket Purchase Agreement (BPA): A simplified procurement method of filling the anticipated repetitive needs for supplies or services through the award of competitive line item contracts or discounts off of a suppliers catalog usually through competition. Used to reduce administrative expense resulting from small, repetitive requirements.

Blind Trust: An independently managed trust in which the beneficiary has no management rights and is not given notice of alterations in, or other dispositions of, the property subject to trust.

Board of Directors (BOD): The top governing body of a corporation, the members of which are elected by the stockholders. *(Business, 2002)*

Boilerplate:
1. A common term used to refer to standard clauses used in a bid or contract document, often prepared as a preprinted insert. The general terms and conditions and instructions to bidders may be sections of a bid document's boilerplate. *Also see General Terms and Conditions and General Provisions.*
2. A colloquialism, used in procurement to identify standard terms and conditions incorporated in solicitations, contracts, or purchase orders and agreements which are often preprinted or incorporated by reference. *Also see Terms and Conditions and General Provisions.* *(Harney, 1998)*

BOM: *See Bill of Materials.*

Bona Fide: In good faith. Bond:
1. A certificate reflecting a firm's promise to pay the holder a periodic interest payment until the date of maturity and a fixed sum of money on the designated maturity date.
2. An interest bearing security issued by governments.

Bonded Carrier: A business transporting goods and operating under a bond to guarantee performance.

Bonded Warehouse:
1. A warehouse under bond to the government for payment of customs duties and taxes on goods stored or processed there.
2. A warehouse insured against damage or loss to goods stored there.

BPA: *See Blanket Purchase Agreement.*

BPI: *See Business Process Improvement.*

Brand: A name, term, symbol, design, or any combination of these that identifies a seller's products and distinguishes them from competitive products. *Also see Brand Name (or Equivalent).* *(Business, 2002)*

Brand Loyalty: The extent to which a customer is favorable toward buying a specific brand to the exclusion of other competitive brands. *(Business, 2002)*

Brand Name: A name that serves to identify a manufacturer's product and may be protected by a trade name or trademark. *Also see Brand.*

Brand Name (or Equivalent) Specification:
1. A descriptive form of specification whereby the commodity or product is described by a unique identifier specific to a particular seller or manufacturer that distinguishes it from its competition. It may be a name, term, symbol, design or any combination thereof.
2. Using one or more manufacturers' brand name, with identifying model numbers, to describe the standards of quality, performance and other characteristics needed to meet the

requirements of the solicitation, and which invites bids for equivalent products from any manufacturer. A requested single brand name tends to limit competition as vendors may not sell that particular brand and all other items will be excluded from further consideration. *Also see Equivalent Items.*

Breach of Contract: Failure by either contracting party to fulfill a contract, wholly or in part, without legal excuse. An action by one party to a contract that violates the terms of the contract thereby permitting the other party to declare the contract in default. The failure of one party to fulfill the terms of a contract when there is no legal reason for that failure. *(Harney, 1992)*

Breach of Warranty: The failure to meet an express or implied agreement as to the title, quality, content, or condition of something sold.

Breakeven Quantity: The number of units that must be sold for the total revenue (from all units sold) to equal the total cost (of all units sold). *(Schiller, 2000)*

Bribe: Money or favor given or promised in order to influence the judgment or conduct of a person in a position of trust.

Bribery: The crime of offering, giving, receiving, or soliciting anything of value to influence action of an official or in the discharge of a public duty. *(Garner, 2004)*

Broker: An intermediary entity that specializes in a particular commodity, represents either a buyer or a seller, and is likely to be hired on a temporary basis.

Budget: A financial statement that projects income and/or expenditures over a specified period, sometimes referred to as a fiscal year. Governmental budgets generally are classified as operating budgets or capital budgets.

Budget Deficit: Amount by which government spending exceeds government revenue in a given time period. *(Schiller, 2000)*

Budget Message: A communication normally written by the chief executive that accompanies the budget estimate. Its purpose is to explain: (1) the main points of the budget; (2) the assumptions under which it was assembled; and (3) the major policy recommendations.

Budget Surplus: An excess of government revenues over government expenditures in a given time period. *(Schiller, 2000)*

Bulk Purchasing: To purchase in volume with the expectation of reducing the unit price of an item. To aggregate quantities of material in hope of achieving deeper discounts and better pricing. *Also see Bundling.*

Bull Market: A market in which average stock prices are increasing or advancing. Market indicators for a bull market trend upward. *Also see Bear Market.* *(Business, 2002*

Bundling: The practice of pooling or grouping smaller purchases to leverage purchasing power thus obtaining the benefits of economies of scale or a reduction in administrative expenses. *Also see Bulk Purchasing.* *(NASPO, 2001)*

Burden: *See Indirect Costs.*

Bureau of Economic Analysis: A federal agency of the U.S. Department of Commerce that generates the gross domestic product (GDP). The Commerce Department also calculates personal income, corporate profits, and the current account balance. For more information: www.bea.gov.

Bureau of Labor Statistics: A federal agency of the U.S. Labor Department that tracks all aspects of the labor market such as employment projections, unemployment numbers, employee compensation reports and a host of other labor related information. For more information: www.bls.gov.

Business: Any corporation, partnership, individual, sole proprietorship, joint stock company, joint venture, or any other private legal entity.

Business Continuity Plan: *See Continuity of Operations Plan (COOP).*

B

Business Cycle: Alternating periods of economic growth and contraction. Sometimes characterized as prosperity, recession, depression and recovery. *(Schiller, 2000)*

Business Interruption Insurance: Commercial insurance protection for a business whose operations are interrupted because of a fire, storm, or other natural disaster. *(Business, 2002)*

Business Plan: A statement of the rationale for a business and a step-by-step explanation of how it will achieve its goals. *(Business, 2002)*

Business Process Improvement (BPI): A systematic approach to help organizations make significant change in the way they do business. *(Business, 2002)*

Business Process Outsourcing: To carve out an internal business process such as IT (Information Technology) or HR (Human Resources) and outsource it to a private entity in an attempt to reduce costs and improve efficiency. *(Miller, 2006)*

Business Valuation: Determines the price that a hypothetical buyer would pay for a business under a given set of circumstances. A business valuation is completed by an appraiser or a Certified Public Accountant using a combination of judgment, experience, and an understanding of generally accepted valuation principles. The two primary types of business valuations that are widely used are income valuations and asset valuations. Income statements and other financial and accounting records provide the basis for most business valuations. *(www.freedictionary.com)*

Buy American:
1. A policy or philosophy usually expressed in law or by executive order which mandates the purchase, at a certain dollar threshold, of products with a substantial percentage of American made components.
2. A preference policy generally adopted by a governmental body that requires the purchase of American-made products or products with a defined percentage of American-made components.

Buy American Act (U.S. Law): Originally enacted in 1933, generally requires that the Federal Government buy for public use only raw materials mined or produced in the United States, and only manufactured items which are made in the United States, "substantially all from" materials or items mined, produced or manufactured in the United States. The act has several important exceptions. The general requirements are inapplicable if the items to be purchased are not available domestically, in commercial quantities of good quality, or if the cost of the domestic items is "unreasonable", or if the head of the department otherwise determines it to be in the public interest to waive the requirement. *(Burt, Dobler, Starling, 2003).*

Buy Local: A bid preference which may be given to vendors doing business in the purchasing jurisdiction. *Also see Bid Preference; Local Preference and Preference.*

Buyer: A purchaser or procurer of products and services. This title may also refer to an individual who is responsible for the procurement activities of an entity. A job title within a procurement organization also commonly referred to as a Purchasing or Procurement Agent. *Also see Agent, Principal and Law of Agency.*

Buyer's Market: An economic condition within a competitive marketplace that occurs when the supply of a product or service exceeds the demand. Generally results in lower prices more favorable to the buyer. *(Harney, 1992)*

Buyer's Option: The contractual right, established in a purchase document, to buy an item or service at a fixed price within a specified time. *Also see Option.*

Buyer's Right of Routing: The right of the buyer to select the carrier to be used for shipment of goods when the buyer pays freight charges; the buyer's right to name the carrier must be made part of the sales contract before shipment of goods if vendor prepays the freight.

Buyer-Seller Relationships: There are three principal relationships between buyers and suppliers: Transactional: An arm's–length relationship wherein neither party is concerned with the well-being of the other. Price is the focus of the relationship. Collaborative: A strategic relationship is created that results in the reduction of risk and uncertainty. This type of relationship creates interdependency and cooperation. Alliance: Relationship is based on institutional trust. Alliance partners share a vision of the future where ethics takes precedence over expediency. *(Business, 2002)*

Buying Allowance: A temporary price reduction to resellers for purchasing specified quantities of a product. *(ISM, 2000)*

Buying Behavior: The decision processes and actions of people who purchase and use products and services. The underlying motivational rationale for an individual's buying decision. *(Business, 2002)*

Buying In: Knowingly submitting an offer or bid below the vendor's anticipated cost with the expectation of increasing the contract amount after award through unnecessary or overpriced change orders. Commonly referred to as "low balling" a price. *Also see Lowball.*

Buying (Seasonal) Calendar: A buying plan which is designed to take advantage of lower seasonal prices, such a road ice chemicals in summer.

By-Law: Most commonly refers to a city or municipal law or ordinance, passed under the authority of a charter or provincial/state law specifying what things may be regulated by the municipality. *Also see Ordinances.*

C

C & F: *See Cost and Freight.*

Calendar of Events: A chronology of dates that is significant to a project. In the procurement of services it reflects key events that will occur between the issuance of the RFP and the award of the contract. *(Harney, 1992)*

Call-Up: CANADIAN A requisition or a request for delivery which is forwarded directly to a supplier to obtain delivery of materiel from a previously negotiated contract, or a standing offer, in accordance with their terms. Also called Drawdown. *Also see Period of Assignment.*

Call up Number: CANADIAN The unique number of a requisition.

Canadian Council for Public-Private Partnerships (CCPPP): An organization promoting the benefits of joint ventures between government and business. *(Summit Magazine, On-Line)*

Canadian General Standards Board (CGSB): A federal government organization that offers client-centred, comprehensive standards development and conformity assessment services in support of the economic, regulatory, procurement, health, safety and environmental interests of our stakeholders—government, industry and consumers. For more information: www.pwgsc.gc.ca/cgsb/home/index-e.html

Canadian Government Catalogue System (CGCS): The official system for civil departments of the Canadian government, by which items of materiel are uniformly named, classified, described, numbered and catalogued; used interchangeably with the NATO Codification System.

Canadian International Trade Tribunal (CITT): The main quasi-judicial institution in Canada's trade remedy system with authority to conduct inquiries into complaints by potential suppliers concerning procurement by the federal government that is covered by the North American Free Trade Agreement, the Agreement on Internal Trade and the World Trade Organization Agreement on Government Procurement. Any potential suppliers who believe they may have been unfairly treated during the solicitation or evaluation of bids, or in the awarding of contracts on a designated procurement, may lodge a formal complaint with the Tribunal. The Tribunal deals with bid challenges on Canadian government contracts, arising under an international agreement. *(www.citt.gc.ca)*

Canadian Public Procurement Council (CPPC): An organization that represents public sector procurement professionals throughout Canada. *(www.ccmp-cppc.qc.ca)*

C

Cancellation of a Contract: Occurs when the authority has determined that the contract should be terminated for cause, default or convenience. *Also see Termination for Convenience and Termination for Default.*

Cancellation Request: A request, by either party to a purchase agreement, to cancel the contract, often at no cost. *Also see Discharge by Mutual Assent, Termination for Convenience and Termination for Default.*

Cannibalize: A term used to describe the disassembly, dismantling, stripping or tearing down of buildings or equipment for salvage components or parts which may be used to repair, assemble, or re-build other equipment. A process used to extend the life cycle of equipment.

Capability: The ability of a bidder to fulfill the contract at time of award.

Capacity: The amount of goods and services that an organization can produce or provide in a given time interval. *(Schiller, 2000)*

Capital:
1. Final goods produced for use in the production of other goods, e.g. equipment, buildings.
2. Wealth in the form of money or property.
3. All buildings, equipment and human skills used to produce goods and services. *(Schiller, 2000)*

Capital Asset: An asset with a life cycle of more than one year with a value of more than a certain prescribed limit set by accounting standards or by governmental policy.

Capital Budget: A financial statement that estimates expenditures for major assets and an entities long-term financing needs. Governmental capital budgets generally reflect large asset expenditures for equipment and buildings over certain dollar thresholds. *(Nash, Schooner, O'Brien, 1998)*

Capital Equipment: Assets listed on an organization's accounting records that have value, usually can be depreciated, and are durable. *(Schiller, 2000)*

Capital Gain:
1. The positive difference between a security's purchase price over the selling price (assuming that the selling price is greater than the purchase price).
2. An increase in the market or accounting value of an asset. *(Schiller, 2000)*

Capital Improvement Plan (CIP): A multi-year plan that forecasts spending for anticipated capital projects and equipment purchases. A typical CIP includes the following steps: identify proposed projects; evaluate proposed projects simultaneously; produce a planning document that considers both financing sources and the timing of the projects; rank the projects based on agency need and perceived community need, determine net present value and/or internal rate of return on the investment; and analyze source of funding for projects, which may include: pay-as-you-go from current income – grants and debt financing – public/private ventures, including privatization or any other financing source. *Also called Capital Improvement Program (CIP).*

Capital Intensive: Production processes that reflect a high ratio of capital to labor inputs. *(Schiller, 2000)*

Capital Lease: *CANADIAN* A lease that transfers substantially all the benefits and risks incident to ownership of the property to the lessee.

Capital Project Funds: Monies from revenues on long-term debt that are used to acquire major assets with a useful life of more than one year, which may be financed by some form of long-term debt.

Cardinal Change: A change that is beyond the scope of the contract, and thus cannot be ordered by the contracting officer under the contract's change clause. Cardinal changes are breaches of contract. They are outside of the scope of the contract.

Cardinal Rule:
1. To give plain meaning to contract terms unless the agency or legislation assigned a special meaning to the term.
2. When silent to an interpretation, cardinal rule allows for the meaning which fits most logically and comfortably into the body of both previously and subsequently enacted law to be utilized.

C

Cargo: A term used to denote goods or produce being transported generally for commercial gain, usually on a ship, plane, train, van or truck. Nowadays containers are used in all intermodal long-haul cargo transport. *(Wikipedia, 2007)*

Carload:
1. The minimum weight, as defined by law, of a shipment entitled to a reduced freight rate.
2. The shipment amount that fills a freight car (or truck).
3. A load that fills the maximum capacity of a transporting unit.

Carrier: A company that transports goods or people, usually over a fixed route and on a fixed schedule. *Also see Common Carrier.*

Carrier's Lien: A carrier's claim on assets pending collection of freight cost or other charges.

Carrying Cost: The cost of keeping inventory on hand including lost opportunity cost, storage cost, handling cost, insurance cost, shrinkage, damage, breakage and obsolescence cost. *Also see Acquisition Cost. (Schiller, 2000)*

Cartage:
1. The act of carting or transporting, generally used to identify local delivery of goods received from a carrier.
2. The cost of such transportation.

Cartel: An organized group (e.g. firms, countries) with an explicit agreement to fix/set prices and output shares in a particular market. Example: OPEC (Oil Producing Exporting Countries). *(Business, 2002)*

Cash Basis Accounting: A financial managing tool that records income when cash is actually received, and records expenses when cash is paid out. Cash basis accounting does not conform with Generally Accepted Accounting Principals (GAAP) and is generally not considered a good financial management tool because there is a time differential between recording the cause of the action (sale or provision of a service) and its results (payment or receipt of money). *Also see Accrual Basis Accounting.*

Cash Discount: A reduction in the full cost of a good or service when payment is made within a specified period of time: e.g. 2% 10 net 30. *Also see Discount, Payment Terms and Prompt Payment Discount.*

Cash Flow: The movement of money through an organization over a daily, weekly, monthly, or yearly basis. The management and monitoring of the cash flow within a business is critical to its financial well being. *(Business, 2002)*

Cash In Advance (CIA): Payment made to a contractor prior to initiating the performance of the contract.

Cash on Delivery (COD): A requirement for full payment for goods and services at time of receipt.

Cash Transfers: Income transfers that entail direct cash payments to recipients, e.g. Social Security payments, welfare, unemployment benefits. *(Schiller, 2000)*

Cataloguing: CANADIAN The various work processes that have to be performed in identifying, classifying, describing, and stock numbering an item of supply.

Cause and Effect Diagrams: Also known as fishbone diagrams, they are a quality control tool which shows the possible cause of a problem. It is an aid to brainstorming and hypothesis generation. *(Business, 2002)*

Caveat Emptor: Latin term which translates to "Let the buyer beware." It implies that the purchaser/buyer is responsible for the quality assurance of a product or service.

Caveat Venditor: Latin term which translates to "Let the seller beware." It implies that the seller/vendor bears responsibility for product defects and inferior quality issues and must satisfy these concerns to the buyer's satisfaction.

CBD: *See Commerce Business Daily.*

CCPPP: *See Canadian Council for Public-Private Partnerships.*

C

Census Bureau: A federal agency of the U.S. Commerce Department that provides access to census figures that can be helpful for supply management strategic planning. It lists a host of demographic data including median household income, education and population statistics. *(www.census.gov)*

Central Accounting System: CANADIAN Part of the Canadian Government accounting system which collects, authenticates, validates, records, and reports all financial transactions of the Canadian Government.

Centralized Purchasing: An organizational structure where all of the rights, powers, duties and authority relating to purchasing are vested in the Chief Procurement Officer (CPO). While the CPO may often delegate some of these powers to others, the final authority nevertheless reside with the CPO. Example: Individual operating departments are permitted to release materials from blanket orders that have been issued by the Purchasing Department or they may use the agency's Procurement Card to make individual purchases for their department. *Also see Decentralized Purchasing.*

Cents per Hundredweight (Cwt.): Transportation/carrier rates are quoted in Cwt. which is determined by dividing the actual weight in pounds by 100.

CERCLA: *See Comprehensive Environmental Response, Compensation and Liability Act.*

Certificate of Compliance: A document submitted by a vendor or manufacturer that provides the buyer with a written assurance that the goods or services delivered fulfill the contractual requirements.

Certificate of Damage: A supply management document prepared by the receiver of goods, establishing that the material delivered and received was damaged and includes a detailed description of the damage and the number of items damaged. May be used to file a damage claim with the carrier.

Certificate of Non-Collusion: A document that may be required, usually by public purchasers, affirming that the bid/offer is made freely and without collusion with another vendor. Sometimes included in the template of the invitation for bids.

Certificate of Origin: A document required by customs officials that identifies the country of origin of the imported goods, and is certified by a U.S. consular official.

Certificates of Deposits (CDs): Savings accounts that guarantee a depositor a set interest rate over a specified interval as long as the funds are not withdrawn before the end of the period—generally six months or one to five years. *(Business, 2002)*

Certification of Cost and Pricing Data: Contractor certification that to the best of the contractor's knowledge and belief, the cost or pricing data submitted was accurate, complete and current as of a mutually determined date prior to the date of the pricing of any contract, change order or modification. Certified Check: A financial instrument whose value is guaranteed by the financial institution upon which the check is drawn. May be required in lieu of a bid bond as a form of bid guarantee.

Certified Professional Contracts Manager (CPCM): A certification issued to qualified individuals by the National Contract Management Association. *(www.ncma.org)*

Certified Professional in Supply Management (CPSM): A certification issued to qualified individuals by the Institute of Supply Management (ISM). The Certified Professional in Supply Management (CPSM) designation is the newest and enhanced designation for supply management professionals replacing the former Certified Purchasing Manager (C.P.M.) designation.

Certified Professional Public Buyer (CPPB): A certification program offered by the Universal Public Purchasing Certification Council (UPPCC). This designation certifies competency in the essential areas of public procurement at the buyer level through application and examination. Unlike other certification programs available in the purchasing field, UPPCC certifications are the only programs designed to meet the needs of purchasing professionals employed in the public sector. *(www.uppcc.org)*

Certified Professional Purchaser (C.P.P.): A designation issued by the Purchasing Management Association of Canada to those who have achieved specified professional qualifications. The Certified Professional Purchaser (C.P.P.) designation sets the national standard for excellence in supply chain management in Canada. *(www.pmac.ca)*

Certified Public Procurement Officer (CPPO): A certification program offered by the Universal Public Procurement Certification Council (UPPCC). This designation certifies competency in the essential areas of public procurement at the supervisory and/or management level through application and examination. Unlike other certification programs available in the purchasing field, UPPCC certifications are the only programs designed to meet the needs of purchasing professionals employed in the public sector. *(www.uppcc.org)*

Certified Purchasing Manager (C.P.M.): A certification issued to qualified individuals by the Institute of Supply Management (ISM). The Certified Purchasing Manager (C.P.M.) designation is globally the most recognized designation for supply management professionals. The program focuses on managerial and leadership skills, plus a variety of specialized functions designed to enhance the value of the profession. *(www.ism.ws)*

CFR: *See Code of Federal Regulations.*

CGCS: *See Canadian Government Catalogue System.*

CGSB: *See Canadian General Standards Board.*

Chain of Command: The line of authority that extends from the highest to the lowest levels of an organization. A hierarchical representation of the organization. May be depicted in an organizational chart. *(Business, 2002)*

Change Order: A written alteration that is issued to modify or amend a contract or purchase order. A bilateral (agreed to by all parties) or unilateral (government orders a contract change without the consent of the contractor) request which directs the contractor to make changes to the contracted scope of work or specifications. In reference to construction contracts, it relates primarily to changes caused by unanticipated conditions encountered during construction not covered by the drawings, plans or specifications of the project. *Also see Amendment, Authorized Deviation, Change Order Authority, Contract Modification and Modification.*

Change Order Authority: Some public agency contracts include the authority to unilaterally modify the current contract without express consent of the contractor. For example, certain supply contracts allow the agency to exceed purchase quantities within an agreed upon percentage range. *Also see Amendment, Authorized Deviation, Change Order, Contract Modification and Modification.*

Changes Clause: A contract clause that specifies the parameters of contract modifications that can be made. Example: Supply contracts typically limit the right to make changes to the method of delivery, place of delivery, or work statements (specifications).

Channel of Distribution (or Marketing Channel): A sequence of marketing organizations that directs a product from the producer/manufacturer to the ultimate user/consumer. *(Business, 2002)*

Charette Process: A public forum where the agency seeks the public's input and to inform them of ideas and plans generally in upcoming construction projects. The public, as well as directly affected stakeholders, have the opportunity to voice their opinions and concerns during the development of the project scope of work and specifications in an effort to arrive at an optimum plan.

Charge-Back: The process of charging the using agency for materials and supplies withdrawn from inventory or from a central stocking location.

C

Chartered Institute of Purchasing and Supply (CIPS): An organization based in the United Kingdom serving the purchasing and supply profession. *(ISM, 2000)*

Chattel: An article of personal, movable property.

Checklist: A form or table included in a solicitation document that identifies all critical information needed to fully comply with all of the requirements of the bidder to make a proper offer. *(Harney, 1992)*

Chief Procurement Officer (CPO): The person holding the position as head of the purchasing office in the agency or jurisdiction.

CI: CANADIAN *See Competitive Intelligence.*

CIA: *See Cash in Advance.*

CIP: *See Capital Improvement Plan.*

CIPS: *See Chartered Institute of Puchasing and Supply.*

Circular A-76 (OMB): The U.S. Office of Management & Budget (OMB) issued Circular A-76 which sets forth a methodology for conducting a make-or-buy decision including how to compute costs and how to make a cost comparison.

CISG: *See United Nation's Convention on Contracts for the International Sale of Goods.*

CITT: *See Canadian International Trade Tribunal.*

Civil Law: A reference to that body of law affecting the relationship among individuals. Contract law is an example of civil law.

Claim: A written assertion or demand, by one of the parties to a contract, which seeks, as a contractual right, payment of money, adjustment of contract terms, or other relief, for injury, loss, or damage arising under or relating to the contract.

Clarification: A communication with an offeror for the sole purpose of eliminating minor irregularities or apparent clerical mistakes in a proposal; may be initiated by either offeror or purchaser; does not give offeror an opportunity to revise or modify its proposal, except to the extent the correction of apparent clerical mistakes results in revision.

Class Award: *See Award by Group.*

Class Code Number: CANADIAN The number that identifies a property class which covers a relatively homogeneous grouping of commodities, grouped together with respect to their similarity of physical or performance characteristics, or grouped together since they are usually requisitioned, stored, and issued together.

Classification: A publication containing a list of items and the classes to which they are assigned for the purpose of applying class freight rates, along with governing rules and regulations.

Classification of Defects: The process of arranging defects in classes or groupings in accordance with a specific schema, for example, by severity of defect such as major, critical, or minor.

Class-Item Code: Part 1 of the NIGP Commodity/Service Code consisting of five digits and containing more than 6000 item descriptions; used to facilitate the open market aspects of the purchasing function.

Class Rate: The transportation charge applicable for groups of similar commodities shipped by common carrier if no specific commodity rate, or exception, has been established. The most expensive LTL (Less than truck load) freight rate. *Also see Commodity Rate, Uniform Freight Classification and National Motor Freight Classification.*

Clawback: Contingent monies or considerations previously disbursed that are returned due to unrealized fulfillment of terms upon which the considerations were distributed.

Clayton Act (The Clayton Anti-Trust Act) (U.S. Law): A 1914 supplement to the Sherman Anti-Trust Act. Regulates general business practices that may be detrimental to fair competition. Some of the business practices regulated by the

Clayton Act are: price discrimination; exclusive dealing contracts; mergers and acquisitions and interlocking directorates. *Also see Sherman Antitrust Act and Price Fixing.*

Clean Bill of Lading: *See Bill of Lading.*

Clerical Mistake: A mistake of a contractor in a bid or proposal that results from a clerical error; often referred to as a "minor irregularity." Such mistakes usually may be corrected within a specified period. Examples may include the misplacement of a decimal point or the reversal of prices.

Click-and-Ship: A sales operation where customers order products online and the product is shipped directly to the customer. On-line ordering of products used to facilitate Just-in-Time procurement. May be referred to as "Point-Click-Buy-Ship". *(Jansen, 2002)*

Client Agency: Identifies the name and address of the organization on whose behalf the bid request has been submitted. *(Summit Magazine, On-Line)*

Client/Server: A relationship in which one computer program requests information from another computer program. The design model for applications running on a network. *(Jansen, 2002)*

Closed Corporation: A corporation whose stock is owned by relatively few people and is not sold to the general public. *(Business, 2002)*

Closing Date/Time: Refers to the date and time for bid closing. The latest date and time a bid will be accepted by the entity. Bids received after the closing time will be rejected as non-responsive.

CMR: *See Construction Manager at Risk.*

COB: Close of business. Refers to the end of business day; sometimes used to specify time by which an event must occur.

COD: *See Cash on Delivery.*

Code of Ethics: A guide to acceptable and ethical behavior as defined by an organization or public body. A standard of behavior adopted by an organization. Written policies or guidelines which apply to the ethical behavior of members of an organization, business or public entity. *(NASPO, 2001)*

Code of Federal Regulations (CFR): The codification of the general and permanent rules published in the Federal Register by the Executive departments and agencies of the United States Federal Government.

Coincident Indicator: A measure of economic activity that changes concurrently with changes in the business cycle. *(ISM, 2000)*

Coinsurance Clause: A part of a fire insurance policy that requires the policyholder to purchase coverage at least equal to a specified percentage of the replacement cost of the property to obtain full reimbursement for losses. *(Business, 2002)*

COLA: *See Cost-of-Living-Adjustment.*

Collaborative Learning System: A work environment that allows problem-solving participation by all team members. Used by procurement managers to obtain a more participatory work environment. *(Business, 2002)*

Collaborative Relationships: A phase in the continuum of Buyer-Seller Relationships whereby the interdependence and necessity of cooperation is the difference between a collaborative and transactional relationship. Lower total costs are the common result of this type of relationship. *(Burt, Dobler, Starling, 2003)*

Collateral:

1. Anything of value that is acceptable to a lender to guarantee repayment of a loan.
2. Real or personal property pledged as security for a loan.

Collective Bargaining: Direct negotiations between employers and unions to determine labor market outcomes. May include wages, benefits, security and safety issues. Usually results in a contract of a specified duration. For more information: www.bls.gov *(US Bureau of Labor Statistics)*

Collusion: When two or more parties act together secretly to achieve a fraudulent or unlawful act. May manifest itself in the form of bid collu-

C

sion when bidders secretly agree to unlawful practices regarding competitive bidding. May inhibit free and open competition in violation of antitrust laws. *Also see Identical Bid.*

Collusive Bidding: A secret agreement among bidders/offerors to circumvent laws and regulation when submitting bids and offers in an attempt to win contracts by illegal means or methods.

Combination Design and Performance Specification: Specifications that incorporate, to the degree necessary, the attributes of both design and performance specifications.

Combustible Liquid: Any liquid having a flash point above 100 and below 200 degrees Fahrenheit as defined by the U.S. Department of Transportation (DOT). May create inventory and supply management issues. *(Miller, 2006)*

Command Economy: A mode of economic organization in which key economic functions (what, how, and for whom) are principally determined by government directive. Sometimes called a centrally planned economy. *(Schiller, 2000)*

Commerce Business Daily (CBD): A daily publication of the United States Department of Commerce listing U.S. Government solicitations, contract awards, subcontracting leads, sales of surplus property and foreign business opportunities. *(U.S. Department of Commerce)*

Commercial Grade Product: A product that has been designed and sold by the manufacturer to be more durable, or more powerful or more longer lasting or having a larger capacity in comparison to its consumer grade product counterpart; designed to meet a more demanding application or operating need or requirements and generally costs more versus the consumer grade product. Generally the internal product's component parts are of a higher quality or more durable materials such as motors, bearings, metal versus plastic which are generally not visible to the end user but result in longer product life expectancy and performance. Example: Maytag Corporation makes a line of consumer grade washing machines for use in the home and it also makes a line of commercial grade product washing machines for use in laundromats, nursing homes and hospitals. *Also see Consumer Grade Product.*

Commercial Law: Principles and rules by which rights and obligations in commercial business transactions are determined, as found in the Uniform Commercial Code. *(NASPO, 2001)*

Commercial Paper: A short–term promissory note issued by a large corporation. *(Ferrell, Hirt, 2003)*

Commission:
1. The compensation of an agent or broker when calculated as a percentage of the amount of the transaction or the profit to the principal.
2. An allowance to a sales representative or agent for services rendered.

Commission Merchant: An agent or broker who buys or sells goods for others in return for a commission.

Commitment Authority: *CANADIAN* The authority delegated to appropriate officers to confirm before a commitment is entered into, as required under financial authority, that there is a sufficient unencumbered balance to discharge such commitment.

Commodity:
1. *CANADIAN* Any moveable, tangible article of trade or commerce.
2. *US* Something useful that can be turned to commercial advantage; anything that can be processed and resold.

Commodity Classification: The schema that identifies commodities according to type, class, size, composition, or manufacturer.

Commodity Code: A system of words and numbers designed to identify and list commodities or services by classes and subclasses. *See the NIGP Commodity/Service Code.*

Commodity Group: A grouping of related items, all of which can be further refined into additional commodity classes within the commodity group.

Commodity Rate: A published tariff applicable to the shipment of a specific commodity in large quantities between selected geographical points. *Also see Class Rate.*

Common Carrier: An entity that, without right of refusal, provides transportation services to the general public as required by law. *Also see Contract Carrier and Private Carrier.* *(Blacks Law Dictionary 275, 1990)*

Common Law:
1. Law based on custom and usage, or confirmed by court decisions, rather than law created by the enactment of legislative bodies.
2. The body of law created by court decisions rendered by judges; also known as case law or judicial law.
3. Principles and rules by which rights and obligations in commercial transactions are determined, found in the Uniform Commercial Code (2) business law.

Common Market: A regional market with common external tariffs and free flow of labor and capital, without internal tariffs. *(ISM, 2000)*

Common Stock: Stock owned by individuals or firms who may vote on corporate matters, but whose claims on profit and assets are subordinate to the claims of others. *(Ferrell, Hirt, 2003)*

Comparable Worth: A concept that seeks equal compensation for jobs requiring the same level of education, training and skills. *(Business, 2002)*

Comparative Advantage: The ability of a country or firm to produce a specific good or service at a lower cost than its rivals or competitors. The ability to produce a specific product or service more efficiently than any other producer. *Also see Absolute Advantage.* *(Ferrell, Hirt, 2003)*

Compensable Delays: Compensation received by a contractor for increased cost as a result of a delay when the agency orders work to be suspended. Example: The agency hires a construction company to begin work on a new highway bridge. During the excavation portion of the project, the contractor found the remains of Indian artifacts and the project was put on hold until archeologists could assess the situation and collect the artifacts. As a result of this delay, which was ordered by the agency, this was a compensable delay to the contractor.

Competent Parties: Persons legally capable of entering into a contract. Must be of legal age, not be insane, etc. For a contract to be valid, both parties must be in a position to enter into a contract and be capable of doing so. *(ISM, 2000)*

Competition: A rivalry among businesses for sales to potential customers. The "invisible hand" (refer to the writings of Adam Smith). The effort of two or more parties acting independently to secure the business of a third party by offering the most favorable terms (including price). *(Ferrell, Hirt, 2003)*

Competition Code: CANADIAN A code describing whether or not the award process was competitive.

Competitive Advantage: The advantage one competitor may have over another due to various factors such as better use of technology, geographic location (resulting in lower transportation costs), more productive employees, etc. While competitive advantage is healthy for the market place, supply managers must be aware of unfair competitive advantage and its various manifestations. *(Ferrell, Hirt, 2003)*

Competitive Bid Solicitation: CANADIAN Solicitation of two or more qualified sources by invitation or public notice for the same requirements.

Competitive Bidding: The process of inviting and obtaining bids from competing sources in response to advertised competitive specifications, by which an award is made to the lowest and best bidder meeting the specifications. The process contemplates giving potential bidders a reasonable opportunity to bid, and requires that all bidders be placed on the same plane of equality. Each bidder must bid on the same advertised specifications, terms, and conditions in all the items and parts of a contract. The purpose of competitive bidding is to stimulate competition, prevent favoritism, and secure the best goods and services at the lowest practicable

C

price, for the benefit of the agency. Competitive bidding cannot occur where contract specifications, terms, or conditions prevent or unduly restrict competition, favor a particular supplier, or increase the cost of goods or services without providing a corresponding benefit to the agency.

Competitive Contract: *CANADIAN* A contract where the process used for the solicitation of bids assures that a reasonable and representative number of suppliers are given an opportunity to bid.

Competitive Intelligence (CI): *CANADIAN* Involves gathering and analyzing information about customers, competitors and the marketplace to support successful business decisions. *(Summit Magazine, On-Line)*

Competitive Market: A particular market in which no buyer or seller has an advantage or possesses market power over a product or service. *(Schiller, 2000)*

Competitive Negotiations: A procurement method for obtaining goods, services and construction for public use in which discussion and negotiations may be conducted with responsible offerors who submit responsive proposals. *Also see Competitive Sealed Proposal.*

Competitive Range: That group of proposals, as determined during the evaluation process for competitive negotiation, which includes only those offerors considered to have a reasonable chance of being selected for award and who are therefore chosen for additional discussions and negotiations. Proposals not in the competitive range are given no further consideration.

Competitive Re-engineering: An outsourcing issue that allows the employees of a public agency the opportunity to re-design their work process in order to achieve efficiency and cost savings. This may be done prior to subjecting the targeted work function to competition against private contractors. *(Business, 2002)*

Competitive Sealed Bidding: Preferred method for acquiring goods, services, and construction for public use in which award is made to the lowest responsive and responsible bidder, based solely on the response to the criteria set forth in the IFB; does not include discussions or negotiations with bidders. *May also be referred to as formal advertised bid. Also see Formal Bid.*

Competitive Sealed Proposals: *See Competitive Negotiation. Also see Competitive Sealed Bidding.*

Completion Bond: *See Performance Bond.*

Completion Payment: Payment made upon successful completion of the work.

Compliance Audit: An audit conducted to determine the degree of compliance with established procedures and policies relative to accounting, financial and business processes.

Composite Sample: A sample obtained by mixing together equal portions from several parts of the lot.

Comprehensive Environmental Response, Compensation and Liability Act (CERCLA): This Act defines hazardous waste as "toxic, ignitable, corrosive, or dangerously reactive substances". Under the CERCLA, a "generator" is an organization that uses or produces hazardous waste. Federal law stipulates that generators are responsible for the safe use and handling from the time the hazardous waste is created until it is completely destroyed. This "cradle to grave" responsibility, which cannot be delegated, includes the packaging used to transport the materials. Under the CERCLA, a "shipper" is a transporter licensed by transportation departments of federal and state environmental protection agencies to dispose of hazardous waste. Example: The proper disposal of old automobile tires, automobile car batteries, fluorescent light tubes, personal computers, televisions, photocopy machines and other hazardous items. This law was originally created to tax the chemical and petroleum industries. The tax is used by a broad federal authority to clean up abandoned or uncontrolled hazardous waste sites. The law provides 1) short term removal and 2) long term remedy that permanently reduces danger. *Also referred to as the Superfund.*

Comptroller: The individual within an organization who is responsible for the organization's accounting and financial management functions.

Computer-Aided Design (CAD): The use of computer systems to assist in the design and development of products. *(Jansen, 2002)*

Computer-Aided Manufacturing (CAM): The use of computer systems to design, plan and control manufacturing processes. *(Burt, Dobler, Starling, 2003)*

Concealed Damage: Damage that may occur during shipment of goods which is not apparent or noticeable.

Conceptual Skills: The ability to think in abstract terms. *(Ferrell, Hirt, 2003)*

Concession Model: Agency contracts with a person, group or company to run a portion of a government-owned facility such as the selling of food at the snack bar in an agency-owned ice skating rink. *Also see Public Private Partnership.*

Conciliation: A form of negotiation used in alternative dispute resolution (ADR). It involves building a positive relationship between the parties to a dispute by using a third party or conciliator. Conciliation may assist in the settling of disputes that have reached an impasse.

Conditional Sale: A sale made with the understanding that title will not pass from the vendor to the purchaser until some prerequisite condition has been met, although possession may be surrendered to the buyer.

Confidential Information: Information, such as trade secrets or test data, which is made known only to those who need to know, only because of a compelling reason. Such information must be protected and is not a matter of public knowledge. Best practice would require that such information be clearly identified and labeled. *Also see Proprietary Information and Trade Secret.* *(Harney, 1992)*

Confirmation Order: A purchase order issued to a supplier, listing the commodities and terms of an order placed verbally, or otherwise, in advance of the issuance of the purchase order. *Also see Confirming Purchase Order.*

Confirming Purchase Order: A purchase order issued after the fact restating the same terms originally placed orally, or by some other informal means. *Also see Confirmation Order.*

Conflict of Interest: A clash between the public interest and the private pecuniary interest of the individual concerned. *(Blacks Law Dictionary, 299, 1990).* The term identifies those situations where contractors or public officials may obtain a benefit from a public contract. Conflicts of Interest may result in a breach of ethics or an ethical code. Actual or Perceived Conflict of Interest: Any action, decision or recommendation by an agent or public official acting in an official capacity, the effect of which could be to the private pecuniary benefit or detriment of the person or person's relative.

Conflict Resolution: A process leading to resolve a contractual conflict or opposition such as the public agency's policy to try to resolve by mutual agreement all contractual issues in controversy. These procedures may include such actions as fact-finding, negotiation, facilitation, mini-trials, mediation or arbitration.

Consequential Damages: The loss of revenues and/or profits incurred by a purchaser as a result of a seller's breach; may involve injury to a person or property, including loss of life or business. *(ISM, 2000)*

Consequentialism: An ethical decision-making model which calls attention to all stakeholders and requires the decision maker to predict the likely results of an act and weigh the good it will produce against the harm it will cause.

Consideration:

1. Something of value which is exchanged by two parties and which serves to form or bind a contract.
2. A type of mutual commitment that must exist to form an express contract.
3. That which is given or promised in order to bring a binding contract into existence.

C

Consignee: A person, company, or government agency, usually the buyer, to whom goods are to be delivered by the consignor.

Consignment: The goods or property shipped via a common carrier from one location to another.

Consignment Buying: A method of procurement in which a supplier maintains inventory on the premises of the purchaser. The purchaser's obligation to pay for the goods begins when goods are drawn from the stock. *(ISM, 2000)*

Consignor: A person or company that ships goods to another (the shipper).

Consolidator: A carrier that collects small shipments from several shippers and consolidates them into larger shipments (truckloads, carloads, containers) for delivery to the consignee.

Consolidated Purchasing: *See Joint Administrative Purchasing.*

Consortium: *See Cooperative Purchasing.* A group of purchasing entities join forces in the purchasing of selected products and services used by the group. The aggregation of need and joint purchase usually results in lower pricing as a result of economies of scale. *Also see Cooperative Procurement.* *(Burt, Dobler, Starling, 2003)*

Construction: The process of utilizing labor to build, alter, repair, improve, or demolish any structure, building or public improvement; generally does not apply to routine maintenance, repair, or operation (MRO) of existing real property.

Construction Management: A method of acquiring construction in which the public agency contracts with a construction manager to assist in project design and construction. The construction manager may act as the agent for the government in assisting in the award of contracts for elements of the project. *(Nash, Schooner, O'Brien, 1998)*

Construction Manager at Risk (CMR): A construction contracting method, often referred to as an alternate construction delivery method, in which the owner enters into separate contracts with the designer and builder, often at or about the same time so that both parties can collaborate. Selection is based on an evaluation of qualifications and price, and the contractor offers a Guaranteed Maximum Price (GMP) instead of a fixed bid. The GMP serves as a ceiling which decreases (in theory) as the design is refined and advanced. The delta between GMP and actual cost is considered savings, which is often shared through an incentive formula. A firm fixed price may be negotiated once the design is advanced to 60% or better. The Construction Manager at Risk is responsible and accepts risk for constructing the entire project for the GMP and the contractor is responsible for assembling the team of suppliers and subcontractors.

Constructive Change: Oral or written communications, an act or omission by the contracting officer or other authorized government official that is construed as having the same effect as a written Change Order. Claims for constructive changes are the primary means used by contractors to obtain additional compensation for performing fixed price contracts. Common types of constructive changes are claims concerning contract interpretation, defective specifications, nondisclosure of information, impracticability of performance, breach of the duty to cooperate and acceleration.

Constructive Suspension: An action in which an agency is responsible for a work stoppage without a contract suspension. Examples include agency convenience, funding delays, and delays that include issuance of the notice to proceed or change orders, site availability, inspection or approvals. A contractor may be entitled to compensation for increased costs after consideration and documentation of a constructive suspension.

Consul: An official appointed by a government to look after its business in a foreign city.

Consular Invoice: An invoice certified by the consulate of the destination country to assure collection of import duties in that country.

Consultant:
1. To work or serve in an advisory capacity.
2. A person or company that possesses unique qualifications which allow them to perform specialized advisory services usually for a fee. *Also see Consulting Services.*

Consulting Services: Services of an advisory nature required to support policy development, decision-making, administration, or management of a business or public entity; generally provided by individuals or organizations who possess specific knowledge, technical skills or unique abilities not usually available in-house or from within the entity. *Also see Consultant.*

Consumable Item: CANADIAN Materiel that is expended or consumed in use and for which no records are maintained after issue.

Consumer: Those individuals that satisfy their wants and desires by consuming a good or a service. *(Schiller, 2000)*

Consumer Grade Product: A product designed and sold by the manufacturer intended to be used for personal use; products intended for intermittent use by the consumer. Example: Conair makes a consumer grade product hair dryer that is intended to be used occasionally by the consumer for up to 20 minutes per day and it also makes a commercial grade product hair dryer that is used professionally by hair cutting salons for frequent and continuous use throughout the 12 hour business day. Manufacturers may indicate "household use only" on the product's label to inform the user of the product's intended use and performance expectancy. *Also see Commercial Grade Product.*

Consumer Price Index (CPI): A measure of changes in the average price of consumer goods and services. A price index constructed monthly by the U.S. Bureau of Labor Statistics that provides a statistical measure of the average change in prices in a fixed market basket of goods and services. It is frequently called a cost-of-living index. For more information: www.bls.gov/cpi.

Consumer Product Safety Commission (CPSC): Independent federal agency created in 1972 to develop and enforce product standards, conduct research, and inform consumers to ensure their safety in the use of consumer products. For recall notices see www.cpcs.gov *(ISM, 2000)*

Consumerism: All activities undertaken to protect the rights of consumers. *(Business, 2002)*

Consumption: Expenditures by consumers on final goods and services. The using up of goods and services by consumer purchasing. Consumer spending on goods and services produced by the economy in a given period. In macroeconomics, the total spending, by individual or a nation, or consumer goods during a given period. *(Schiller, 2000)*

Consumption Rate: The pace at which items are used or expended during a given time interval.

Container: A truck trailer body that can be detached from the chassis for loading onto a vessel, a railcar, or stacked in a container depot. They come in various lengths between 20' and 53'. *(Business, 2002)*

Containerization: The process of packing goods in very large, separate containers (sometimes referred to as "cubes") for shipment to a final destination. Container shipment may be via ship, rail or truck.

Contingency Planning: Planning that applies to issues resulting from a crisis, emergency or interruption of a critical service.

Contingent Fee: A commission, percentage or other fee that is conditional upon the success that a person or concern has in securing a contract.

Continuity of Operations Plan (COOP): A detailed strategy developed to ensure the continuation of essential functions during an emergency that result in the inability of the organization to provide essential services to its constituents. The COOP must be a fluid and dynamic plan capable of being immediately adjusted and modified depending on the situation. A well-developed COOP addresses the people, processes, systems, and infrastructure elements that will be needed to continue to perform essential functions during a disaster or emergency situation. *Also referred to as Business Continuity Plan.*

Continuous Improvement: A process for improving an organization's performance along several criteria, particularly quality, over a period of time. An outcome generally included in a total quality management program. *Also see Total Quality Management (TQM).* (Burt, Dobler, Starling, 2003)

Contract:
1. A contract is an obligation, such as an accepted offer, between competent parties upon a legal consideration, to do or abstain from doing some act. The essentials elements of a contract are: an offer and an acceptance of that offer; the capacity of the parties to contract; consideration to support the contract; a mutual identity of consent; legality of purpose; and definiteness.
2. A legally binding promise, enforceable by law.
3. An agreement between parties with binding legal and moral force, usually exchanging goods or services for money or other considerations.
4. Under the Canadian Government Contracts Regulations, a contract means a construction contract, a goods contract, a service contract, or a lease entered into by or on behalf of Her Majesty by contracting authority.

Contract A – Bid Contract: *CANADIAN* A legally binding obligation formed between an "owner" (purchaser) and a bidder based on the submission of a responsive bid in a competitive process. *Also known as submission of price.*

Contract B – Traditional Contract: *CANADIAN* Formed between the government or agency (Owner) and the successful bidder when the agency formally accepts a Bid.

Contract Acquisition Plan: *See Contract Administration Plan (CAP).*

Contract Adjusted Amount: *CANADIAN* The dollar value for a contract reflecting adjustments made for changes such as foreign currency fluctuations or inflation.

Contract Administration: Following the award of a contract, the management actions that must be taken to assure full compliance with all of the terms and conditions contained within the contract document, including price. Action steps that assure that the contractor is in full compliance with the entire contract. Contract administration activities include payment, monitoring of progress, inspection and acceptance, quality assurance, monitoring and surveillance, modifications, negotiations, contract closeout, and other activities. *Also see Contract Management and Surveillance.*

Contract Administration Plan (CAP): A planning tool that provides the framework for effective contract administration with an emphasis on process, output and outcome. The length and detail of the CAP depends on the complexity and potential risk of the contract. *Also referred to as Contract Acquisition Plan.*

Contract Administration Team: A cross-functional team comprised of such members as the procurement contracting officer, subject matter expert, IT, engineering, legal advisers, price and cost analysts, quality assurance specialists, contracting officer's representative who all offer their expertise to the contract. Such a team is generally used on complex projects. This team may also assist in resolving conflict that arises during the contract performance.

Contract, Amended Amount: *CANADIAN* Total cost in Canadian dollars of the contract reflecting the cumulative impact of the original amount and all contract amendments.

Contract Amendment: *CANADIAN* An agreed addition to, deletion from, correction or modification of a contract. *Also see Contract Modification.*

Contract Amount/Value: *CANADIAN* Total dollar amount negotiated between buyer and seller and identified in the contract for purchase of services.

Contract Award: The final agreement on the terms and conditions of a contract between a buyer and seller.

Contract Carrier: A person or company that is under contract to transport people or goods for individual contract customers only. *Also see Common Carrier and Private Carrier.*

Contract Ceiling: Maximum amount available for payment of cost and fee, which the contractor cannot exceed without approval of the purchasing authority.

Contract Commencement Date: The date on which all parties accept a contract thereto; the date of contract award. Maybe referred to as contract date. *(Harney, 1992)*

Contract Completion Date: CANADIAN The date that the contract was closed in the financial accounts.

Contract Extension: An action to change and extend a contract termination date pursuant to a provision in the scope of work and upon written mutual agreement by both parties. Reasons for a contract extension include: an excusable delay, a contractor's acceptable performance record, unused allocated funding, or agency need for continued service until a new contract is in place. Extension should be based on sound legal advice so as to avoid challenges by other interested vendors. A contract extension is not the same as a contract renewal. Also called Extension of Contract.

Contract Goals: A term generally used in construction projects in seeking a good faith effort on the part of the prime contractor to have a certain level of minority subcontracting participation in the agency's project. *Also see Goals and Set-Asides.*

Contract Management: The overarching process that a governmental agency will use to ensure that the contractor has performed in accordance with the performance standards contained within the statement of work (SOW) or the Performance Work Statement (PWS). A quality assurance plan contained within the contract. May include: 100% Inspection, Random Sampling, Periodic Inspection, Customer Input, as well as other methodologies. May also be referred to as Surveillance. *Also see Contract Administration and Surveillance.*

Contract Management: CANADIAN Pertains to the activities of the contracting or purchasing authority and centers around such areas as issuance of a request for proposal, tendering activities, contract award and subsequent amending activities.

Contract Modification: Any written alteration in specifications, delivery point, frequency of delivery, period of performance, price, quantity, or other provisions of the contract, accomplished by mutual agreement of the parties to the contract. *Also see Amendment, Authorized Deviation, Change Order and Contract Amendment.*

Contract Number: An alpha-numeric code which uniquely identifies a contract

Contract Original Amount: CANADIAN The original award value for a contract.

Contract Planning: The process by which the efforts of all personnel responsible for an acquisition are coordinated and integrated through a comprehensive plan for fulfilling the needs of the government in a timely manner and at a reasonable cost. *(Federal Acquisition Institute, 1999, p.6-6)*

Contract Rates: Agreed upon transportation rates between a shipper and a carrier. *(NASPO, 2001)*

Contract Record: A report providing detailed information regarding the orders or releases placed for delivery of goods against a contract so the volume of contract purchases can be determined.

Contract Renewal: A renewal clause allows an agreement to continue for a defined period if the existing agreement isn't renegotiated within a specified time measured from the expiration of the current contract. The term of renewal depends on the specific contract language, but such clauses generally provide that the contract shall be automatically renewed for the same period (or some lesser term) unless either party, at some stipulated and predetermined time (i.e., 60 days before expiration), gives notice to the other of its desire to end the agreement.

Contract Signing Authority: CANADIAN The authority delegated to occupy a position, that is, the incumbent of a position, to sign on his/her behalf contract, contract amendment or Standing Offer documents after ascertaining that the approval authority has been duly granted and ensuring that the terms and conditions written in the documents reflect those approved by the contract approval authority. *(Summit Magazine, On-Line)*

Contract Status Code: CANADIAN A code assigned to each milestone in the procurement process.

Contracted Delivery Date: CANADIAN The date agreed to under the terms and conditions of a contract.

Contracting Authority: CANADIAN The authority delegated to persons for entering into and approving contracts and arrangements.

Contracting Officer: A person with the authority to enter into, administer, and/or terminate contracts, and make related determinations and findings.

Contracting Out: The process of having services performed by private contractors rather than by employees of the public agency. *Also see Outsourcing and Insourcing.* *(Harney, 1992)*

Contractor: Any individual or business having a contract with a governmental body to furnish goods, services, or construction for an agreed-upon price.

Contracts Canada: CANADIAN An inter-departmental initiative to improve supplier and buyer awareness and simplify access to Federal Government purchasing information. *(Summit Magazine, On-Line)*

Contractual Arrangement: CANADIAN An agreement between a contracting authority and entity of the Crown (e.g. Crown corporations, provincial governments or municipalities) to provide a good, perform a service, construct a work or to lease real property, for appropriate consideration. These types of agreements are not contracts in the true sense but are still subject to certain limits or constraints imposed by the Treasury Board.

Controlled Items: CANADIAN Items of supply that are both accountable items or non-accountable items, which for administrative purposes, require special controls beyond those normally employed.

Convenience Product: A relatively inexpensive, frequently purchased item for which buyers want to exert only minimum effort to obtain. *(Schiller, 2000)*

Conversion: The transformation of materials into economic goods and services. Manufacturing is a conversion activity. *(Schiller, 2000)*

Conversion Costs (One-Time Conversion Costs): Costs that are incurred due to change in service delivery from in-house to a privatized contract. They may be either personnel related or material related. Personnel related costs can include accrued annual and sick leave benefits owed public employees and any other severance type costs. Material related costs can include costs associated with the preparation and transfer of facilities or equipment to the contractor or other costs such as: penalties for terminating leases and the costs of maintaining underutilized facilities or equipment until they are sold or leased.

Convertibility: The ability to exchange a country's currency for currencies of other nations. *(Schiller, 2000)*

Conveyance:

1. A formal written instrument, usually called a deed, by which title or other interest in real property is transferred from one person to another.
2. A means of transporting goods or people; a carrier such as a railroad, car, truck, vessel, barge, or airplane.

COOP: *See Continuity of Operations Plan.*

Cooperative Agreement: A federal grant to support a joint federal/state program in which the grantor (Federal Government) and the grantee (state government) share in the management decisions about the funded activity.

Cooperative Problem-Solving: An alternative dispute resolution (ADR) technique which is one of the most basic methods of dispute resolution. This informal process usually does not use the services of a third party and typically takes place when the concerned parties agree to resolve a question or issue of mutual concern. It is a positive effort by the parties to collaborate rather than compete to resolve a dispute.

Cooperative Procurement (Purchasing):
1. The action taken when two or more entities combine their requirements to obtain advantages of volume purchases including administrative savings and other benefits.
2. A variety of arrangements whereby two or more public procurement units purchase from the same supplier or multiple suppliers using a single IFB or RFP.
3. Cooperative procurement efforts may result in contracts that other entities may "piggyback". *Also see Consortium.*

Cooperative Supply: CANADIAN Federal, provincial or local governments may, where it is advantageous for them to do so, provide goods and services to each other. *(Summit Magazine, On-Line)*

Copyright:
1. The exclusive right to publish, perform, copy, or sell an original work. The length of copyright protection is based on the author's life plus 70 years. *(Copyright Act of 1976)*
2. The legal right to exclusive publication, production, sale or distribution of a literary or artistic work. Provides its holder the right to restrict unauthorized copying and reproduction of an original expression. *(www.encyclopedia.thefreedictionery.com)*
3. CANADIAN An exclusive statutory right of those such as authors, publishers, composers, etc. to control the publication/dispositions of their works of art, literature, music, films, pictures, etc., which is protected by the Copyright Act of Canada, under the Geneva Convention of 1952 to which Canada became a party in 1962. *(Summit Magazine, On-Line)*

Core Competencies: Those functions of an organization in which the business is most competent. The critical areas of expertise within the organization. *(Business, 2002)*

Corporate Bond: A corporation's written pledge that it will repay a specified amount of money, with interest. *(Business, 2002)*

Corporate Charter: A contract between the corporation and the state, in which the state recognizes the formation of the corporation as being endowed by law with the rights and liabilities of an individual. *(Ferrell, Hirt, 2003)*

Corporate Culture: The rites, rituals, heroes, stories, history and values of an organization. *(Business, 2002)*

Corporate Officers: The chairman/chairwoman of the board, president, executive vice presidents, corporate secretary, and treasurer, or any other top executives appointed by the board of directors. *(Business, 2002)*

Corporate Stock: Shares of ownership in a corporation. *(Business, 2002)*

Corporation: A body formed and authorized by law to act as a single person, with most of the legal rights of a real person, including the rights to start and operate a business, to buy or sell property, to borrow money, to sue or be sued, and to enter into binding contracts. A legal entity owned by stockholders whose liability is limited to the value of their stock. *(Business, 2002)*

Correction (Prison) Industries: An organization established to sell/market products manufactured, fabricated or assembled by incarcerated persons in penal systems operated by a public entity.

Cost: The actual expenses incurred in delivering a product, service, or construction; includes both direct and indirect costs, but does not include fee or profit for the vendor.

Cost Adjusted: CANADIAN The dollar value of materiel items adjusted for upgrades, deterioration in condition, or other changes.

C

Cost Analysis: The review and evaluation of cost data for the purpose of arriving at costs actually incurred or estimates of costs to be incurred. A cost analysis should be employed when price analysis is impractical or does not allow a purchaser to reach the conclusion that a price is fair and reasonable. Cost analysis is most useful when purchasing nonstandard items and services. *Also see Cost Breakdown.* *(Burt, Dobler, Starling, 2003)*

Cost and Freight (C & F): A quoted price that includes both the cost of an item and transportation charges to the destination; commonly used when shipping via ocean freight.

Cost Avoidance: Actions taken to avoid having to pay some sort of cost – this could be financial (i.e. by negotiating an extension to current prices when the entity becomes aware that price increases are likely to occur) or in resource terms (i.e. the use of cooperative arrangements mean the organization "avoids" the time and work involved in completing a bidding or contracting exercise on its own behalf). Well defined specifications and value analysis will help to avoid extraneous costs. *(Spikes Cavell, 2011)*

Cost-Based Pricing: A method in which a fixed sum or percentage of the total cost is added as an income or profit to the cost of the product to arrive at its selling price.

Cost-Benefit Analysis (Study): A comparative evaluation of the trade-off between the cost of a good or service and the value or benefit to be obtained in order to choose among alternatives. *(Business, 2002)*

Cost Breakdown: The detailed analysis of the contractor's pricing that may include overhead and profit. *Also see Cost Analysis.* *(Burt, Dobler, Starling, 2003)*

Cost Containment: A detailed plan to hold costs and purchase prices within certain target limits over a period of time. *(ISM, 2000)*

Cost Contract: A cost-reimbursement contract in which the contractor receives no fee. *See Cost-Reimbursement Contract.*

Cost (Pricing) Data: Factual information about the actual or estimated costs of labor, material, overhead and other cost elements which are expected to be incurred by the contractor in performing the contract and which are allowable and allocable.

Cost Drivers: The factors and forces that influence the nature and level of cost incurred by an enterprise. *(ISM, 2000)*

Cost Element: A direct or indirect cost of providing a good, service, or construction, such as labor, materials, fringe benefits, or travel.

Cost Estimate: A forecast amount as distinguished from an actual outlay, based upon related cost information available at the time and anticipated future conditions. The process of calculating the probable cost of a job.

Cost, Insurance, Freight (c.i.f.): A quoted price that includes marine insurance in addition to the cost of the item and transportation charges to destination; commonly used when shipping via ocean freight.

Cost, Labour: *CANADIAN* An expenditure for manual labour measured by the amount paid.

Cost Objective: A function, organizational unit, or contract for which costs are to be determined and cost data accumulated.

Cost of Goods Sold: The dollar amount equal to beginning inventory plus net purchases less ending inventory. *(Schiller, 2000)*

Cost-of-Living-Adjustment (COLA): An automatic adjustment of nominal payment tied to the rate of inflation. *(Schiller, 2000)*

Cost or Pricing Data: All facts which prudent purchasers and vendors would reasonably expect to affect price negotiations significantly.

Cost Ordering: *CANADIAN* In calculating economic order quantity, the costs which increase with the number of orders placed; includes costs related to the clerical work of preparing, issuing, following and receiving orders, physical handling of goods, inspection, and machine set-up costs, if the order is being manufactured.

C

Cost, Original: The original cost for which a good or service was acquired; for equipment purchases it may include shipping, installation and other associated costs.

Cost Plus Award Fee Contract (CPAF): A cost reimbursement contract that provides for a base fee amount fixed at inception of a contract, and an additional fee to be determined at time of fee award that is based on an evaluation by the purchaser as to the quality of the contract performance, and the evaluator's assessment as to the fee amount necessary to motivate the contractor toward excellence.

Cost Plus Fixed Fee Contract (CPFF): A contract whereby the contractor is reimbursed for its actual incurred cost for material, labor and other agreed to incidentals, plus a fixed sum established in the contract. *(Harney, 1992)*

Cost Plus Incentive Fee Contract (CPIF): A contract whereby the contractor receives additional compensation for keeping the total amount expended below the agreed-upon maximum contract amount or for achieving certain pre-specified goals during the performance of the contract. Often used in construction contracts in order to assure completion of the building project prior to the targeted completion date.

Cost Plus Percentage of Cost Contracts: An agreement on a construction project in which the contractor is provided a specified percentage profit over and above the actual costs of construction. These contracts are considered poor business practice because the contractor has little incentive to hold down costs. This type of costing method is prohibited in Federal purchasing. A cost-plus-fixed-fee contract is a better approach.

Cost Principles: The regulatory principles used to determine the allowability of incurred costs for the purposes of reimbursement under the provisions of the contract.

Cost Realism: A factor considered during cost analysis of a proposal to determine if the costs proposed are realistic in light of historical experience, costs on similar projects, market conditions over the life of the proposal, or other factors.

Cost Reduction: Generally realized when a manufacturer is able to lower the material or labor costs used to make its products; interchangeably used to indicate a lower price paid by the buyer from what was previously paid. *Also see Price Reduction, Cost Savings.*

Cost-Reimbursement Contract: Reimburses the contractor for all incurred costs which are allowable and allocable under the terms of the contract and applicable laws and regulations; may include profit or fee. May also be referred to as a Cost Plus contract. *Also see Cost Contract.*

Cost Replacement: ***CANADIAN*** The cost at current prices which is expected to be incurred to replace an item.

Cost Savings: A realized and measurable reduction in material, resource, or labor expense(s) associated with the production and delivery of an item or service. Primarily associated in the manufacturing of an item; interchangeably used to indicate a lower price paid by the buyer from what was previously paid. *Also see Price Reduction, Cost Reduction.*

Cost Sharing: A type of contract that is used when it is impossible to firmly estimate costs and there is a high probability that the contractor will receive a substantial present or future commercial benefit. This type of contract may be used in research and development areas, as well as public-private partnerships.

Council of Logistics Management: A professional and educational organization whose goal is to promote the understanding and development of the logistics concept.

Council of State Governments (CSG): The premier multibranch organization forecasting policy trends for the community of states, commonwealths and territories on a national and regional basis. CSG alerts state elected and appointed officials to emerging social economic and political trends; offers innovative state

C

policy responses to rapidly changing conditions; and advocates multistate problem solving to maximize resources and competitiveness. CSG promotes excellence in decision-making and leadership skills and champions state sovereignty. *(www.csg.org/about/faqs.aspx)*

Counteroffer: An adjusted proposal made in response to another offer, by the one who rejected the initial offer.

Countertrade: An international barter transaction in which payment is made partially or fully with goods instead of money. A quid pro quo absent monetary exchange. For example, trading military hardware for oil or trading wheat for beef. *(Ferrell, Hirt, 2003)*

Country of Origin: The country where the goods are grown, produced or manufactured.

Covenant: An agreement or promise of two or more parties, in writing, stipulating that something is done, or shall be done, or as to the truth of certain facts.

Cover: A remedy, (in accordance with Section 2-711 of the Uniform Commercial Code) that permits the buyer to seek the reasonable purchase of substitute goods resulting from the seller's breach of contract.

CPAF: *See Cost Plus Award Fee Contract.*

CPCM: *See Certified Professional Contract Manager.*

CPFF: *See Cost Plus Fixed Fee Contract.*

CPI: *See Consumer Price Index.*

CPIF: *See Cost Plus Incentive Fee Contract.*

CPM: *See Critical Path Method.*

C.P.M.: *See Certified Purchasing Manager.*

CPO: *See Chief Procurement Officer.*

C.P.P.: *See Certified Professional Purchaser.*

CPPB: *See Certified Professional Public Buyer.*

CPPC: *See Canadian Public Procurement Council.*

CPPO: *See Certified Public Procurement Officer.*

CPSM: *See Certified Professional in Supply Management.*

Cradle-to-Grave: A representation of the life cycle of a given system, from concept through development, acquisition, operations phases and final disposition. This term is also used when speaking about the generation and disposal of hazardous waste. *Also called womb-to-tomb and referred to as the purchasing cycle.* *(Nash, Schooner, O'Brien, 1998)*

Credible: Plausible or believable.

Credit: In monetary theory, the use of someone else's assets in exchange for a promise to pay (usually with interest) at a later date. The major examples are short-term loans from a bank, credit extended by a supplier, and commercial paper. In balance of payment accounting, an item such as exports that earns a country foreign currency. *(Schiller, 2002)*

Credit Memo: A method of correcting an overcharge, paying a trade rebate, or crediting the value of goods returned.

Creditor: A lender, whether by making a loan, buying a bond or allowing money owed now to be paid. *(Schiller, 2000)*

Critical Path Method (CPM): The sequence of production activities that takes the longest time from start to finish. This technique is useful for planning, scheduling and monitoring complex projects composed of a large number of interrelated and interdependent activities. It is often used in construction procurement to sequence critical timeline events.

Crosby, Philip: An American quality guru who rose to international fame as a management consultant. Crosby is best known for his zero defects standard and popularizing many slogans, such as "Do it right the first time." For more information: *Quality is Free*, (NY, 1979). *(Miller, 2006)*

Crowson Decision: City of Richmond v. J.A. Crowson Co. was a legal case in 1989 in which the United States Supreme Court held that the City of Richmond Virginia's minority set-aside program, giving preference to minority business enterprises (MBE) in the awarding of municipal contracts, was unconstitutional under the Equal Protection Clause. This court case prompted public sector agencies to move toward using the term, "contract goals" in its construction projects in seeking a good faith effort on the part of the prime contractor to have a certain level of minority subcontracting participation in the project.

Cross-Docking: A distribution system in which freight moves in and out of a distribution center or point without ever being stored there. *(ISM, 2000)*

Cross-Functional Team: A group of employees from different departments who work together on a specific team usually to accomplish a specific task. The team may be permanent or ad hoc and may include vendors and customers as appropriate. Examples of procurement specific teams may include: Commodity Procurement Strategy Team; Sourcing Team; Supplier Performance Evaluation Team; Supplier Certification Team.

Cross-Organizational Synergies: Proactive activities by supply management in order to identify opportunities to share best practices or coordinate sourcing programs to reduce costs, usually accomplished through cross-functional teams.

Crowdsourcing (otherwise known as Cyberspace Outsourcing): A form of institutional outsourcing which solicits a large group of people who are not directly employed by, or who lack a contract with the originating institution. Solicitations are typically put out in the form of a wide call on the Internet, and the chosen work-product may or may not yield compensation. Crowdsourcing is an innovative way to leverage distributed knowledge on the Internet so that highly intractable problems can be solved in a low-cost manner, typically by shifting time costs to the experts who are interested in helping to the solve the quandary. This frees up institutional employees to focus on core competencies.

Crown Property: CANADIAN Property to which title is vested in the Crown. This includes Crown-owned property usually in the care, custody and control of contractors. Examples of Crown property usually in the custody of contractors are: capital assistance assets, special production tooling, special test equipment, equipment undergoing repair and overhaul, contract issue materials and equipment, work-in-process and finished work to which title is vested in the Crown as a result of progress payments, accountable advances or by any other means. *(Summit Magazine, On-Line)*

CSG: *See Council of State Governments.*

CSIG: *See United Nations' Convention on Contracts for the International Sale of Goods.*

Cultural Diversity: Ethnic, gender, racial, and socioeconomic variety in a situation, institution, or group; the coexistence of different ethnic, gender, racial, and socioeconomic groups within one social unit. *(Webster's New Millenium Dictionary of English)*

Cumulative Average Cost Curve: Used in price and cost analysis, this curve plots cumulative units produced against the average direct labor cost or average labor hours required per unit for all units produced. *(Schiller, 2000)*

Cure Notice: A delinquency notice that must be issued prior to termination for default of a supply or service contract before the contract's delivery date. Failure to issue a cure notice when required may result in an invalid termination for default. *(Nash, Schooner, O'Brien, 1998)*

Cure Period: CANADIAN When a contractee is in default of the deliveries in a contract, the cure period is the period of time that the contractor can give to the contractee to make good on the services required to be delivered, or additional time for the product contracted for to be delivered. The period of time is ultimately up to the contractor. The cure period would come before the contractor deems the contract to be terminated for reasons of default. *(Summit Magazine, On-Line)*

D

Currency Depreciation: A fall in the price of one currency relative to another. *(Business, 2002)*

Currency Devaluation: The reduction of the value of a nation's currency relative to the currency of other countries. *(Business, 2002)*

Current Account: International cash flows in payment for exports; part of a nation's balance of payments. *(Schiller, 2000)*

Current Assets: Assets that can be quickly converted into cash or that will be used in one year or less. *(Ferrell, Hirt, 2003)*

Current Funding: The current sum of money assigned to a contract.

Current Liabilities: Debts that will be repaid in one year or less. *(Ferrell, Hirt, 2003)*

Current Ratio: A financial ratio computed by dividing current assets by current liabilities. *(Ferrell, Hirt, 2003)*

Current Stock Level: The quantity currently on hand in the warehouse or storage depot.

Current Yield: The rate of return on a bond; the annual interest payment divided by the bond's price. *(Schiller, 2000)*

Custodian: CANADIAN The authorized officer who is accountable for the use and condition of a materiel item.

Customer Code: CANADIAN A five digit code utilized by the Supply and Services Canada Customer Address Directory to identify the using agency that issued the requisition; also indicates shipping and invoicing addresses.

Customs: Taxes, tolls, or duties levied upon goods which pass a frontier: generally an import duty. A customs duty is a tariff or tax on the import of or export of goods.

Customs Broker: A highly trained import professional, licensed by the U.S. Customs Service. *(ISM, 2000)*

Customs Tariff: A schedule of charges assessed by a government on goods moving in or out of a country. *(ISM, 2000)*

Cwt: *See Cents per Hundredweight.*

Cyberspace: Refers to a virtual reality within the world's computers and networks. The word was coined by William Gibson, the Canadian science fiction writer. *(Jansen, 2002)*

Cycle Counting: A physical stock checking system in which the inventory is divided into groups which are physically counted at predetermined intervals, depending on their ABC classification. Thus, the physical inventory counting goes on continuously without interrupting operations or storeroom activities. *(ISM, 2000)*

Cycle Time: The time required to complete a process, such as replenishing inventory. *(ISM, 2000)*

Cyclical Deficit: That portion of the budget deficit attributable to unemployment or inflation. *(Schiller, 2000)*

Cyclical Unemployment: Unemployment attributable to a lack of job vacancies, that is, to an inadequate level of aggregate demand. *(Schiller, 2000)*

D

Damages: A monetary settlement awarded to a party that is injured through a breach of contract. Compensation, usually monetary, for injury to goods, persons or property. *Also see Liquidated Damages and Penalty Charge.* *(Harney, 1992)*

Dangerous Goods: Articles or substances which are capable of posing a significant risk to health, safety or property, and which when transported, are subject to special regulations.

DAR: *See Defense Acquisition Regulations.*

Database: A single collection of data stored in one place that can be used by personnel throughout the entire organization to make decisions and assist in analysis. *(Jansen, 2002)*

Data Deliverables: Information organized for analysis. This Information can refer to technical data, cost data and administrative reports as determined by the contract. The request for data deliverables must be included as part of the contract. The contract administrator or designee and supplier must be aware of data requirements stated in the contract so compliance provides effective management of the contract.

Data Warehouse: A technology term that refers to a collection of data received from various transaction systems, which are accessible to various personnel throughout the organization. *(ISM, 2000)*

Date of input (forecast last amended): CANADIAN Date of last amendment entered. Date input entered into the system.

Davis-Bacon Act: A Federal Law (1931) which requires contractors who perform public works construction projects that are federally funded to pay their workers the prevailing wage rate paid in the area for similar work, as set by the Secretary of Labor.

DDN: *See Defense Data Network.*

Debarment:
1. To prohibit a seller/contractor from bidding on future requirements for cause for a certain period of time.
2. A sanction brought against a seller whereby they may not engage in future procurement actions.
3. To exclude or shut out of future solicitations and contracting opportunities. *Also see Suspension.*

Debit Card: A card, similar to a credit card, that electronically subtracts the amount of a purchase from a bank account at the moment the purchase is made. A pre-determined amount is debited to an account before a transaction is made and a declining balance is maintained as purchase transactions are recorded. *(Miller, 2006)*

Debriefing: A practice used primarily during the Request for Proposal process, whereby the contracting authority will meet with those parties whose proposals were not deemed appropriate for award. It is viewed as a learning process for proposers who may gain a better understanding regarding perceived deficiencies contained within their submitted proposal.

Debt Capital: Borrowed money obtained from loans of various types generally used to capitalize a business and allow it to meet operating expenses. *(Business, 2002)*

Debt Ceiling: An explicit, legislated limit on the amount of outstanding national debt. *(Schiller, 2000)*

Debt Service: The interest required to be paid each year on outstanding debt. *(Schiller, 2000)*

Debt Service Funds: Receive resources from other funds, taxes, grants or proceeds from long-term debt and are used to pay the principal and interest on the debt.

Debt-To-Owners' Equity: A financial ratio calculated by dividing total liabilities by owners' equity. *(Schiller, 2000)*

Decentralized Organization: An organizational design in which authority is widely distributed to lower levels of the organization. Broadly based organizational decision making within and among lower levels of the organization. *(Business, 2002)*

Decentralized Purchasing: An organizational structure in which designated personnel/operating departments from within the organization have the delegated authority to decide on sources of supply and contract directly with vendors without consulting or receiving the approval from the Chief Procurement Officer (CPO). It should be noted that the scope and degree, if any, of decentralized purchasing varies from agency to agency. Example: In one agency, all of the IT (Information Technology) software and hardware decisions and purchases are unilaterally made by the Chief Information Technology Officer and in other agencies all of those IT purchases are directly made by the Purchasing Department. *Also see Centralized Purchasing.*

Decisional Role: A role that involves various aspects of management decision making. *(Business, 2002)*

Decision Tree: A decision-making tool that maps alternative courses of action and their related consequences. Many components may be included such as decision forks, outcome forks, outcome probabilities, outcome rewards, and expected values. *(Business, 2002)*

Declared Value:
1. The monetary value placed on a shipment of goods by the shipper when delivered to the carrier.

2. The value placed upon imported goods by the importer for clearance through customs.

Default:

1. The omission or failure to perform a legal or contractual duty, to observe a promise or discharge an obligation, or to perform an agreement. *(Black's Law Dictionary, 417, 1990)*
2. Failure to make scheduled payments of interest or principal on a loan, bond, or other types of debt.

D

Defect: The absence of something that is necessary for completeness or perfection, or a deficiency in something essential to a thing's intended or proper use. A product is defective if it is not fit for the ordinary purposes for which it is sold and used. Defects are generally of two types, latent (not apparent to the buyer by reasonable observation) and patent (a defect that is apparent on normal inspection). *Also see Latent Defect.* *(Black's Law Dictionary, 1126, 1990)*

Defects-Per-Hundred Units: The number of defects found in any quantity of a product, divided by the total number of units then multiplied by one hundred; the average number of defects per hundred.

Defense Acquisition Regulations (DAR): A subset of the Federal Acquisition Regulations (FAR) that directly apply to the U.S. Department of Defense (DOD).

Defense Data Network (DDN): Internet linkages to U.S. military bases and defense contractors around the world. *(Jansen, 2002)*

Deficit Spending: The use of borrowed funds to finance government expenditures that exceed tax revenues. *(Schiller, 2000)*

Definiteness: The important or material terms of an agreement that are specifically expressed. Under common law, an offer must include the important, or material, terms of the proposed agreement so that, when a party accepts the offer, a resulting agreement is enforceable. Important terms include: subject matter, price, payment terms, quantity, quality, duration and the scope of work to be done. If the parties purport to agree on a material term but do so in a vague manner, as contrasted from omitting the term altogether, there is no agreement because it is too indefinite.

Deflation: A decrease in the average level of prices of goods and services. *Also see Inflation.* *(Schiller, 2000)*

Delay Claim: A claim filed by a contractor or an owner for unanticipated delays to a project. Delay claims require significant documentation and are based in part on cost accounting concepts. When the contractor delays the project, the owner can recover one of two types of damages: Liquidated damages or Actual damages. The components of a contractor delay claim include: (1) indirect costs that occurred during the extended performance period; (2) home office overhead that was incurred during the extended performance period; (3) increased material direct costs that occur during the delay; (4) lost productivity caused by the delay and (5) other damages directly related to and attributable to the delay. *(library.findlaw.com)*

Delegated Purchase: Authorized or appointed individuals, outside the purchasing department, are delegated authority under the entity's rules and procedures that allow them to make small dollar purchases on behalf of the agency.

Delegation of Authority: The conferring of authority by someone who has it, to another person, in order to accomplish a task.

Deliverable: The completion of a milestone or the accomplishment of a task. Used to measure successful performance. *Also see Milestones.* *(Harney, 1992)*

Delivery: The physical transfer of possession from one person to another, as from a carrier, vendor, or contractor to the purchaser. *Also see various Free on Board (F.O.B.) descriptions.*

Delivery Date: A single date, phased date and/or date of a contract.

Delivery/Definite: Terms utilized when a specific requirement quantity and delivery date have been established. This is the most common type of delivery requirement. Common examples include one-time purchase orders and capital outlays.

Delivery/Indefinite: Terms suitable for commodity purchases because the products purchased are standard throughout the industry, with numerous vendors. All of the indefinite delivery types of clauses should be used only with fixed firm price or fixed price with escalation pricing contracts. The following are three variations of indefinite delivery contracts:
- **•Indefinite delivery with a definite quantity** occurs when a quantity of supplies or services is specified, but the time of delivery is flexible. Used when requirements are definite or have a short lead time.
- **•Indefinite quantity and delivery** is used to establish a minimum and maximum quantity that can be ordered within a definite delivery period. This contract requirement is flexible in terms of both quantity and delivery schedule.
- **•Requirement delivery** is used when the public entity agrees to purchase all requirements for a certain period of time from the supplier. Used when the quantity of items and the number of deliveries is unspecified; thereby differentiating it from a definite type of contract, since specific quantities have not been established.

Delivery Order Contract: An indefinite delivery/indefinite quantity contract for supplies or services that provides for the issuance of orders for services or supplies during the contract period. May also be referred to as a task order contract.

Delivery Required By: The requested date by which all goods have to be delivered.

Delivery Schedule: A delivery plan indicating the time of beginning and completion of each delivery.

Delivery Terms: Conditions in a contract regarding freight charges, place and time of delivery, or method of transportation. *Also see various Free on Board (F.O.B.) definitions.*

Delphi Method: A forecasting method that utilizes a panel of experts who are polled repetitively in writing or over the Internet to develop a consensus prediction of future anticipated conditions. *(Business, 2002)*

Demand: The willingness and ability to buy specific quantities of goods at alternative prices in a given time period. *(Schiller, 2000)*

Demand Analysis: An all-inclusive method conducted to quantify, with reasonable accuracy, the anticipated agency material requirements that will be needed to support the agency's operations. *Also see Market Analysis and Supplier Analysis.*

Demand Contract A binding legal agreement that links spend data by dates and allows for rebates and discounts through automated contract management systems. Pricing is based on historical usage. A contract under which a contractor/vendor agrees to provide goods or services to a purchaser on a demand basis. *Also see Blanket order.*

Demand Curve: A curve describing the quantities of a good a consumer is willing and able to buy at alternative prices in a given time period. *(Schiller, 2000)*

Demand Deposit: An amount on deposit in a checking account. *(Schiller, 2000)*

Demand Elasticity: An economic term used to describe the sensitivity of demand to price changes. An example is the price escalation in petroleum products beginning in 2003. *(Schiller, 2000)*

Demand Level: The amount of inventory required for a given item.

Deming, W. Edwards: Most influential quality guru of the last century. Best known for his 14 points summarizing the philosophy of quality management he developed while working with Japan following WWII. *(Burt, Dobler, Starling, 2003)*

Demurrage: A fee charged by a carrier against a consignee, consignor, or other responsible party to compensate for the detention of the carrier's equipment in excess of allowable free time for loading, unloading, re-consigning, or stopping in transit. The term is also used by suppliers of material delivered in a variety of returnable containers, such as gas cylinders, rail containers and equipment.

D

Demobilization: The effort of a construction contractor in leaving the site after the contract work is completed. *Also see Mobilization.* *(American Purchasing Society, Glossary of Purchasing)*

Departmental Individual Standing Offer (DISO) Number: *CANADIAN* The serial number of a departmental individual standing offer arranged with one or more vendors, against which DSS (Department of Supply & Services) only may issue call-ups, upon receipt of funded customer requisition.

Dependent Demand: Derived from or contingent upon the demand for another component or a finished product. An example is the demand for automotive tires is dependent on the demand for automobiles by the consumer. *(Schiller, 2000)*

Depreciation:

1. An accounting term which denotes a loss or decrease in the acquired value over a specified period of time. Usually applies to a loss of value of a fixed asset (capital equipment).
2. The systematic transfer of the cost of a capital expenditure (an asset on the balance sheet) to expense (on the Income Statement).
3. To diminish in price or value.
4. The consumption of capital in the production process.
5. The wearing out of plant and equipment over a specified time.

Depression:

1. A phase of the economic cycle which follows a recession.
2. A drastic decline in the economy that includes high unemployment and wage stagnation. *(Schiller, 2000)*

Descriptive Literature: Information, such as charts, illustrations, brochures, and technical data, furnished by a bidder, on request as part of a bid, to describe the items offered; shows the characteristics or construction of a product, or explains its operation to determine the acceptability of the item.

Designation of Special Purpose: Identifies items created by modification of standard commercial products to meet special needs, such as equipment modified to meet the needs of the physically challenged.

Design-Bid-Build: The traditional delivery method for construction projects where design and construction are sequential and contracted for separately with two contracts. *(ISM, 2000)*

Design-Build: A delivery method for construction projects that combines the architectural, engineering, and construction services required for a project into a single contractual agreement. *(ISM, 2000)*

Design-Build-Finance-Operate: An Alternate Project Delivery Method (ADPM) demonstrating a design-build concept where the owner and designer/contractor work as a team to ensure that the owner's requirements are met during design and construction. A complex and innovative approach developed through "private public partnerships" where there is much greater involvement of private financing and often combines construction and management or operations contracts. (Examples: Building and operating a county amusement park, ice skating rink, golf course).

Design Deficiency: A condition which prevents a product from being useful, the correction of which would require a design change.

Design Specification: A specification that establishes the characteristics an item must possess, including detail indicating how it is to be manufactured. May include engineering plans or drawings and blueprints. It tells the contractor in very prescriptive terms, what they are to provide the buyer. *Also see Performance Specifications.*

Designee: A duly authorized representative.

Destination: The place to which a shipment is consigned. The final delivery point to which a shipment is routed. A delivery point where title passes from seller to buyer.

Detailed-Item Description Code: Part II of the NIGP Commodity/Service Code which expands the class-item code into 11 digits with more than 140,000 item descriptions; used in the areas of inventory, warehousing, and cooperative purchasing operations.

Determination and Findings: A legal document prepared by a purchasing official to justify a decision to take a certain action; includes conclusion, or determination, and the reason or findings of fact.

Devaluation: An abrupt depreciation of a currency whose value was fixed or managed by a government. An indicator of a troubled economy. *(Schiller, 2000)*

Deviation:
1. To differ or move away from an established course.
2. To offer an alternative product, service or business solution from what has been established or specified. *(TheFreeDictionary.com)*

Dictum Meum Pactum: Latin phrase that means "My word is my bond." It reflects the public trust of those in positions of authority in public procurement. *(Miller, 2006)*

Differential Exchange Rates: Different exchange rates imposed by a country's government depending upon the nature of the goods imported. *(ISM, 2000)*

Digital Signature: The ability to transpose a signature via the Internet. A piece of code that can be attached to an email message on an online transaction to provide authentication. An important component of ePurchasing/eCommerce. *(Jansen, 2002)*

Direct Cost: The cost of materials or services identified with only a single cost objective.

Direct Delivery: The shipment of goods directly from the source to a user; frequently used where a third party acts as purchasing agent for the user.

Direct Labor Hours: The labor portion of a contract that denotes the time spent working solely to satisfy the specific requirements of the contract as detailed in the specifications or statement of work.

Direct Selling: The marketing of products and services to the ultimate customer through face-to-face sales presentations at home or in the office. *(Business, 2002)*

Directed Contract (marché prescrit): CANADIAN A contract awarded to a pre-selected contractor in circumstances where the contracting authority has justifiably set aside the requirement to solicit bids under the provision of one or more of the exceptions to competitive solicitation in Section 6 of the Government Contracts Regulations. Contracting authorities are strongly encouraged to provide public notification of these contracts through an Advance Contract Award Notice (ACAN) using the electronic bidding methodology. If this is done and if there are no valid challenges received to the ACAN within 15 days, the directed contract is deemed to be competitive and may be awarded using the higher electronic bidding contracting authority levels. *(www.tbs-sct.gc.ca/pubs_pol/dcgpubs/Contracting/contractingpol_a_e.asp)*

Directive: CANADIAN A statement indicating the mandatory features of a policy. In those cases where the Treasury Board is prepared to permit deviations, departments must obtain prior approval by means of submissions. Directives are characterized by the use of the verbs shall, must, and will and appear in bold Italics throughout the manual.

Disadvantaged Business: A business owned or controlled by a majority of persons who are determined to have been deprived of the opportunity to develop and maintain a competitive economic position because of specified social disadvantage. *Also see Minority-Owned and Women-Owned Business Enterprises (MBE and WBE), and Historically Underutilized Businesses (HUB).* *(Harney, 1992)*

Discharge By Mutual Assent: Termination of a contract by mutual agreement of all parties. *Also see Cancellation Request, Termination for Convenience and Termination for Default.* *(Garner, 2004)*

Discount: An allowance, reduction or deduction from a selling price or list price extended by a seller to a buyer in order for the net price to become more competitive. More common forms of discounts include trade discounts, quantity discounts, seasonal discounts and cash discounts. *Also see Cash Discount, Payment Terms and Prompt Payment Discount.*

D

Discount-From-List: Mathematical calculation to determine the buyer's price from a manufacturer's price list. On non-automated term contracts the manufacturer must submit a printed price list/catalog from which prices are to be figured. Prices in this category cannot be increased for a specified time after the contract begins, unless otherwise noted in the contract.

Discount Rate: The interest rate that the Federal Reserve System charges for loans to member banks. *(Schiller, 2002)*

Discount Schedule: A listing of various discounts offered to the buyer for varying amounts of goods or services. May be requested as part of a bid or a request for proposal.

Discrepancy:
1. A deviation between the contract or purchase order and the material or services received or delivered.
2. A variance or difference in identification, condition, or quantity between the supplies or services delivered and the contracting documents.

Discretion: A power or right, conferred on procurement officers by law, to act officially in certain circumstances, according to the dictates of their own judgment and conscience and uncontrolled by the judgment or conscience of anyone else. *Also see Best Interest. (Black's Law Dictionary 466-67, 1990)*

Discretionary Fiscal Spending: Those elements of the federal budget not determined by past legislative or executive commitments. *(Nash, Schooner, O'Brien, 1998)*

Discretionary Income: Disposable income less savings and expenditures on food, clothing and housing. *(Schiller, 2000)*

Discriminatory Price: A pricing scenario in which a supplier offers similar or identical items for sale, in identical quantities, at different prices to different buyers. *(Business, 2002)*

Discussions: Formal or informal communication involving an oral or written exchange of information for the primary purpose of obtaining information essential for determining the acceptability of a proposal. To provide the offeror an opportunity to revise its proposal. Usually includes negotiation used in competitive negotiation, emergency and sole source procurement.

DISO: CANADIAN *See Departmental Individual Standing Offer.*

Disparagement: Making malicious or false statements of fact as to the quality or performance of an organization's product. *(Business, 2002)*

Disposable Income: After tax income of households; personal income less personal taxes *(Schiller, 2000)*

Disposal:
1. To remove an item of inventory or a capital asset from an organization in accordance with disposal and accounting procedures.
2. The disposition of assets or inventory.

Disposal Cost: The expense of removing inventory or assets from an organization. *(ISM, 2000)*

Disposal Value:
1. The estimated value of excess or surplus property prior to actual disposal.
2. The proceeds obtained from a sale of surplus property.

Disposition: Transferring, trading-in, selling, or destroying goods that are excess property, surplus property, or scrap.

Dispute:
1. A contractual disagreement or misunderstanding between contracting parties specific to contract provisions or language. Resolution is generally through pre-established administrative procedures or agreed upon alternative dispute resolution provisions.
2. A difference between a contractor/seller and a buyer over a bid, solicitation or contract calling for appropriate administrative action with the intent of achieving a remedial or amicable resolution. When a resolution cannot be achieved the parties may resort to alternative dispute resolution or litigation. *Also see Bid Protest and Protest.*

Dispute Panels: A form of ADR (alternative dispute resolution) which uses one or more neutral or impartial individuals who are available to the parties as a means to clarify misperceptions, fill in information gaps, or resolve differences over data or facts.

Disputes Resolution Officer (DRO): Designated individual within the agency to resolve business disputes between the agency and its bidders and vendors.

Distance Learning: Also known as eLearning or online training. Taking a class or obtaining training via the Internet. Classes may be sponsored by a university, college or other educational venue. ISM and NIGP provide distance learning classes for professional development. *(Miller, 2006)*

Distribution:
1. The movement of goods from the seller to the buyer.
2. The logistical aspects involved in the transfer of goods from manufacturer to user.

Distributor: An individual or business that buys and sells products from a manufacturer. Generally a wholesaler who may represent various manufacturers and maintains an inventory of material.

Diversion: The act of changing the route or destination of goods in transit from the original destination to a new destination.

Diversity (in the workplace): The attempt by organizations to recruit and retain a multicultural, multi-talented workforce. Embracing many dimensions of difference and creating a culture of inclusion in the workplace. Business success requires that managers create a culture of inclusion, trust and mutual respect. *(Business, 2002)*

Diversity Suppliers: Business entities including individuals that have challenges in becoming successfully established and gaining economic representation proportional to their demographic representation. Usually applicable to certain ethnic groups as well as the physically challenged and women-owned businesses. *(ISM, 2000)*

Dividend: Amount of corporate profits paid out for each share of stock. A distribution of earnings to the stockholders of a corporation. *(Business, 2002)*

Dockage: A charge for the use of a dock.

Document Identifier: CANADIAN Unique code showing requisition status.

Document Management: The computerized administration of electronic and paper-based documents. A document management system generally includes a scanner and an optical character recognition (OCR) program for converting paper documents into electronic form. *(Jansen, 2002)*

Domestic Corporation: A corporation in the state in which it is incorporated. *Also see foreign corporation.* *(Business, 2002)*

Door-To-Door: A transportation term used to indicate through transportation of a container and its contents from the consignor to consignee. *(ISM, 2000)*

Double Sampling: The inspection of a second sample when the first sample does not lead to a decision to accept or reject.

Downsizing: A deliberate management strategy to create a new organizational structure that will result in fewer employees on the payroll. This strategy may include outsourcing, eliminating redundant positions, layoffs and terminations. *(Business, 2002)*

Draft: A written order drawn by a creditor directing a debtor to pay a sum of money to a third party or to the bearer.

Drawback: A refund of money paid. For example, a refund of customs duties paid on imported material if the material is later exported.

Drawdown: CANADIAN *See Call-Up.*

Draw Off Order: The amount to be delivered by the contractor to the users under a blanket order as authorized or arranged for by the purchasing office. May also be referred to as a sub-order release.

Drayage: A charge for hauling something between various locations by a transportation company.

Drill Down: Clicking on various links within a program or Web site to obtain additional information contained therein. *(Jansen, 2002)*

DRO: *See Disputes Resolution Officer.*

Drop Shipment: A shipment made directly from a manufacturer or direct provider of goods to a buyer or purchaser in response to a request by the vendor who has received an order but does not carry the merchandise in inventory.

Due Diligence: A business and legal term which refers to research and inquiry made prior to committing to a purchase or making a major business decision. A thorough investigation into the performance and background of a business entity prior to making a decision to purchase. *(Business, 2002)*

Due Process of Law:

1. A guarantee, found in the Fifth and Fourteenth amendments of the U.S. Constitution, of fundamentally fair treatment by the Government. Substantive due process requires that no person be arbitrarily denied life, liberty or property by Government action. *(Black's Law Dictionary, 500-01, 1990)*
2. In government contracting, the issue of due process arises whenever a contractor claims that it has been denied a liberty or property right without proper procedures. *(Nash, Schooner, O'Brien, 1998)*

Dues In: CANADIAN The recorded quantity of an item to be received from all outstanding procurement documents, and all materiel expected to be returned.

Dues Out: CANADIAN The recorded quantity of an item to be issued on receipt of issuable materiel.

Dumping: Exportation of large quantities of a product at a price lower than that of the same product in the home market. The sale of goods in export markets at prices below domestic prices. *(ISM, 2000)*

Durables: Consumer goods expected to last longer than three years. *(Schiller, 2000)*

Dutch Auction: A type of online auction where a seller offers multiple copies of the same item, and the winning bidders pay the amount of the lowest winning bid. *(Jansen, 2002)*

Dutiable Goods: Imported or exported goods upon which duties are to be imposed.

Duties: Customs charges imposed on taking articles out of, or into, a country.

E

Earned Value Management: An integrated management tool that examines cost, progress and the original project schedule to determine variances from planned profiles. Its purpose is to allow for the prediction, with some degree of certainty, actual cost and schedule at completion of a project, given cost and progress at certain intervals of contract performance.

Earnest Money: Something of value paid as a pledge to bind an agreement or contract, typically money paid by a seller to a buyer.

Earnings Per Share: A financial ratio calculated by dividing net income after taxes by the number of shares of common stock outstanding. *(Business, 2002)*

Easement: A right held by a person to some limited and specified use of land held by another person.

eAuctions: *See Reverse Auction.*

eBay (eBay Inc.): A company with an on-line auction site that enables people and businesses to buy and sell goods and services on a local, national, and international basis. Founded by Pierre Omidyar in 1995 it transacts billions of dollars in gross merchandise sales over the Internet. *(Jansen, 2002)*

eBusiness: A business that is deriving some or all of its revenue via the Internet. A business that has an online business strategy. A business that generates sales via the Internet and embraces other Internet based business strategies. *(Jansen, 2002)*

ECCMA: *See Electronic Commerce Code Management Association.*

eCommerce (Electronic Commerce): All forms of business processes conducted via the Internet. Creating online business opportunities that are global in nature. (Jansen, 2002) *Also referred to as Electronic Sourcing (eSourcing).*

Economic Community: An organization of nations formed to promote the free movement of resources and products among its members and to create common economic policies. Example: European Union. (Schiller, 2000)

Economic Growth: An increase in output (real GDP); an expansion of production possibilities. (Schiller, 2000)

Economic Indicators: Economic activities that change relative to the economy. Examples include: imports, exports, unemployment, housing starts. (Schiller, 2000)

Economic Interregnum: A gap in economic continuity, the outcome of which cannot be predicted. A discontinuity in the global economy, thereby making future predictions uncertain. (Business Week, 12.20.04)

Economic Object: CANADIAN Code which classifies expenditures according to type of goods and services acquired or transfer payments made to measure the impact of government transactions on the economy.

Economic Order Quantity (EOQ): An inventory calculation used to determine stock-level reorder point. The calculation is based on costs of acquisition, storage, handling and inventory investment to determine the most cost-effective time and quantity to reorder.

Economically Disadvantaged Individuals: Socially disadvantaged individuals whose ability to compete in the free enterprise system is impaired due to diminished opportunities to obtain capital and credit as compared with others in the same line of business that are not socially disadvantaged. *Also see Small Disadvantaged Business, Historically Underutilized Business (HUB), Minority-Owned Business (MBE) and Women-Owned Business Enterprises (WBE).* (FAR 19.001)

Economies of Scale:
1. Reductions in minimum average costs that come about through increases in the size (scale) of plant and equipment.
2. A reduction in selling price as a result of an increase in the quantity ordered.
3. The aggregation of quantities to obtain certain economic advantages. *Also see Quantity Discount, Volume Discount and Volume Leveraging.* (Business, 2002)

Economy: The system through which a society answers the two economic questions-how wealth is created and distributed. (Schiller, 2000)

ECOTS: CANADIAN *See Electronic Catalogue and Order Taking System.*

ECP: CANADIAN *See Environmental Choice Program.*

EDI: *See Electronic Data Interchange.*

EDP (Electronic Data Processing): *See Automated Data Processing.*

EEO: *See Equal Employment Opportunity.*

Effectiveness: A measure of the quality of the output. It helps to determine the degree of customer satisfaction. (Business, 2002)

Efficiency:
1. The ratio between inputs and outputs. When outputs are increased and inputs are decreased, more efficiency is generated.
2. Getting the most out of the resources used.

(Business, 2002)

EFT: *See Electronic Funds Transfer.*

EIN: *See Employer Identification Number. Also see FEIN (Federal Employer Identification Number).*

Electronic Catalogue and Order Taking System (ECOTS): CANADIAN A system that allows clients to send requisitions electronically to Supply and Services Canada to obtain requisition status information and to browse, select and download catalogue information.

Electronic Commerce (eCommerce): The integration of electronic data interchange, electronic funds transfer, and similar techniques into a comprehensive electronic-based system of procurement functions; could include the posting of IFB's and RFP's on electronic bulletin boards, the receipt of bids via electronic data interchange, notification of award by email, and payment via electronic funds transfer. *Also referred to as Electronic Sourcing (eSourcing).*

E

Electronic Commerce Code Management Association (ECCMA): Formed in 1999, ECCMA has brought together thousands of experts from around the world and provides them a means of working together to build and maintain the global, open standard dictionaries that are used to unambiguously label information. *(Jansen, 2002)*

Electronic Data Interchange (EDI):
1. The electronic transfer and exchange of business documents, such as bid requests, quotations, purchase orders, invoices and payments, from one computer directly to another computer, using established technical standards.
2. The transfer of data between two or more companies, using networks and the Internet. *(Jansen, 2002)*

Electronic Funds Transfer (EFT): The direct payment to contractors and businesses through electronic transfer of funds between financial institutions. Payment by paper check is eliminated. *(Business, 2002)*

Electronic Procurement: *See eProcurement. (Also called ePro)*

Electronic Sourcing (eSourcing): *See Electronic Commerce (eCommerce).*

Electronic Signatures in Global and National Commerce Act (E-Sign): Signed on June 30, 2000, by President Bill Clinton, an act that made contracts sealed by a computer as binding as those signed in pen and ink. Online contracts have the same legal force as equivalent paper contracts.

Embargo: A prohibition on exports or imports. May create supply shortages of certain commodities that are available from global sources. *(Schiller, 2000)*

Emergency Purchase: A purchase made due to an unexpected and urgent request where health and safety or the conservation of public resources is at risk. Usually formal competitive bidding procedures are waived.

Employee Stock Ownership Plan (ESOP): An individual stock bonus plan designed specifically to invest in the stock of the employer company. *(Business, 2002)*

Employer Identification Number (EIN): The number assigned to a business unit or individual for purposes of withholding tax; used by many purchasing organizations as a vendor identification number. In governments entities referred to as FEIN (9-digit Federal Employer Identification Number).

Empowerment: Allowing employees to participate in the decision-making process. The outcome of an employee participation process. *(Business, 2002)*

Enabling Legislation: Legislation which provides purchasing authority to an official or department. The primary sources of enabling legislation in any governmental jurisdiction are: Written Law; Administrative Law; and Common Law. *(Garner, 2004)*

Encoding: The process of rewriting or transferring media sources from one format to another. *(Jansen, 2002)*

Encryption: The process of protecting information as it moves from one computer to another. A way of making data unreadable to everyone except the receiver and it is an increasingly common way of sending credit card numbers over the Internet when conducting eCommerce transactions. *(Jansen, 2002)*

Encumbrance: The commitment of appropriated funds to purchase an item or service. To encumber funds means to set aside or commit funds for a specified future expenditure.

End Item: A manufactured product that can be sold, distributed, or used, without any additional work being done on it.

Energy Conservation:
1. A deliberate approach to the efficient use of energy to preserve natural resources.
2. A strategic plan that includes various elements of energy efficiency and energy reduction in all applicable areas of the supply chain.

Energy Efficiency Standards: A performance standard for products that consume energy prescribing a minimum level of energy efficiency, or low rate of energy consumption for a given output.

Energy Star: A federal standard applied to office equipment for the purpose of rating the energy efficiency of the equipment. Energy Star rated-computers, monitors, and printers save energy by powering down when not in use, resulting in a reduction in electrical bills and pollution levels. *(Miller, 2006)*

Engineer: An individual, partnership, or corporation that performs professional engineering services for the agency as an independent contractor. A registered, Professional Engineer is an individual who works to develop economical and safe solutions to practical problems by applying mathematical and scientific knowledge while considering technical constraints. Engineers design materials, structures, machines and systems while considering the limitations imposed by practicality, safety and cost while adhering to local and national building codes. Engineers are required to have Errors and Omissions Insurance.

Engineering Estimate: A cost estimate prepared by the engineering department or an outside engineering firm, to enable the purchasing official to determine a potential estimated cost of a project and establish a budget range.

Enterprise Funds: A type of proprietary fund used to account for fees charged in exchange for goods and services. A criteria to determine enterprise funds is 1) generates revenue, 2) provides goods or services or 3) operates as a stand-alone or is self-supporting. Funds which control various utilities such as water, water reclamation, storm water, electric and other entities providing service financed through user charges. *Also see Internal Service Fund and Proprietary Fund.*

Enterprise Resource Planning (ERP): A business process software system that manages multiple management systems. May include finance, accounting, human resources, purchasing, inventory control and other activities. Deploying ERP is generally an enterprise-wide process, involving analysis, replacement of legacy systems and the development of new work procedures. *(Jansen, 2002)*

Entrepreneur: A person who risks time, effort and money to start and operate a business. *(Business, 2002)*

Entrepreneurship: The assembling of resources to produce new or improved products and technologies. *(Business, 2002)*

Environmental Choice Program (ECP): CANADIAN An eco-labeling program of Environment Canada that promotes the use of environmentally responsible goods and services, encouraging consumers, organizations and government to buy environmentally preferable items. *(Summit Magazine, On-Line)*

Environmental Compliance: Procurement decisions that impact the environment such as energy consumption, recycled products and waste disposal. Governmental buying decisions should also incorporate environmental and societal costs and benefits not contained in the purchase price of a product or service, such as the pollution produced or avoided when using a particular product or service. *(Miller, 2006)*

Environmental Protection Agency (EPA): A Federal Government agency established to implement and enforce federal laws relating to clean air, clean water, waste disposal and related environmental issues.

Environmentally Preferable Product (EPP): A product or service that has a lesser or reduced impact on human health and the environment when compared to competing products or services that serve the same purpose. Such products or services may include, but are not limited to, those which contain recycled content, minimize waste, conserve energy or water, and reduce the amount of toxics either disposed or consumed. *Also see Sustainability.*

E

Environmentally Preferable Purchasing: An attempt to address environmental challenges by taking advantage of government's vast purchasing power to create strong markets for environmentally friendly products and services. Purchasing goods and services in a way that does not harm the environment. *Also known as Green Purchasing.* (Miller, 2006) *Also see Sustainable Procurement.*

EOQ: *See Economic Order Quantity.*

EPA: *See Environmental Protection Agency.*

EPP: *See Environmentally Preferable Product.*

eProcurement (Electronic Procurement): Conducting all or some of the procurement function over the Internet. Implies that point, click, buy and ship Internet technology is replacing paper-based procurement and supply management business processes. *Also called ePro.* (Miller, 2006)

Equal or Approved Equal: Used to indicate that an item may be substituted for a required item if it is equal in quality, performance and other characteristics. (NASPO, 2001)

Equal Employment Opportunity Commission: A government agency with the power to investigate complaints of employment discrimination and power to sue firms that practice it. (Business, 2002)

Equal (Employment) Opportunity (EEO): Policies and procedures of the jurisdiction to ensure non-discrimination and equal opportunity to all employees, especially women, minorities, and persons with disabilities. (Business, 2002)

Equilibrium Price: The market clearing price at which the quantity demanded by buyers equals the quantity supplied by sellers. The point of intersection on a supply and demand curve. (Schiller, 2000)

Equipment: Major items that are not expendable except through depreciation or wear and tear and which, although they may be fixed or positioned in prescribed places, do not lose their identity or become integral parts of other items or installations.

Equipment Condition Codes: CANADIAN Specific categories or grades assigned to materiel based upon its further usefulness, as to whether it is serviceable, repairable, or condemned.

Equity: Justice according to natural law or right; freedom from bias or favoritism.

Equivalent Items: Items that without actually being identical have sufficient in common to be capable of being used for the same purpose. *Also see Brand Name (or Equivalent) Specification.*

Ergonomics:
1. The applied science of product/equipment design intended to reduce operator fatigue and discomfort.
2. To design the physical environment to enable the worker to work more effectively and safely.

ERP: *See Enterprise Resource Planning.*

Errors and Omissions Insurance: A professional liability insurance that protects companies and individuals against claims made by clients for inadequate work or negligent actions. Errors and omissions insurance often covers both court costs and any settlements up to the amount specified on the insurance contract. (Investopedia)

Escalator (Escalation) Clause: Allows the contract price to be adjusted up or down in direct relationship to a defined market indicator such as the Consumer Price Index.

Escrow: A sum of money, bond, piece of property, or deed delivered into the keeping of a third party by one party to a contract, to be returned only when an obligation is fulfilled, or conditions of a contract are met.

eSign: *See Electronic Signatures.*

ESOP: *See Employee Stock Ownership Plan.*

Established Catalog Price: Price included in a catalog, printed price list, schedule, or other form which is regularly maintained by a manufacturer or contractor, either published or otherwise available for inspection by all customers, which states prices currently in effect for the general buying public for the given supplies or services.

Established Due Date: The date and time specified in the IFBs and RFPs for submission of initial bids or proposals.

Estimated Contract Date: *CANADIAN* The estimated date of the acknowledgement of the offer.

Estimated Cost: The cost to be used as the basis of the sourcing decision. It is representative of all known work and expected unscheduled work arising out of the requirements, i.e. the total estimated contract value.

Estoppel: A legal principle that prevents a person from asserting a position that is inconsistent with his or her prior conduct, if injustice would thereby result to a person who has changed position in justifiable reliance upon that conduct. For example a landlord might inform a tenant that rent has been reduced, for example, if there is construction or a lapse in utility services. If the tenant relies on this advice, the landlord could be estopped from collecting rent retroactively.

Ethics:
1. A principle of right or good conduct or a body of such principles.
2. A system of moral principles or values.
3. A code of conduct.
4. Prohibits breach of the public trust by any attempt to realize personal gain by a public employee through conduct inconsistent with the proper discharge of the employee's duties. Strong ethical principles are required for public procurement personnel and both the National Institute of Governmental Purchasing (NIGP), Inc. and the Institute of Supply Management (ISM) have articulated ethical codes for their membership. The Universal Public Procurement Certification Council (UPPCC) has also published a Code of Ethics. *Also see Integrity and Norm.*

Euro: The European Monetary Unit (EMU) launched on January 4,1999 initially with eleven EU member countries. *(Business, 2002)*

European Community (EC): Formerly the European Economic Community, this is the part of the European Union under which public procurement legislation is enacted, and is referred to as EC Directives. *(Business, 2002)*

European Union (EU): A union of European nations established in 1992 with the Maastricht Treaty, to promote trade among its members; one of the largest free trade markets in the world. *(Business, 2002)*

Evaluation: A review process used to make a determination. In service contracting, a methodology used to determine the successful proposer/offeror which may include subjective criteria and scoring.

Evaluation Committee/Team:
1. A component of the Request For Proposal (RFP) process, whereby a committee is established to conduct interviews and negotiations during proposal evaluation for a specific product or service. Usually is composed of representatives from the functional area identified in the Statement of Work (SOW) and may be chaired by a procurement representative.
2. A group of individuals established to conduct interviews and negotiations during proposal evaluation for a specific product or service. The teams typically represent the functional areas to be addressed in the discussions with a purchasing representative chairing the team. *Also see Negotiation Team.*

Evaluation Criteria: Generally used in the Request For Proposal (RFP) method. Qualitative factors that an evaluation committee will use to evaluate/score a proposal and select the most qualified proposer/offeror. May include such factors as past performance, references, management and technical capability, price, quality and performance requirements. *(Harney, 1992)*

Evaluation Factors: In competitive negotiations, those factors specified in the RFP that will be considered in determining to whom a contract will be awarded.

Evaluation of Bids: The examination of bids after opening to determine the bidder's responsibility, responsiveness to requirements and other aspects of the bid to determine the successful bidder.

Evergreen Contracts: Contracts with automatic renewal clauses or provisions for renewals for a specified number of years. This has the benefit of allowing suppliers and agencies to establish longer-term working relationships. *(Harney, 1992)*

E

Excess Property:
1. Any supplies or equipment, other than expendable supplies having a remaining useful life, which are no longer required by the agency in possession of the material.
2. Material and supplies that are acquired by a government agency but are not required or can no longer be used by the agency and it may or may not have a residual value.

Exchange Rate: The price of one country's currency expressed in terms of another's; the domestic price of a foreign currency. A major cost factor in the sale of goods and services in the global marketplace. *Also called Rate of Exchange.* *(Schiller, 2002)*

Excise Taxes: Taxes levied on a specific good or service, such as cigarettes, alcohol or fuel, and are set by unit (for example, a gallon of gas) rather than by purchase price. They are sometimes referred to as "selective sales taxes." *(Schiller, 2002)*

Exclusive Distribution: The use of only a single retail outlet or distributor for a product in each geographic area. *(Business, 2002)*

Exculpatory Clause: A contract clause stating that one of the contracting parties is not liable upon the occurrence of some specified event. These clauses are most frequently used in an attempt by a public procurement agency to relieve itself of liability for defective specifications. *(Nash, Schooner, O'Brien, 1998)*

Excusable Delays: A contract clause that provides the contractor with protection from sanctions for late performance, such as default termination, liquidated damages, actual damages and excess costs due to delays. An excusable delay must meet two general requirements: The delay must be beyond the control of the contractor; The delay must be without the contractor's fault or negligence.

Ex Dock: Vendor bears cost and responsibility for placing goods on the dock at the port of destination; all costs from that point are on the buyer.

Exhaustion of Administrative Remedies: A legal doctrine which requires a complaining party to seek administrative remedy from designated administrative bodies before looking at the courts for relief.

Exigency purchase: *See Emergency Purchase.*

Expectancy Theory: The assumption that motivation depends not only on how much a person wants something but also on how likely he or she is to get it. *(Business, 2002)*

Expedite: The effort to assure delivery of goods purchased in accordance with a time schedule. An attempt to rush or improve a pre-established delivery date.

Expendable Items or Supplies: Denotes supplies or equipment that are normally consumed during use and have a very short life cycle.

Ex Point of Origin: In foreign trade, quotation or bid that does not include cost of exportation, such as transportation costs, export permit fees or export duties.

Export Bill of Lading: Issued by a carrier covering the transportation of goods from a domestic point of origin to a foreign destination.

Export License: A permit from a host country government, enabling organizations to take goods out of a country. *(ISM, 2000)*

Export Permit: A document issued by the government of the exporting country granting an exporter permission to export the merchandise described in the document.

Exports: Goods and services sold to foreign buyers. *(Schiller, 2000)*

Express Authority: That authority that is explicitly given in direct language, rather than inferred from conduct. *Also see Implied Authority and Inherent Authority.*

Express Contract: Those contracts, either written or oral, in which all of the formal elements for contract creation exist.

Express Language Rule: This rule states that when there is only one reasonable interpretation, that interpretation shall prevail. This is a secondary rule of determining the intent of the contracting parties during a dispute. The express language in the contract overrules the behavior of the parties prior to the dispute. Note that the burden of proof rests with the party to show that they actually relied on the interpretation language in the contract.

Express Warranty: A written explanation of the responsibilities of the seller in the event that the product is found to be defective or otherwise unsatisfactory. *Also see Implied Warranty.*

Extended Price: The price for the total number of items ordered, calculated by multiplying the quantity ordered by the unit price.

Externalities: Costs or benefits of a market activity borne by a third party; the difference between the social and private costs and benefits of a market activity. *(Schiller, 2000)*

External Procurement Authority: Any buying organization not located in the state or jurisdiction which, if located in the state or jurisdiction, would qualify as a public procurement unit.

Extranet: Also referred to as an "external network". The connection of two or more intranets for sharing information between a business and its clients and suppliers. *(Jansen, 2002)*

Ex Warehouse: Vendor makes delivery at port of origin, and all risks and costs from that point on are the purchaser.

F

Facilitation: An ADR process which involves the use of techniques to improve the flow of information between parties to a dispute. The technique may also be applied to decision-making meetings where a specific outcome is desired. Is generally successful when the parties or issues are not extremely polarized.

Facilities: Buildings, land, equipment and any tangible capital asset, wherever located, whether owned or leased.

Fact-Finding: An ADR technique that uses an impartial expert (or group) selected by the parties with the authority to appoint a fact-finder in order to determine what the "facts" are in a dispute.

Factor: A finance company to which businesses sell their accounts receivable—usually for a percentage of the total face value. *(Schiller, 2000)*

Factors of Production: Resource inputs used to produce goods and services e.g. land, labor, capital, entrepreneurship. *(Schiller, 2000)*

FAI: *See Federal Acquisition Institute.*

FAI: *See First Article Inspection.*

Fair and Reasonable Price: A price that is fair to both contracting parties, considering the agreed upon conditions, promised quality, and timeliness of contract performance. Purchasing officials may use a variety of techniques to assure a fair and reasonable price, such as, sealed competitive bidding, competitive proposals, price and cost analysis, and benchmarking to other contracts.

Fair and Reasonable Price Block: *CANADIAN* Certification as to method of solicitation and price acceptability.

Fair Market Value: The price for an item upon which purchaser and vendor agree in an open market when both are fully acquainted with market conditions.

Fair Trade Statute: A law, in some states, which allows a manufacturer to set a minimum retail price on their products. Such a law is a violation of federal anti-trust law if it affects interstate commerce.

Fair Use: Use of a work that is not an infringement of a copyright because it is used for the purpose of criticism, comment, news reporting, teaching, scholarship, or research. *(Nash, Schooner, O'Brien, 1998)*

F

False Claims Act: Provides for the recovery of damages and remedies upon proof of loss to the government, sustained through fraud in the award or performance of government contracts.

FAQ (Frequently Asked Questions): An eCommerce initiative which is widely used in various marketing and sales promotion applications. They are designed to help customers understand and feel comfortable with the product or service. *(Schiller, 2000)*

FAR: *See Federal Acquisition Regulations.*

FAS: *See Free Alongside Ship.*

Fast Track Construction: A method of construction contracting under which the contractor begins building as soon as the foundation plans are ready and a foundation permit has been issued, despite the fact that the architect-engineer has not finished designing the project. Throughout performance, the architect-engineer must keep ahead of the contractor's progress in order to supply the necessary plans and drawings before each stage of the construction is reached. *(Nash, Schooner, O'Brien, 1998)*

FCC: *See Federal Communication Commission.*

FCM: *See Federation of Canadian Municipalities.*

FED: *See Federal Reserve System.*

Federal Acquisition Institute (FAI): FAI promotes the development of a professional acquisition workforce. In addition, FAI collects and analyzes acquisition workforce data, coordinates government-wide research and studies to improve the procurement process, and assists agencies with recruitment of qualified candidates for acquisition fields.

Federal Acquisition Regulations (FAR): The primary document in the Federal Acquisition Regulations System, containing uniform policies and procedures that govern the acquisition activity of all federal agencies. The FAR is prepared, issued and maintained jointly by the Secretary of Defense, the Administrator of General Services and the NASA Administrator. *(Nash, Schooner, O'Brien, 1998)*

Federal Communication Commission (FCC): An independent Federal Government agency that regulates interstate and international communications by radio, television, wire, cable and satellite. It was created by an act of Congress and is independent of the executive departments. *(www.fcc.gov)*

Federal Deficit: A shortfall created when the Federal Government spends more in a fiscal year than it receives. *(Schiller, 2000)*

Federal Employer Identification Number (FEIN): In government entities the 9-digit number assigned for purposes of withholding tax; used by many purchasing organizations as a vendor identification number. *Also see Employer Identification Number (EIN).*

Federal Register: A daily publication available from the Government Printing Office, that lists and discusses the regulations of federal agencies, makes the regulations available for public comment before they are made final, and publishes all final rules and regulations. *(www.gpoaccess.gov/fr)*

Federal Reserve System (FED): The central bank and monetary authority of the United States. Established in 1913 and popularly known as "The Fed", the system divides the United States into 12 Federal Reserve districts, each with its own regional Federal Reserve Bank. *(www.federalreserve.gov)*

Federal Standard 1037: Entitled, Telecommunications: Glossary of Telecommunication Terms, it is a Federal Standard issued by the General Services Administration pursuant to the Federal Property and Administrative Services Act of 1949. The document provides federal departments and agencies a comprehensive source of terms used in telecommunication by international and U.S. Government telecommunication specialists. *(Jansen, 2002)*

Federal Supply Service: The U.S. General Services Administration Federal Supply Service provides federal customers with the products, services, and programs to meet their supply, service, procurement, vehicle purchasing and leasing, travel and transportation, and personal property management requirements.

Federal Trade Commission (FTC): A five-member committee charged with the responsibility of investigating illegal trade practices and enforcing anti-trust laws. *(www.ftc.gov)*

Federal Trade Commission Act (U.S. Law): Passed by the U.S. Congress in 1914, this Act established the Federal Trade Commission as an independent regulatory agency of the Federal Government empowered to enforce the Clayton Antitrust Act and the Robinson-Patman Act.

Federation of Canadian Municipalities (FCM): Promotes a strong, effective and accountable municipal government. *(www.fcm.ca)*

Fee:
1. A sum of money paid for some service.
2. A charge or payment, usually for professional or technical services.

FEIN: *See Federal Employer Identification Number. Also see EIN (Employer Identification Number).*

FFE: *See Furniture, Fixtures, Equipment.*

FFP: *See Firm Fixed Price Contract.*

Fidelity Bond: Insurance against losses due to the dishonesty of an employee.

Fiduciary Duty: An individual's obligation to serve the best interests of selected stakeholders, especially those of their employer. *(www.american-purchasing.com/glossary)*

Fiduciary Funds: Monies used to account for assets held in a trustee or agency capacity for others and which cannot be used to support the agency's own programs.

Field Purchase Order (FPO): A type of purchase order with a pre-approved maximum value used to expedite the acquisition of non-recurring goods and services necessary for business operations. An FPO is used for occasional, unexpected business expenditures i.e., the breakdown of a company vehicle in the middle of a delivery trip.

FIFO: *See First In-First Out.*

Final Cost Objective: A cost objective whose costs are not assigned to any other cost objective, and is therefore one of the final points for accumulating costs in the accounting system.

Final Inspection: A review or examination of a product, service or construction by the purchaser to assure that the seller/contractor has conformed to all applicable specifications and requirements before making final payment.

Final Payment: Payment made for completed services after all offsets are calculated and claims are completed.

Financial Audit: An audit conducted to determine whether all financial transactions are recorded and shown accurately in accounts, to verify the accuracy of financial statements, and the fairness of the facts they represent.

Financial Coding: ***CANADIAN*** Coding which identifies a financial account and is used as part of a system of accounts.

Financial Interest:
1. Ownership of any interest in, or involvement in any relationship which, or as a result of which, a person has recently received, or will receive, a sum of money (or something of value).
2. Holding any position in a business or any position of management.

Financial Lease: A lease used to obtain financial leverage and related long-term benefits. Generally long-term, for a fixed period of time just short of the approximate life of the equipment being leased. Usually of two types: full payout (the lessee pays the full purchase price plus interest charges plus maintenance, insurance and administration costs) and partial payout (gives the lessee credit for the residual value of the leased item after the lease period is complete). *Also see Operating Lease.* Financial Ratio: A number that shows the relationship between two elements of a firm's financial statement. *(Schiller, 2000)*

Finished Goods: Goods that have completed the manufacturing or assembly process and are ready for sale to external customers. *(ISM, 2000)*

Firewall: A specially programmed computer system that stands between an organization's LAN and the Internet. A security measure used to prevent hackers and other unauthorized users from accessing internal networks. May also be created to protect the security of servers. *(Jansen, 2002)*

Firm: A partnership or business unit of two or more persons not recognized as a corporation.

Firm Bid: A bid that binds a bidder until a specified time of expiration.

Firm Fixed Price (FFP) Contract: A type of contract providing for a price that is not subject to adjustment on the basis of the contractor's cost experience in performing the contract. FFP contracts place maximum risk and full responsibility on the contractor for all costs and resulting profit or loss. They provide maximum incentive for the contractor to control costs and perform effectively and impose a minimum administrative burden upon the contracting parties unless changes are issued or unforeseen events occur during performance. *(Nash, Schooner, O'Brien, 1998)*

First-Article Inspection (FAI): A term usually used in the purchase of custom-made goods (design specification). A qualitative method by which the vendor must provide a final production item for the purchaser's review and approval before the balance of the production run is made and shipped by the vendor. *Also known as First-Article Testing.*

First-Article Testing: *See First-Article Inspection.*

First In-First Out (FIFO): An inventory costing method in which stock acquired earliest is assumed to be sold (issued) first, leaving stock acquired more recently in inventory. Under FIFO, inventory is valued near current replacement costs. Provides for a physical rotation of the stock so that the oldest stock is used first. *Also see Last In-First Out (LIFO). (Nash, Schooner, O'Brien, 1998)*

Fiscal Policy: Government influence on the amount of savings and expenditures; accomplished by altering the tax structure and by changing the levels of government spending. The Federal Reserve impacts fiscal policy by their actions to raise or lower interest rates and to monitor and control inflation. *(Schiller, 2000)*

Fiscal Restraint: Tax hikes or spending cuts intended to reduce aggregate demand. *(Schiller, 2000)*

Fiscal Stimulus: Tax cuts or spending hikes intended to increase aggregate demand. *(Schiller, 2000)*

Fiscal Year: The 12-month period used for accounting purposes. Generally begins July 1 or October 1 for governments (October 1 for the Federal Government).

Fit, Form and Function: Physical, functional, and performance characteristics or specifications that uniquely identify a component or device and determine its interchangeability in a system or piece of equipment. Used especially when considering the suitability of a suggested alternate or "equal".

Fixed Asset: Physical assets such as property, plant and equipment.

Fixed Costs: Costs of production that don't change when the rate of output is altered, e.g., the cost of basic plant and equipment. *(Business, 2002)*

Fixed Period Average: A mathematical calculation used to divide the total usage for a fixed period (generally 12 months), usually using the last fiscal calendar, by the number of months involved (generally 12). The resulting average is the forecast for the entire comparable future period. This is a straight mathematical calculation which ignores current trends.

Fixed-Price Contract: A contract providing for a firm price, or a price that may be adjusted only in accordance with contract clauses providing for revisions of the contract price under stated circumstances.

Fixed-Price Contract with Escalator (Economic Adjustment Clause): A contract under which the contractor is reimbursed at a fixed price for all services and material provided that allows for periodic price increases or decreases at one or more stated intervals during the contract term. The amount of increase or decrease is based on the movement of an independent price index (escalator) for goods, services, or labor. *(Harney, 1997)*

Fixed-Price Contract with Price Redetermination: A fixed-price contract that provides a firm fixed price for an initial period of performance, after which the price may be recalculated for subsequent periods of performance based on experience during the initial period.

Fixed-Price Incentive: A fixed-price contract that provides an incentive to reduce cost by allowing for the adjustment of profit and establishing the final contract price by a formula based on the relationship of final negotiated cost to total target cost.

Fixed-Price Level-of-Effort: A fixed-price contract that requires the contractor to provide a specified level of effort for a specified period of time for work which can only be described in general terms.

Fixed Unit Price: CANADIAN A method of pricing in which the total payable is calculated by multiplying the number of identical units of work or items delivered by a fixed price per unit or item.

Fixed Weights: A numerical system used to evaluate proposals. Weights are assigned to each evaluation criteria by percentage distribution.

Flexible Manufacturing Systems (FMS): A single production system that combines robotics and computer aided manufacturing. *(Business, 2002)*

Flextime: A system in which employees set their own hours within employer determined limits. May also include a four-day workweek schedule. *(Business, 2002)*

Floater: An insurance policy that covers a changing, dynamic liability, such as the inventory of a store or warehouse, moveable property, or goods in transit.

FMS: *See Flexible Manufacturing Systems.*

F.O.B.: *See Free On Board.*

Follow-Up: To review the status of a transaction; in connection with purchasing transactions.

Force Majeure: Unexpected or uncontrollable events, including those caused by nature that can impact the contracts price, terms and conditions. These events are not due to contractor negligence and may excuse contractor performance during the events and under certain conditions caused by them. Acts of God or disruptive conditions for which a contractor or carrier will not be held responsible.

Forecasting: A tool used to determine future needs. An ongoing assessment to examine opportunities and is an essential element of strategic planning. It requires procurement professionals to keep abreast of the market and surveys and understand various indicators, business cycles, indexes, lead times, and price histories of commodities and services.

Foreign Corporation: A corporation in any state in which it does business except the one in which it is incorporated. *Also see Domestic Corporation. (Schiller, 2000)*

Foreign-Exchange Markets: Places where foreign currencies are traded. *(Business, 2002)*

Foreign Trade Zone (FTZ): A designated area for holding goods pending customs clearance; legally duty free storage space. Property set aside at or near a port or airport, under the control of the U.S. Customs Service. *(Schiller, 2000)*

Forfeiture of deposit or bond: A loss of bid bond, bid deposit, or performance bond resulting from non-performance of the obligation the bond was to insure by one's own act, negligence, or fault.

Form, Fit, and Function: *See Fit, Form and Function.*

Formal Bid: A bid which must be submitted in a sealed envelope and in conformance with a prescribed format to be opened in public at a specified date and time. *Also see Competitive Sealed Bidding.*

Forward Purchasing: The purchasing of supplies and materials in quantities exceeding the immediate needs, often in anticipation of a price increase, strike threat, or future supply disruption.

Forward (Supply) Contract: A contract for future supply of definite quantities of supplies or services. *Also see Futures and Spot Price.*

F

FPO: *See Field Purchase Order.*

Franchise: A license to operate an individually owned business as though it were part of a chain of outlets or stores. A franchisor is an individual or organization granting a franchise and a franchisee is a person or organization purchasing a franchise. *(Business, 2002)*

Fraud: An intentional perversion of truth for the purpose of inducing someone to rely upon it and part with something of value or surrender a legal right. The three necessary elements of a cause of action for fraud are (1) false representation of a present or past fact on the part of the defendant, (2) a plaintiff's action in reliance upon that misrepresentation, and (3) damage resulting to the plaintiff from the action that was based on the misrepresentation. *(Black's Law Dictionary, 660, 1990)*

Free Alongside Ship (FAS): A price that includes the cost of transportation and delivery to the side of the vessel, within reach of its loading tackle, at the specified port of shipment, with the purchaser's liability beginning at that point.

Free Astray: A shipment misrouted or unloaded at a wrong destination that is forwarded to the correct destination free of extra charges.

Freedom of Information Acts: Designed to make government bodies more open (by requiring release of information collected by the public body) and, at the same time, more accountable (by controlling what information may be released). *Also known as Freedom of Information Legislation (FOIL). (www.american-purchasing.com/glossary)*

Free Enterprise: The system of business in which individuals are free to decide what to produce, how to produce it, and at what price to sell it. *(Business, 2002)*

Free on Board (F.O.B.) Destination: Title changes hands from the supplier to the public entity at the destination of the shipment when the public entity signs for the goods; the supplier owns the goods in transit, assumes responsibility for carrier selection, and files any claims for damages incurred during this period. It does not address the responsibility for the cost of transportation (freight charges) which must be specified with the inclusion of additional language. See further definitions below which must state who is responsible for freight charges.

Free on Board (F.O.B.) Destination, Freight Collect: Title passes at destination, and buyer pays the freight.

Free on Board (F.O.B.) Destination, Freight Collect and Allowed: Title passes at destination, and buyer pays the freight and deducts it from the seller's invoice.

Free on Board (F.O.B.) Destination, Freight Prepaid and Added: Title to the goods passes from the supplier to the agency at the point of destination and supplier pays the freight expense and then adds the freight expense to the agency's invoice. Supplier owns goods in transit and files claims, if any.

Free on Board (F.O.B.) Destination, Freight Prepaid and Allowed: Title passes at destination, and seller pays the freight.

Free on Board (F.O.B.) Origin: Title changes hands from the supplier to the public entity at the origin of the shipment. In this scenario, the public entity owns the goods in transit, assumes responsibility for carrier selection, and files any claims for damages incurred during this period. It does not address the responsibility for the cost of transportation (freight charges) which must be specified with the inclusion of additional language. See further definitions below which must state who is responsible for freight charges.

Free on Board (F.O.B.) Origin, Freight Collect: Title passes at origin, and the buyer pays the freight.

Free on Board (F.O.B.) Origin, Freight Prepaid and Added: Title passes at origin, and seller pays the freight and then collects the charges from the purchaser by adding them to the invoice.

Free on Board (F.O.B.) Origin, Freight Prepaid and Allowed: Title to the goods passes from the supplier to the agency at point of origin and supplier pays and bears the freight expense. Agency owns goods in transit and files claims, if any.

Free on Board (F.O.B.) Origin, Freight Prepaid and Charged Back: Title passes at origin, seller pays the freight and adds it on to the seller's invoice.

Free Rider: The name given to individuals who reap direct benefits from someone else's purchase or consumption of a public good. *(Schiller, 2000)*

Free Trade: The uninhibited flow of goods and services across international borders. *(Schiller, 2000)*

Freeware: Free software available on the Internet for downloading. Used and redistributed at no cost to the user. *Also see shareware.* *(Jansen, 2002)*

Freight:
1. Supplies, goods, and transportable property being moved between locations.
2. Compensation paid for the transportation of goods or for the use of a carrier.

Freight Bill Audit: A review of freight bills to determine if the assessed charges were correct. It checks the classification, rating, or extension either by a third party or an inside auditor. *(Miller, 2006)*

Freight Classification: A list of articles, their assigned classification, the applicable freight rate, and freight rules and regulations.

Freight Forwarder: A person or company whose business is to act as an agent on behalf of the shipper. *(Business, 2002)*

Frictional Unemployment: Brief periods of unemployment experienced by people moving between jobs or into the labor market. *(Schiller, 2000)*

Friction-Free Market: A term used to describe a market in which there is little differentiation between the various products sold to the same target market thus resulting in a high degree of customer choice. Example: Beverages and cereal. *(Business, 2002)*

Fringe Benefits: Non-salaried incentives and rewards used to recruit and retain employees. An area that is negotiated by unions in their labor contracts with employers. May include health, life insurance, deferred compensation, childcare, and a variety of other benefits. *(Business, 2002)*

Front-End Loading: The inclusion in a bid or proposal of inflated prices on items to be delivered early in the performance of the contract and unduly low prices on later items. It is a form of unbalanced bidding that is aimed at enabling the bidder to recover money in advance of the performance of the work. *Also see Unbalanced Bid.* *(Miller, 2006)*

FTC: *See Federal Trade Commission.*

FTZ: *See Foreign Trade Zone.*

Full and Open Competition: The process by which two or more vendors attempt to secure the business of a third party by offering the most favorable price, quality, delivery terms, or service. The concept of competition presumes the existence of a marketplace in which there is more than one vendor supplying similar goods and/or services.

Full Employment: The lowest rate of unemployment compatible with price stability; variously estimated at between 4 and 6 percent unemployment. *(www.bls.gov, US Bureau of Labor Statistics)*

Full-Time Equivalent Position (FTE): The baseline is a full-time position. All part-time positions are converted to the decimal equivalent of a full-time position based on 2,080 hours per year. For example, a part-time typist working 20 hours per week would be the equivalent to .5 of a full-time position.

Full Warranty: A warranty as to full performance covering both labor and material; the warrantor must remedy the product within a reasonable time and without charge after notice of a defect or malfunction.

Functional Specification: A specification setting forth the results required from the supply or service.

Functions of Money: The roles played by money in an economy. These roles include the medium of exchange, standard of value, and the store of value. (Schiller, 2000)

Funds (Budgetary/Governmental): An independent legal fiscal entity with assets, liabilities, reserves, a residual balance, or equity, and revenues and expenditures for undertaking activities. Funds may be expendable, meaning the authorization for spending expires at the end of the fiscal period; or non-expendable or revolving, meaning that spending beyond the fiscal year is allowed without reauthorization. Governmental funds generally finance the activities most citizens associate with general-purpose governments, e.g. police, fire, public works and procurement. Governmental funds may be subdivided into four categories: General Fund; Special Revenue Funds; Capital Project Funds; Debt Service Funds – each described separately in this dictionary.

Furniture, Fixtures and Equipment (FFE): A supply management term that refers to commodity designations often procured by a buying team that specializes in this area. Relates to new construction and the commodities needed to furnish the structure. (ISM, 2000)

Future Option: A contract entered into to buy or sell a currency, security or commodity at a fixed price for delivery sometime in the future at a date to be determined. (Business, 2002)

Futures: Contracts for immediate purchase or sale of something to be delivered at a definite time in the future at a specified price. Used as a hedging device against market price fluctuations or unforeseen supply shortages. *Also see Forward Contract and Spot Price.*

G7 – G8 Summit: The seven major industrial nations that meet to discuss economic issues. The group includes the United States, Canada, France, Germany, Italy, Japan and the United Kingdom. The eighth country is Russia. (Business, 2002)

GAAP: *See Generally Accepted Accounting Principles.*

Gain Sharing: A team building and quality effort to achieve improvements by empowering employees to find creative ways to save dollars, improve profit, increase productivity and efficiency. Employees come together as a group or team and are rewarded if their efforts prove successful. Rewards may be monetary or non-monetary. (Business, 2002)

Gantt Chart: A graphic scheduling device that displays the tasks to be performed on the vertical axis and the time required for each task on the horizontal axis. Gantt charts are the simplest of the various charting techniques for planning and controlling major projects and the materials deliveries that flow from them. (Burt, Dobler, Starling, 2003)

GASB: *See Governmental Accounting Standards Board.*

Gatekeeper: A role that contributes to the positive functioning of a group. A relations-oriented team role that encourages communication and participation from all team members; invites and clarifies ideas; and focuses on the assigned task.

GATT: *See General Agreement on Tariffs and Trade.*

GBL: *See Government Bill of Lading.*

GC: *See General Contractor.*

GDP: *See Gross Domestic Product.*

General Agent: An agent who has much broader powers and more latitude in using their own judgments to carry out duties assigned to them by their principals; they act on behalf of the principal on a continuous basis. Example: Purchasing Agents for a governmental agency have broad powers to contract for goods and services within the scope of their procurement authority and responsibilities.

General Agreement on Tariffs and Trade (GATT): A trade agreement originally signed by 23 nations in 1947, that provided a forum for tariff negotiations and a place where international trade problems could be discussed and resolved. *(Schiller, 2000)*

General and Administrative (G & A) Expense: An indirect cost including any management, financial or other expense which is for the management and administration of the business unit as a whole, and which cannot be identified with a smaller business unit.

General Contractor (GC): A contractor with the entire responsibility for performing a construction contract. A contractor that bids for a construction contract and bears the entire risk if the contract cannot be performed at the contract price. *(Nash, Schooner, O'Brien, 1998)*

General Fund: Used to track revenues and expenditures that support all services not assigned to other funds.

General Ledger: A book or computer file with separate sections for each financial account. *(Business, 2002)*

General Obligation Bond: A bond backed by the full faith, credit, and unlimited taxing power of the government agency that issued it. *(Schiller, 2000)*

General Provisions: That part of the contract (bid, proposal) that contains all of the standard clauses and requirements. *Also see Boilerplate.*

General Terms and Conditions: The section of a solicitation that contains clauses that deal primarily with the contractual obligations of the parties to a contract; a part of the boilerplate of a bid or contract document. *Also see Boilerplate.* *(Harney, 1992)*

Generally Accepted Accounting Principals (GAAP): CANADIAN Those accounting principles which have been given formal recognition or authoritative support in any particular Canadian jurisdiction. *(Summit Magazine, On-Line)*

Generally Accepted Accounting Principals (GAAP): Uniform minimum standards for financial accounting and recording, encompassing the conventions, rules and procedures that define accepted accounting principles.

Generic (Name): Related to or characteristic of a whole group or class; not protected by trademark registration. *(Business, 2002)*

Gift: Something of economic value given to a public official or the public official's relative without valuable consideration of equivalent value.

G.I.P.P.E.R Canadian: *See Governments Incorporating Procurement Policies to Eliminate Refuse.*

Global Positioning System (GPS): Composed of a series of geosynchronous earth-orbiting satellites that continuously transmit signals that help determine actual geographic location. *(Jansen, 2002)*

Globalization: Oversees business expansion and operation on a world-wide level. The Internet and other technology developments have facilitated this concept. Specific to public procurement, purchasers are part of a global economic community and products and services are now provided globally. *(Miller, 2006)*

GMIF: CANADIAN *See Green Municipal Investment Fund.*

GNP: *See Gross National Product.*

Goals:
1. Observable and measurable end results that help to further define an organization by giving it direction; long term target and vision of the future.
2. A contract term often used in seeking MBE/WBE (Minority and Women Owned Business Enterprises) participation. A level of expectation that a vendor will make a good faith effort to achieve the pre-determined percentage of this participation upon award. *Also see Contract Goals and Set-Aside.*

Go, No-Go: An evaluation technique that may be used to score proposals. It can be applied to major areas and elements of management, operational suitability and other criteria, when identified for evaluation. Generally applied to technical and management areas.

Golden Parachute: A clause that is inserted in the contract of employment generally for top management employees that creates a financial package payable if the employee is dismissed and provides a measure of financial security. It may also protect the employee if mergers or takeovers take place or if the employee is dismissed due to poor corporate performance. *(Business, 2002)*

Goods: Anything purchased other than services or real property. Objects that can satisfy people's wants.

Goods and Incidental Services: *CANADIAN* Materiel items and the services needed to acquire, operate and maintain them; represent the end products of materiel expenditures.

Goods and Services Identification Number (GSIN): *CANADIAN* An alphanumeric code used to categorize goods and services for the allocation of requisitions, identification of source lists, and coding of contracts. Number is allocated systematically by Supply and Services Canada.

Goods and Services Tax (GST): *CANADIAN* The tax charged by the Canadian Government on the purchase of goods and services in Canada. A Canadian tax levied at the manufacturer's level. GST is levied on all goods manufactured or produced in Canada, as well as those imported into Canada unless an exemption applies.

Goodwill: An intangible asset of a company that includes factors such as reputation, contacts, and expertise for which a buyer of the company may have to pay a premium. *(Business, 2002)*

Government Bill of Lading (GBL): A bill of lading used by the United States Government for shipment of government-owned property or for goods being delivered to the government.

Government Performance and Results Act (GPRA) (Public Law 103-62): Adopted in 1993, requires that all programs in all federal departments and agencies report annually to the U.S. Congress on their performance. Requires federal agencies to "establish performance indicators to be used in measuring or assessing the relevant outputs, service levels and outcomes of each program activity." *(www.whitehouse.gov/omb/mgmt)*

Government Property: All property owned by or leased to a government entity or acquired by the government under the terms of a contract, including property made available for the use of the contractor during the term of the contract.

Governments Incorporating Procurement Policies to Eliminate Refuse (G.I.P.P.E.R): *CANADIAN* This guide serves as a tool to assist purchasers to incorporate environmental considerations into the procurement process.

Governmental Accounting Standards Board (GASB): The organization that establishes generally accepted accounting principles for state and local governments. *(www.gasb.org)*

Governmental Body: Any department, commission, council, board, bureau, committee, institution, legislative body, agency, Government Corporation, or other establishment, or official of the executive, legislative, or judicial branch of the jurisdiction.

Government-Wide Information: *CANADIAN* Information to be provided by all departments and agencies to meet either the statutory requirements of Parliament or the corporate information requirements of central agencies.

GPO: *See Group Purchasing Organization.*

GPRA: *See Government Performance and Results Act.*

GPS: *See Global Positioning System.*

Grandfather Clause: A contractual provision that protects the existing interests of affected parties. *(ISM, 2000)*

Grant:
1. A transfer of Federal Government funds to state or local governments to support or stimulate programs authorized by federal or state laws, to accomplish objectives that are locally defined and managed under a broad federal or state program.
2. The furnishing of assistance by a jurisdiction whether financial or otherwise, to any person to support a program authorized by law; does not include an award whose primary purpose is to procure supplies, services or construction.

Grantee: An entity, an agency that receives a grant of monetary funds from a grantor. *Also see Third Party.*

Grantor: An entity which makes a grant of monetary funds to the grantee; generally a federal or state government is the grantor.

Grapevine: An informal channel of communications, separate from management's formal, official communication channels. *(Business, 2002)*

Gratuitous Offer: An uninvited condition or provision submitted by a bidder or offeror; an unnecessary or unwarranted submission.

Gratuity: Something given voluntarily or beyond obligation usually for some service (i.e. Tip).

Green Municipal Investment Fund (GMIF): *CANADIAN* A revolving fund providing financial services (including loan guarantees and interest-bearing loans) that allow Canadian municipalities to fund projects that protect the climate and improve air, water and soil quality. *(Summit Magazine, On-Line)*

Green Purchasing: *See Environmentally Preferable Purchasing.*

Green Seal: A non-profit environmental organization that offers expertise in green purchasing, operations and plant improvement. This organization has helped prepare environmentally responsible criteria including specifications for many products including paint, adhesives, degreasers, paper towels and napkins just to name a few. *(www.greenseal.org)*

Grey Market Goods: Usually refers to the flow of new goods through distribution supply channels other than those authorized or intended by the manufacturer or producer. For example, goods intended to be only sold in Europe but eventually find their way for sale and use in the United States market. Goods being sold outside of normal distribution channels by companies which may have no relationship with the producer of the goods. Typical grey market goods include electronics, cameras, and watches. The original manufacturer may not honor the product warranty on grey market goods.

Gross Domestic Product (GDP): The total market value of all final goods and services produced within a nation's borders in a given time period. *(Schiller, 2000)*

Gross Income: Revenues minus the cost of goods sold required to generate the revenues. *(Schiller, 2000)*

Gross National Product (GNP): A measure of the country's economic performance. It is calculated by adding to the GDP the income earned by residents from investments abroad, less the corresponding income sent home by foreigners who are living in the country. *(Bishop, 2004)*

Gross Negligence: Actions that display a complete disregard for life or safety. A deliberate indifference to the rights of others. A failure to act in a prudent manner or to take reasonable precaution. *(Harney, 1992)*

Gross Weight: Weight of an item including the container and the packing materials. Group Purchasing Organization (GPO): An organization created by groups of purchasers in related areas of endeavor who come together and form a purchasing consortium in order to achieve aggregated volume thus achieving economies of scale. Hospitals, universities, school districts and airports are examples of GPO groups.

Groupthink: A phenomenon that occurs during decision making or problem solving when a team's desire to reach an agreement overrides its ability to appraise the problem properly. *(Business, 2002)*

Groupware: Software that allows individuals to share documents and work collaboratively. *(Jansen, 2002)*

Growth Rate: Percentage change in real output from one period to another. *(Schiller, 2000)*

GS1 US BarCodes and eCom: The organization dedicated to supporting the adoption and implementation of the GS1 System (formerly the EAN.UCC [Uniform Code Council, Inc.] System) in the United States. The BarCodes and eCom Group works with industry to solve supply chain problems through solutions based on the standards of the GS1 System. The GS1 System - the world's most accepted standards system - standardizes identification numbers, Electronic Data Interchange (EDI), Business Message Standards using Extensible Markup Language (XML) and other supply chain solutions for more efficient business. The GS1 System is currently used by more than one million member companies worldwide. For more information: http://barcodes.gs1us.org/About/BarCodesandeComFAQs/tabid/142/Default.aspx. (Jan 2007)

GSIN: CANADIAN *See Goods and Services Identification Number.*

GST: CANADIAN *See Goods and Services Tax.*

Guarantee: To warrant or insure performance or quality. A warranty. A written assurance attesting to the quality or durability of a product.

H

Haggle: To negotiate a price with a buyer or seller by the gradual raising of offers and lowering of asking prices until a mutually agreeable price is reached. *(Business, 2002)*

Hand-To-Mouth Buying: Frequent purchases in small quantities to meet only immediate, short-term requirements. *(ISM, 2000)*

Hard Bargaining: A term used in negotiation strategy. It is the last resort and involves take-it-or-leave-it tactics. Its use is limited to one-time or adversarial situations in which long-term or collaborative relationships are not an objective. *(Burt, Dobler,Starling, 2003)*

Hard Currency: Any national currency widely accepted in payment in international markets. Examples: Dollar, Euro, Yen. *(Schiller, 2000)*

Hawthorne Experiments: A series of studies undertaken at the Hawthorne plant of Western Electric in the United States from which Elton Mayo concluded that an approach emphasizing employee participation can improve productivity. They began in 1924 as a study conducted by the National Research Council into the relationship between workplace lighting and employee efficiency, and was then extended to include wage incentives and rest periods. *(Business the Ultimate Resource, Bloomsbury Publishing, 2002)*

Hazardous Material (HAZMAT): Any material that, under the conditions of transportation or storage, is capable of posing an unreasonable risk to health, safety, or property. Includes material classified as explosive, flammable, corrosive, combustible, poisonous, toxic, biological or radiological and compressed gases. May be referred to as HAZMAT. *Also see Waste.*

Hedging (Currency): Hedging protects the buyer against major swings in the value of the dollar against foreign currency. The buyer can achieve this via forward or futures contracts or via currency options. The buyer would enter into contracts to sell dollars for foreign currency at the time the supplier is paid. There is a profit or loss on a currency hedge contract that takes place behind the scenes. An important issue for those involved in global selling. *(Burt, Dobler, Starling, 2003)*

Herzberg, Frederick: Psychologist who found that job satisfaction and job dissatisfaction acted independently of each other. Two Factor Theory states that there are certain factors in the workplace that cause job satisfaction, while a separate set of factors cause dissatisfaction. Herzberg divided these into two factor groups: Hygiene factors (dissatisfiers) i.e., working conditions, salary, polices and procedures, etc.

and Motivator factors (satisfiers) i.e., recognition, achievement, advancement, job challenge, etc. Herzberg's factors represent the things people want from their workplace (motivators). He coined the term "job enrichment" to describe the process of redesigning work in order to build in the motivators needed to keep people interested in their jobs. *Also see Hygiene Factors.*

Hierarchy of Interpretation: Contract rendition and supplementation classified according to rank, capacity or authority; order is conventionally conceived of as a multi-stage process, in which various sources, including express terms, course of performance, course of dealing, trade usages, default rules, and general standards of reasonableness, are sequentially resorted to. The decision maker should not turn to any particular source before exhausting the previous ones, and in case of inconsistency, each source trumps the following ones.

Historically Underutilized Business (HUB): Generally refers to minority, women-owned, and small businesses. *Also see Economically Disadvantaged Individuals, Small Disadvantaged Business, Minority-Owned Business (MBE), and Women-Owned Business Enterprises (WBE).*

Hold Back: A public sector regulatory requirement primarily appearing in construction solicitation projects; it is designed to retain a predetermined monetary amount of the full payment or a stated length of time after the project is completed before agency payment is made to the prime contractor in order to ensure that sub-suppliers have been paid for their work and materials. *Also see Retainage.*

Hold Harmless: A clause that requires the contractor to assume liability for damages resulting from an action taken by the contractor and absolves the government or other contracting body from any responsibility for the consequences of the action. *(Harney, 1992)*

Holding Cost (Inventory): Expenses related to the risk of keeping inventories. May include overhead expenses, labor, equipment, administration, shrinkage and other costs such as repair of equipment, workers compensation, etc. *(Schiller, 2000)*

Hollow Corporation: A business entity that has outsourced most of its internal support operations such as payroll, purchasing, human resources, IT, etc. *(Business, 2002)*

Homogenization: The removal of characteristics differences between separate markets and cultures. *(Business, 2002)*

Honorarium: A token of appreciation in recognition of acts or professional services.

Horizontal Integration: The merging of functions or organizations that operate on a similar level. Involves the union of companies producing the same kinds of goods or operating at the same stage of the supply chain. A strategic plan where most business functions are outsourced except a few core activities. *(Business the Ultimate Resource, Bloomsbury Publishing, 2002)*

Horizontal Training: Broad-based training to develop employee diversification and focus on special skills. Training that provides experiences with those who can share the corporate knowledge base needed to continue the evolution of the profession. Also known as cross training.

Hourly Rate: The amount charged for an hour of labor; includes wages, all indirect costs, and profit. Canadian The hourly rate of pay for the classification as established in the standing offer.

HTML: *See Hypertext Markup Language.*

HUB: *See Historically Underutilized Business.*

Human Capital: The knowledge and skills possessed by the workforce. The health, strength, education, training, and skills which people bring to their jobs. *(Schiller, 2000)*

Human Resources:

1. The quantity and quality of human effort directed toward producing goods and services *Also called labor.*

2. The physical and mental abilities that people use to produce goods and services. *(Business, 2002)*

Hurdle Rate: Also referred to as "minimum cost differential", it is a predetermined amount of cost savings that must be achieved before a change in service delivery (e.g. moving from government service delivery to outsourcing) is considered warranted.

Hybrid Contracts: Contracts containing both services and product and are usually governed by the "predominant purpose" doctrine in order to determine whether the contract is one for goods or services.

Hygiene Factors: Aspects of Herzberg's theory of motivation that focus on the work setting and not the content of the work; these aspects include adequate wages, comfortable and safe working conditions, fair company policies and job security. *Also see Herzberg, Frederick.* *(Business, 2002)*

Hyperinflation: Inflation rate in excess of 200 percent and lasting for at least one year. *(Schiller, 2000)*

Hypertext Markup Language (HTML): The standard for publishing hypertext on the Web. It is a mark-up language not a programming language that uses tags to structure text into headings, paragraphs, links and lists. It tells a Web browser how to display text and images. *(Jansen, 2002)*

Hypothecate: A finance, banking and accounting reference to the use of property as collateral for a loan. *(Schiller, 2000)*

Hypothesis Testing: A statistical process of testing sample data from a statistical study to determine whether it is consistent with what is known about the sample population. *(Business, 2002)*

I

IATA: *See International Air Transport Association.*

ICC: *See Interstate Commerce Commission.*

ICE: *See Independent Cost Estimate.*

ICMA: *See International City/County Management Association.*

ID/IQ Contracts: *See Indefinite Delivery and Indefinite Quantity Contracts.*

Identical Bid: A bid that is exactly the same in all respects with another bid submitted at the same time and for the same requirements. Bids that are the same price but submitted by two or more bidders. In some cases terms and conditions may be the same. Identical bids may raise an antitrust concern when there is reason to suspect collusion between the bidders. *Also see Collusion.*

IFB: *See Invitation for Bids.*

IFPSM: *See International Federation of Purchasing and Supply Management.*

IMF: *See International Monetary Fund.*

Immaterial Defects: A tangential flaw having no material body or form that may be corrected without prejudice to other bidders. Example: Submission of two copies of a catalog when three copies were requested.

Imperfect Competition: A condition that exists when the marketplace is dominated by only one or possibly a few sellers. This is referred to as an Oligopoly. *Also see Oligopoly.*

Implied Authority: Authority that is not defined expressly, but is only determined by inferences and reasonable deductions arising out of the conduct of the principal toward the agent and the agent's actions. *Also see Express Authority and Inherent Authority.*

Implied Contract: A contract not created or evidenced by an explicit agreement of the parties, but inferred, as a matter of reason and justice, from the parties' act or conduct.

Implied contracts are sometimes divided into two categories: (1) those implied in fact and (2) those implied in law. Often referred to as "quasi-contracts". *(Black's Law Dictionary, 754, 1990)*

Implied Warranty: A warranty not specifically written into a contract but implied to be valid through law. *Also see Express Warranty.*

Implied Warranty of Fitness for a Particular Purpose: A warranty that applies to an instance where the seller, at time of contracting, has reason to know that the buyer wants the goods for a particular purpose and the buyer is relying on the seller's skill or judgment to select or furnish suitable goods. Example: A sawmill operator described in detail the mill's hydraulic system and asked a major oil company's representative to recommend proper oil. After some time, the operator discovered that the oil was not the proper product and was the cause of the hydraulic system's frequent breakdowns. The oil company's representative had to pay damages to the mill operator due to a breach of the implied warranty of fitness for a particular purpose.

Implied Warranty of Merchantability: A promise, arising by operation of law, that something that is sold will be merchantable and fit for the purpose for which it is sold. Implied warranties come in two general types: merchantability and fitness.

Imports: Goods and services purchased from international sources that flow into a country. *(Schiller, 2000)*

Imprest Fund: A petty cash fund. A cash reserve for expenditures made in accordance with established policies and controls.

Improper Influence: Any influences that induce or tend to induce a government employee or officer to give consideration to or act regarding a government contract on any basis other than the merits of the matter. *(FAR 3.401)*

In Bond: The state of goods that are manufactured, stored, or transported under the care of a bonded agency until duties or taxes are paid on the goods.

Incentive Contract: Any contract that includes a means to reward the contractor for reaching certain predetermined goals to reduce cost, reach a level of performance above the level contracted for or produce results that are beneficial and exceed contract requirements. *(Harney, 1992)*

Income Redistribution: An economic term that refers to a government policy to redirect income to a targeted sector of a country's population, for example, by lowering the rate of tax paid by low income earners. *(Schiller, 2002)*

Income Statement: A financial report that shows an organization's profitability over a period of time- months, quarter or year. *(Business, 2002)*

Incompatible Items: ***CANADIAN*** Certain materiel or substances which cannot be stored or shipped together or in close proximity to one another because they are likely to react to each other owing to their chemical composition.

Incoterms: *See International Commercial Terms.*

Incurred Costs: Actual costs rather than Estimated Costs.

Indefinite Delivery (ID) Contract: A type of contract in which the time of delivery is unspecified in the original contract but established by the procurement officer during contract performance.

Indefinite Delivery with a Definite Quantity: *See Delivery/Indefinite.*

Indefinite Quantity and Delivery: *See Delivery/Indefinite.*

Indefinite Quantity (IQ) Contract: A type of contract that provides for the delivery of indefinite quantities, within stated limits, of supplies or services to be furnished during a fixed period, with deliveries or performance to be scheduled by placing orders with the contractor.

Indemnification: The agreement of a contracting party to hold the other party harmless, to secure the other party against loss or damage, or to give security for the reimbursement of the other party in case of an anticipated loss. *(Black's Law Dictionary, 769,1990)*

Indemnify:
1. To protect against hurt or loss; to exempt from incurred penalties or liabilities.
2. To compensate or pay for damage.

Independent Contractor: A worker hired by a business or public entity to accomplish a given result who has the right to control or direct his or her own work as to the details and means by which the desired results are achieved.

Independent Cost Estimate (ICE): Generally refers to the Project Manager and/or Consultant's cost estimate for the pending project which reflects anticipated project costs for budgetary funding purposes, etc.

Indexation: The linking of a rate to a standard index of prices, interest rates, share prices, or similar items. This is what occurs on contracts where the pricing is tied to an index. *(Miller, 2006)*

Indirect Channel: The selling and distribution of products to customers through intermediaries such as wholesalers, distributors, agents, dealers and retailers. *(Business, 2002)*

Indirect Costs: Costs incurred that are not directly related to service delivery such as insurance and employee benefits. Costs that do not relate directly to performance such as overhead costs incurred in the normal course of business. *(Harney, 1992)*

Indirect Labor: Personnel not directly engaged in the manufacturing of products or the provision of services. Includes white-collar workers and office and support staff. *(Business, 2002)*

Industrial Engineering: An applied science discipline concerned with the prediction, planning, evaluation, and improvement of company effectiveness. The purpose of industrial engineering is to maximize efficiency, quality, and production through the best use of personnel, materials, facilities, and equipment. *(Business, the Ultimate Resource, 2002)*

Industrial Espionage: The practice of spying on a business competitor in order to obtain their trade or commercial secrets. *(Business, the Ultimate Resource, 2002)*

Industrial Goods: Goods produced for industry, which include processed or raw materials, goods used to produce other goods, machinery, components and equipment. *(Schiller, 2000)*

Industrial Revenue Bond: A bond that a private company uses to finance construction. *(Business, the Ultimate Resource,2002)*

Ineligible Bidder/Offeror: An individual or business entity who does not meet the stated qualifications for responding to a bid/offer or has been disqualified, suspended or debarred. *(Harney, 1992)*

Inflation: An increase in the average level of prices of goods and services usually measured incrementally over a given time period. *Also see Deflation.* *(Schiller, 2000)*

Inflation Index: **CANADIAN** A statistical table which reflects trends of inflation or deflation for classes of materiel items; can be used to forecast replacement costs.

Inflation Rate: The annul percentage rate of increase in the average price level. *(Schiller, 2000)*

Informal Bid/Proposal: A competitive bid, price quotation or proposal for supplies or services that is conveyed by a letter, fax, e-mail or other manner that does not require a formal sealed bid or proposal, public opening or other formalities. Generally relegated to requirements that may be considered low value or fall under a stipulated price/cost threshold.

Informalities/Irregularities: A submission of a bid or offer which contains minor defects or variations from the exact requirements of the solicitation that do not affect price or other mandatory requirements. Generally a matter of form rather than substance. Following legal review may sometimes be corrected within a certain time period. *Also see Irregularities and Informalities.* *(Harney, 1992)*

Information Technology (IT): An all encompassing term that refers to the devices used for creating, storing, using, or exchanging information, and to the design and practical application of the devices themselves. May refer to a group within the organization that is responsible for managing, evaluating and upgrading the various forms of technology the organization is using. *(Jansen, 2002)*

Infrastructure:
1. The physical facilities that support a country's economic activities, such as railroads, highways, ports, airports, schools, hospitals, communication systems and commercial distribution systems.
2. The transportation, communication, education, judicial and other institutional systems that facilitate market exchanges. *(Schiller, 2000)*

Inherent Authority: Authority based on a government's sovereignty, to enter into contracts, although not explicitly authorized. *Also see Implied Authority and Express Authority.*

Inherently Governmental Functions: A nebulous term that has been defined as those governmental functions or services which are so intimately related to the public interest as to mandate performance by government employees. These functions include those activities that require either the exercise of discretion in applying governmental authority or the making of value judgments in making decisions for the government.

In-House Bidding: The practice of allowing public agencies to compete against private providers of services. When a decision is made to contract out a service, the public service provider submits an offer/proposal to perform the services just as a private provider would. *(Harney, 1992)*

Initial Public Offering (IPO): The first issuance to the general public of stock in a corporation. *(Business, 2002)*

Initial Training: A method of training typically provided to new employees to expose them to the body of knowledge which includes agency policies and procedures that will be required to comprehend and perform the duties of their position.

In-Process Inspection: Inspection performed at the seller's site usually during the manufacturing or repair process to ensure work to date complies with specifications and contractual agreements; has the potential to identify defects which could not be seen during final inspection.

Inside Information: Information that is of advantage to investors that gives them unfair advantage over other investors and the general public. *(Business, 2002)*

Insolvency: The inability to pay debts when they become due. Insolvency will apply even if total assets exceed total liabilities, if those assets cannot be readily converted into cash to meet debts as they mature. *(Business, 2002)*

Insourcing (in-house): Moving an outsourced business operation in-house. *Also see Outsourcing and Contracting Out.*

Inspection: Examining and testing supplies or services to determine whether they conform to contract requirements. Comparing material and services received to the specifications. The buyer's legal right to inspect goods is stated in the Uniform Commercial Code (U.C.C.), Section 2-513(1).

Inspection Level: The quantity level at which samples are to be inspected, as well as the size of the sample.

Inspection Report: The result of an organized examination. A document made as a result of an analysis, informing the purchasing authority of a product's compliance with advertised specifications.

Installment Sale: A contractual exchange made with the agreement that the purchased goods will be paid for in fractional amounts over a specified period of time.

In-State Preference: A bid preference given to vendors/bidders doing business in the state.

Institute of Supply Management (ISM): Founded in 1915, ISM's mission is to lead the supply management profession through its standards of excellence, research, promotional activities, and education. ISM's membership base includes more than 45,000 supply management professionals with a network of domestic and international affiliated associations. ISM is a not-for-profit association that provides opportunities for the promotion of the profession and the expansion of professional skills and knowledge. Formerly National Association of Purchasing Management (NAPM).

Insurance: A contract between an insurance company and a person or group which provides for a monetary payment in case of a covered loss, accident, death or other insurable exposure. A form of risk mitigation.

Intangible Asset: An asset such as intellectual property or goodwill that is not physical. *(Business, the Ultimate Resource, 2002)*

Integrity: Personal adherence to a strict moral or ethical code of conduct. The National Institute of Governmental Purchasing has published an ethical code of conduct for its membership and a guide to those in the public purchasing profession. *Also see Ethics. (Miller, 2006)*

Intellectual Property: Includes inventions, patents, copyrights, trade secrets, trademarks, technical data, industrial designs that are generally protected and proprietary. *(Business, 2002)*

Interest Rate: The price paid for the use of money. Since most businesses borrow money, the interest rate is factored into their cost of doing business and may be reflected in the selling price of commodities and services. *(Schiller, 2000)*

Interested Party: *See Legal Standing.*

Intergovernmental Contract: An agreement in which one government contracts with another for the delivery of goods and services. *Also see Shared Services. (Harney, 1992)*

Intergovernmental Cooperative Purchasing: A variety of arrangements under which two or more governmental entities pool their commodity and/or service requirements to purchase aggregated quantities thus achieving economies of scale. The process usually involves a single combined bid or request for proposal in which all of the participating entities are named or their participation implied.

Interlocking Directorates: A provision of Section 8 of the Clayton Antitrust Act that prohibits corporations from reducing competition by having the same directors or officers. Sometimes called Interlocking Agreements. *Also see Clayton Act (The Clayton Anti-Trust Act).*

Intermediate Goods: Goods or services purchased for use as input in the production of final goods or services. *(Schiller, 2000)*

Intermodal: More than one mode of transportation is involved, i.e. air, rail, truck. *(ISM, 2000)*

Internal Rate of Return: An efficiency measure of return promised by an investment project over its useful life. It is some time referred to simply as yield on a given project. The internal rate of return is computed by finding the discount rate that equates the present value of a project's cash outflow with the present value of its cash inflow. In other words, the internal rate of return is that discount rate that will cause the net present value of a project to be equal to zero.

Internal Repairs: A rebuild/remanufacture process the extent and cost of which cannot be determined until the item is disassembled and evaluated. By definition, an internal repair must contain labor and parts.

Internal Service fund: A type of proprietary fund which accounts for the financing of goods or services provided by one department or agency to other departments or agencies of the governmental unit, or to other governmental units, on a cost-reimbursable basis. Some examples of internal service funds could include: self-insurance funds, central warehousing and purchasing, central data processing and central printing and duplicating. *Also see Enterprise Fund and Proprietary Fund.*

International Air Transport Association (IATA): A non-political international organization, with headquarters in Geneva. Membership is open to all scheduled airlines registered in countries that hold membership in the International Civil Aviation Organization. IATA promotes the standardization of air transportation rates and promotes safety and efficiency among commercial air carriers. *(www.iata.org)*

International City/County Management Association (ICMA): Established in 1914, ICMA is the professional and educational organization for chief appointed managers, administrators, and assistants in cities, towns, counties, and regional entities throughout the world. *(www.icma.org)*

International Commercial Terms (Incoterms): Terms published by the International Chamber of Commerce (ICC) which are globally recognized terms for moving goods internationally. These terms define the responsibilities and risks of both the buyer and seller including while the merchandise is in transit. Incoterms apply to goods that cross national borders.

International Federation of Purchasing and Supply Management (IFPSM): The union of 42 National Purchasing Associations worldwide. Within this circle, about 200,000 purchasing professionals can be reached. It is a non-profit organization registered in Aarau, Switzerland. (www.ifpmm.org)

International Monetary Fund (IMF): An organization established in 1947 to promote trade among member nations by eliminating trade barriers and fostering financial cooperation. There are 184 member countries working together to foster global monetary cooperation, secure financial stability, facilitate international trade, promote high employment and sustainable economic growth, while reducing poverty. For more information: www.imf.org.

International Organization for Standardization (ISO): Headquartered in Geneva Switzerland, it is an international body composed of members representing standards organizations. The objective of the organization is to promote the development of standards, testing and certification in order to encourage the international trade of goods and services. As of 2002, ISO reports that its standards have resulted in certification of over 400,000 organizations around the world. ISO has concentrated on quality improvement and has issued the ISO 9000 series of quality system standards. ISO 14000 standards certify an organization's environment performance. For more information: www.iso.ch.

Internet: Originally designed by the U.S. Department of Defense so that a communication signal could withstand nuclear war and serve military installations worldwide. A network of computer networks that is international in scope. It facilitates data transfer and communication services. The Internet is a valuable resource for public procurement personnel which facilitates research, benchmarking, networking, eProcurement and a host of other applications. *(Jansen, 2002)*

Internet Merchant: Specific to eCommerce, a business person or entity that sells a product or service over the Internet. *(Jansen, 2002)*

Inter-Program Efficiency: A method to determine the most efficient program, when competing programs exist, that are designed to meet the same objective. This analysis is conducted by using the measures of cost and anticipated benefits of the competing programs to determine which program produces the greatest net benefits. Then funds (budget) may be allocated appropriately to that most beneficial program. Example: If the goal is reducing juvenile crime activities, should the Police Department budget for youth activities be increased, decreased or eliminated when compared to youth programs in Recreation Departments or vice versa?

Interrogatory: Specific to legal matters; a written question or questions submitted to the other party involved in litigation usually under oath. Interrogatories are usually performed by attorneys representing the parties. *(Garner, 2004)*

Intersector Efficiency: A method of analysis that determines whether or not the cost of government activity yields more benefits to society than if it remained in the private sector. A typical example is daycare. Should it be provided by the agency as a government service, or should it be left to the private sector?

Interstate Commerce Commission (ICC): Created by the Government in 1887. Until 1996 it was the dominant regulatory agency that controlled the movement of goods between the states, regulated rates and granted operating authority to carriers. It ceased to exist upon enactment of the ICC Termination Act of 1995. *(Miller, 2006)*

Interstate Commerce Commission Termination Act of 1995: Eliminated the ICC; Surface Transportation Board was established within the Department of Transportation to take over the ICC functions.

Intranet: A private network of computers within a company or organization, that serves shared applications intended for internal use. (Jansen, 2002)

Intrapreneurs: Individuals in large firms who take responsibility for the development of innovations within the organization. (Business, 2002)

Intra-Program Efficiency: A method to determine the most efficient service delivery alternative, when several service delivery alternatives exist, to support a successful program. This analysis is done by using the measures of cost and anticipated benefits for competing service delivery alternatives used to support the program which service delivery alternative (or combination thereof) will provide the maximum net benefits. Then funds (budget) may be allocated appropriately to the alternative(s) that best support the success of the program. Example: If the program is supporting elder well-being through home delivery of nutritious meals should the meals be cooked by volunteers or a catering service? Should employees or taxi drivers deliver the meals?

Inventory: A detailed list of articles of property or goods held for sale or lease or furnished under service contracts, or raw materials or work in process or materials used or consumed. (Black's Law Dictionary, 824, 1990) A stockpile of goods which are physically recorded by item, value, quantity, volume, and description.

Inventory Control: Supervision and management of the supply, storage and accessibility of items held in inventory to insure an adequate supply of available material without excessive oversupply, back orders or stock outages.

Inventory (Holding Cost): *See Holding Cost (Inventory).*

Inventory Reconciling: CANADIAN Comparing the physical inventory figures with the perpetual inventory record and making any necessary corrections.

Inventory Shrinkage:
1. The loss of inventory value due to various factors such as breakage, evaporation, deterioration, theft or scrap.
2. A deliberate management attempt to downsize inventory value.

Inventory Turnover: The ratio of the costs of goods sold or used to the average inventory value to determine the number of times in a year that the entire inventory is issued and replaced.

Inventory Valuation: CANADIAN The determination of the acquisition cost, or market value portion of this cost, or market value assignable to on-hand raw materials, goods in process, finished stock, merchandise held for resale and supplies.

Inventory (Vendor Managed): A form of outsourcing whereby a contract is initiated with a private business to manage and control the inventory of the public entity. The contractor is responsible for all inventory functions which may include re-ordering. *Also called Vendor Managed Inventory.* (Miller, 2006)

Investment:
1. Expenditures on new plant, equipment, and structures in a given period plus changes in business inventory.
2. The purchase of something of value that will generate a return.
3. The purchase of a security, such as a stock or bond. (Business, 2002)

Investment Recovery Initiatives (IRI): Systematic efforts to manage materials and equipment surplus in order to recover as much of the original cost and investment as possible. May involve life cycle cost analysis. (ISM, 2000)

Invitation for Bid (IFB): All documents used to solicit competitive or multi-step sealed bids. *Also known as Invitation To Bid (ITB).*

Invitation to Negotiate (ITN): A competitive negotiation process that is used when the procurement authority deems it is in their best interest to negotiate with offerors to achieve "best value". A form of source selection that is similar to the Request for Proposal process. A short list of acceptable proposers is created. Two negotiation methods are allowed: single negotiation and concurrent negotiation. For more information: Journal of Public Procurement, Volume 3, Issue 3, 301-319-2003; Florida Department of Transportation-ATIS case study-6/24/99.

Invitation to Tender (ITT): CANADIAN A formal bid solicitation document when the estimated value of the requirement exceeds the threshold for formal bidding; two or more sources are considered capable of supplying the requirement; the requirement is adequately defined in all respects to permit the evaluation of tenders against clearly stated criteria; tenders can be submitted on a common pricing basis; and it is intended to accept the lowest-priced responsive tender without negotiations.

Invoice: A written account or itemized statement, addressed to the purchaser, of merchandise shipped or services performed, together with the quantity and the prices and other charges. An invoice is the sellers bill or written request for payment of work or services performed under the contract. *(Nash, Schooner, O'Brien, 1998)*

IPO: *See Initial Public Offering.*

IRI: *See Inventory Recovery Initiatives.*

Irregularities and Informalities: Defects or minor non-compliance contained within a response to a bid. A defect which is easily correctable. Deviations from the exact requirements of the solicitation that do not affect the price, terms or conditions of the bid document. A minor informality or irregularity is one, which is merely a matter of form and not of substance or pertains to some immaterial or inconsequential defect or variation of a bid from the exact requirement of the IFB, the correction or waiver of which would not be prejudicial to other bidders. Example: Failure to execute a required certificate. *Also see Informalities/Irregularities.*

ISM: *See Institute of Supply Management.*

ISO: *See International Organization for Standardization.*

ISO 9000, ISO 14000: Families of standards and guidelines relating to quality management systems and processes. ISO 9000 is primarily concerned with quality; ISO 14000 is primarily concerned with environmental management. Developed by the International Organization for Standardization. *(ISM, 2000)*

Issue: CANADIAN The release of materiel pursuant to a properly authorized requisition or instruction.

ITB: *See Invitation to Bid.* Sometimes referred to as Invitation for Bid (IFB). Item Description: CANADIAN The minimum data necessary to establish the identity of an item of supply for material management purposes.

ITN: *See Invitation to Negotiate.*

ITT: CANADIAN *See Invitation to Tender.*

J

Jawboning: The use of verbal encouragement or discouragement by political and economic leaders to achieve a targeted outcome or a particular result. It is an attempt to change public sentiment and move the economy in a certain direction without implementing formal economic policies. *(Schiller, 2000)*

JIT: *See Just In Time.*

Job Analysis: A review and determination, through observation and study, of pertinent information about a job - including specific tasks and necessary abilities, knowledge and skills. *(Business, the Ultimate Resource, 2002)*

Job Description: A formal, written explanation of a specific job, usually including job title, tasks, relationship with other jobs, physical and mental skills required, duties, responsibilities and working conditions. *(Ferrell, 2002)*

Job Enrichment: To include various motivational factors, such as opportunity for achievement, recognition, responsibility, and advancement into a job. An attempt by management to make a job more interesting and exciting. *(Ferrell, 2002)*

Job Order Contracting (JOC): Based on a competitively bid indefinite delivery-indefinite quantity (IDIQ) contract between a facility owner and a construction contractor. The contract typically has a base year with 2 to 4 option years. The contract sets parameters such as the types of work that can be done, location of work, design criteria and maximum amount of work to be awarded. The contract also has a unit-price book (UPB) that establishes a unit price to be paid for each of a multitude of construction line items. The contract's price is put in terms of a coefficient, which is a multiplier that covers the contractor's overhead and profit as well as any adjustments between the UPB and actual local prices. *(Burt, Dobler, Starling, 2003)*

J

Job Rotation: Movement of employees from one job to another in an effort to relieve the boredom often associated with job specialization as well as exposing the employee to other jobs in order to achieve cross-training and upward mobility opportunities. *(Business, 2002)*

Job Shadowing: The pairing up of a less-experienced employee with a veteran employee to transfer knowledge. The veteran is asked to share knowledge (and perhaps hands-on practice) in dealing with everyday issues or tasks in addition to the most difficult situations he or she has faced on the job.

Job Sharing: Performing one full-time job by two part-time employees. *(Ferrell, 2002)*

JOC: *See Job Order Contracting.*

Joint Administrative Purchasing: An arrangement under which part or all of the purchases of two or more governmental units are made by a joint purchasing office. *Also referred to as consolidated purchasing.*

Joint Bid Method: A form of intergovernmental cooperative purchasing in which two or more public procurement agencies agree on specifications and contract terms and conditions for a given item of common usage and combine their requirements for these items in a single request for competitive sealed bids. Once bids have been received and discussed by the participants, each public procurement agency issues and administers its own purchase order or contract.

Joint Ownership: Ownership by more than one party, each with equal rights in the item owned. Frequently applied to the ownership of property or other assets. *(Business, 2002)*

Joint Purchasing Office: A shared administrative agency created to perform the purchasing function for two or more governmental units in a joint administrative purchasing arrangement.

Joint Solutions Procurement (JSP): Partnering the supply community with the procurement agency where the supply community provides input to establish appropriate specifications, project designs, and deliverables prior to posting a solicitation for formal bids or proposals. These acquisitions normally involve high dollar value/high risk procurements.

Joint Venture: The coming together of two or more parties who combine their resources in response to a solicitation for bids or proposals (IFB/RFP). The relationship that is created is for the sole purpose of responding to the solicitation. *(Harney, 1992)*

Joint-Use (Agreements): Agreements between various government agencies that may involve the joint-use of public property such as buildings and equipment. For example, a public school district may share the use of a high school swimming pool with a county recreation and parks agency.

Judgmental Forecasting Method: A prediction tool that incorporates intuitive judgments, opinions and probability estimates. These forecasts are very subjective and are considered qualitative issues with no absolute resolutions. Generally this situation occurs when either the organization infrequently procures the product or service or if the product or service is relatively new or in a dynamic environment. An example is the rapid increase in demand for hybrid automobiles.

Junk Bonds: A special type of high-interest-rate bonds that carry higher inherent risks. *(Business, 2002)*

Juran, Joseph: Published the Quality Control Handbook in 1951. Developed the quality trilogy, which consisted of quality planning, quality control, and quality improvement. *(Business, 2002)*

Just-in-Time (JIT): A quality concept first perfected by the Japanese. Its basic tenet is the elimination of waste: the waste of overproduction, unneeded motion, transportation, excessive inventory and production and labor time. The term has been adapted to mean that previously held MRO inventory items are outsourced to JIT suppliers who may provide next day delivery. JIT generates best value through supplier partnerships which generate savings through labor, inventory, production and processing costs. *(Business, 2002)*

K

Kaizen: An approach to total quality management (TQM) originating in Japan. It is the Japanese word for "improvement". It can be described as continuously improving by making small improvements, mainly in process type improvements. If effectively practiced, it eliminates waste and generates dramatic improvement and cost savings. During the TQM revolution, many organizations practiced Kaizen in their manufacturing operations. *(Business, the Ultimate Resource, 2002)*

Kanban: A Japanese production management technique that uses cards attached to components to monitor and control workflow in a factory. It was first developed by the car manufacturer Toyota. Its theory became part of the total quality management movement. *(Business, the Ultimate Resource, 2002)*

KD: *See Knocked Down.*

Keiretsu: A Japanese loose conglomerate company that promotes interdependencies between firms with interlocking interests in each other and is characterized by close internal control, policy coordination and cohesiveness. Keiretsu business groups are alliances between firms that share close buyer-supplier relationships. *(Business, the Ultimate Resource, 2002)*

Kickback: The payment of something of value to an individual with the goal of persuading or influencing his or her decision or performance in a certain situation. May be in the form of cash or favors and is usually unethical.

Knocked Down (KD): A requirement that goods be shipped disassembled to reduce space required for transportation and storage or to achieve economies by having the product or goods assembled on-site. *(ISM, 2000)*

L

Labor Force: All persons over the age of 16 who are either working for pay or actively seeking paid employment. *(Schiller, 2000)*

Labor-Hour Contract: A variation of the time-and-materials contract differing only in that materials are not supplied by the contractor. Provides for the acquisition of services on the basis of direct labor hours at specified fixed hourly rates; is generally used when it is not possible to estimate the extent or duration of required work.

Labor Surplus Area: An area designated by the Secretary of Labor as having concentrated unemployment or underemployment in comparison with other areas. Used as one of the criteria for designating economically disadvantaged vendors/suppliers.

Lagging Indicator: A measure of economic activity that tends to change after the state of the general economy has changed. *Also see leading indicators.* *(ISM, 2000)*

Laissez Faire: A French phrase meaning "let it be". An economic doctrine that opposes government involvement in business and commerce. The philosophy of "leave the economy alone" of non-intervention by government in the market mechanism. *(Schiller, 2000)*

Landed Item Cost: The total external item-related costs incurred by the purchaser in obtaining an item from the vendor; i.e. sum of the individual directly-related costs such as the expenses (if any), taxes, custom duty fees, etc. This is especially helpful to the agency in determining its total cost to procure that specific item. It does not include any internal agency costs such as salary and overhead expenses, etc.

Last In-First Out (LIFO): A warehousing inventory term used to indicate that the latest acquired materials are assumed to be physically used first and the remaining materials acquired earlier in date time are assumed to be still on hand in inventory. The LIFO methodology does not rotate inventory therefore it tends to result in aged and outdated materials remaining in inventory; An accounting technique where the highest price is selected from a range of prices that have been paid for the item over a period of time, thus lowering the average cost per unit remaining in inventory while simultaneously increasing the cost of goods sold. The LIFO accounting technique tends to be more popular during inflationary periods, especially in private sector organizations, because of tax considerations. *Also see First in-First Out (FIFO).*

Late Bid/Proposal: A bid, proposal, withdrawal, or modification received, at the designated place for receipt, after the established due date and time. Procurement policies should be established in order to provide guidance regarding how late bids/proposals are handled administratively. In most public entities, late bids/proposals are not opened and may be returned to the bidder/proposer advising that the bid was received late (after the due date and time) and cannot be accepted.

Latent Defect: A defect, deficiency or imperfection that is not detected or discovered using generally accepted inspection methods. A defect that surfaces after final acceptance. It is not concealed damage. *Also see Defect.* *(NASPO, 2001)*

Law of Agency: The law of agency states that an agent is someone who acts on behalf of a principal. A product of common law that focuses not only on the creation of agent relationships but also the liability for losses suffered by others who deal with agents. There are two ways to create an agency relationship - by agreement between principal and agent or by law. *Also see Agent, Buyer and Principal.*

Law of Demand: The quantity of a good demanded in a given time period increases as its price falls. *(Schiller, 2000)*

Law of Supply: The quantity of a good supplied in a given time period increases as its price increases. *(Schiller, 2000)*

LBO: *See Leveraged Buyout.*

LCC: *See Life Cycle Cost.*

Leadership in Energy and Environmental Design (LEED) Certification: A certification issued by the U.S. Green Building Council (USGBC). It is a voluntary, consensus-based rating system, which delivers a sound and certifiable basis for identifying buildings that represent leadership in the use of sustainable building practices and design. Referred to as LEED Certification. *(www.usgb.org)*

Lead Time: The period of time from date of ordering to date of delivery, including the time required for the vendor to manufacture or prepare the goods for shipment; may include the time needed by the procurement function to process the purchase request, issue a solicitation, evaluate bids and award a contract. *Also see Supplier Lead Time.*

Leading Indicators: An economic term also referred to as cyclical indicators, these are groups of statistics that point to the future direction of the economy and the business cycle. May be helpful when performing price or supply forecasts. *(ISM, 2000) Also see Lagging Indicator.*

Lean Thinking: An organizational culture that is characterized by a comprehensive effort to identify and remove waste and thus improve efficiency in all areas including time, materials, people, money, facilities, quality, schedules, policies, customers, transportation and logistics.

LEAP (Learning and Education to Advance Procurement): Educational services offered by NIGP that offer opportunities for purchasing interns, practitioners and scholars to elevate professional recognition. The curriculum provides foundation courses leading to professional certification and advanced courses leading to an Executive Certificate in Public Procurement.

Learning Curve: A concept that originated in the observation that individuals performing repetitive tasks tend to improve incrementally the more frequently the task is performed. A technique that is used for projecting or estimating the amount of direct labor and material that will be used to manufacture a product on a repetitive basis. *(ISM, 2000)*

Lease: A contract by which one party (lessee) enters into a contract with a second party (lessor) for possession and use of property (equipment) for a specified period of time at a predetermined cost. There are two primary lease categories: Operating and Financial. Major benefits of a lease are: Obsolescence can be minimized or eliminated; Avoidance of large capital outlays; Maintenance problems may be reduced; The Lessee's working capital is not consumed and may be utilized for other projects.

Lease or Buy Decision: A decision based on the results of a cost/benefit analysis of the costs to own, costs to lease, and the advantages and disadvantages of any relevant qualitative factors. *(ISM, 2000)*

Lease-Purchase Agreement: A lease in which the lease payments are applied, in whole or in part, as installment payments for equity or ownership upon completion of the agreement.

Lease to Own/Purchase: CANADIAN The conveyance, by a lessor to a lessee, of the right to use a tangible asset usually for a specified period of time in return for rent. At a specified period of time the lessee may purchase the equipment outright by paying an additional specified sum.

LEED Certification: *See Leadership in Energy and Environmental Design (LEED) Certification.*

Legacy Costs: An economic term applied to those costs incurred by a business that apply to on-going contractual obligations resulting from agreements with collective bargaining units. Examples include pension and retiree benefits. *(Schiller, 2000)*

Legacy System: Any outdated computer/software system that remains in use despite the availability of more current technology. It usually is an archaic data management platform that may contain proprietary custom designed software. An old database management system running on mainframes. May run financials, payroll, human resources, purchasing, supply management, inventory control and other business processes. The name given to a "home grown" technology-database management system. *(Business, 2002)*

Legal Barriers: Refers to the effect that existing laws, statutes, or ordinances may have on governmental decision making or the lack thereof. *(Business, 2002)*

Legal Notice: A public notice required by law, ordinance or executive order. Generally placed in a newspaper of general circulation or may be posted on a web-site, magazine or other media, depending on the specific legal requirements.

Legal Standing: In common law, and under many statutes, standing is the ability of a party to demonstrate to the court sufficient connection to and harm from the law for action challenged to support that party's participation in the case. *Also reference Interested Party.*

Legality of Purpose: To be valid and enforceable, a contract must be consistent with federal, state or local law and cannot violate legal statutes of public policy. *(ISM, 2000)*

Legally Flawed: A document or situation that contains terms or conditions that are contrary to law which may make an award impossible.

Legislative Law: A source of public procurement law that may include written constitutions, statutes, ordinances, and charters.

Lessee: The party to whom a lease is granted.

Lessor: The party who owns the property in question and grants the lease.

Less-Than-Carload (LTC): A quantity of freight less than the amount necessary to constitute a full carload. A transportation/freight term that refers to a freight rate that is usually higher than for a full carload. *(ISM, 2000)*

Less-Than-Truckload (LTL): A quantity of freight less than the amount necessary to constitute a full truckload.

Letter Contract: Typically, a quickly crafted document, where exigency requires an immediate binding agreement so work can begin, but time does not permit the development of a definitive contract. An interim contractual agreement.

Letter of Credit: A document issued by a bank or lending institution authorizing the bearer to draw a specific amount from the bank or its agents. A letter extending credit up to a given amount at a certain affiliated bank for a person who has paid or guaranteed that amount to the issuing bank. This may be considered in lieu of a Performance Bond. *(ISM, 2000)*

Letter of Intent (LOI): A letter customarily employed as a preliminary understanding of parties that intend to enter into a contract. *(Black's Law Dictionary, 904, 1990)*

Letter of Interest (LOI): *CANADIAN* Letter sent to the buyer to measure interest in receiving feedback from suppliers. This may lead to re-opening or re-issuing of the opportunity for an open tender at a later date. An LOI or a Request for Information (RFI) is not open for bidding. *(Summit Magazine, On-Line)*

Level of Contractor: *CANADIAN* The identification of an individual contractor in the contracting organization's hierarchy as the prime contractor, subcontractor or other. The individual contractor's designation in the hierarchy determines the legal responsibility of that contractor and reporting structure relative to the customer (Owner).

Level-of-Effort (LOE) Contract: A type of contract stating the work in terms of an amount of effort (usually labor-hours or labor-years) to be performed by specified classes of employees over a given period of time. *(Nash, Schooner, O'Brien, 1998)*

Leveraged Buyout (LBO): A purchase in which a group of investors borrow money from banks and other institutions to acquire a company, using the assets of the purchased company to guarantee repayment of the loan. *(Business, 2002)*

Liability: A debt or an obligation to make future payment. *(Business, 2002)*

License: A legal instrument granting permission to do a particular thing, to exercise a certain privilege, to carry on a particular business, or to pursue a certain occupation. When granted by an appropriate government body, licenses are permits allowing a person, firm, or corporation to pursue some occupation or business, subject to regulation. *(Black's Law Dictionary, 919-20, 1990)*

Lien: The right exercised by one party to take or keep possession of or to control the property of another for the purpose of satisfying a debt or obligation. *(Harney, 1992)*

Life Cycle Cost (LCC): The total cost of ownership over the life span of the asset. An analysis technique that takes into account operating, maintenance, the time value of money, disposal and other associated costs of ownership as well as the residual value of the item.

Life Cycle Management: Includes the four phases of procurement and associated costs of owning assets, namely the acquisition planning phase, the procurement phase, the in-life-use phase and the disposal phase of the asset.

Life Expectancy: The number of years during which the asset is expected to remain in active use.

LIFO: *See Last In–First Out.*

Limitation of Cost: A provision that limits the total costs for which a contractor can be reimbursed under the terms of a cost reimbursement contract.

Limited Liability Company (LLC): A form of business ownership that provides limited liability and taxation like a partnership but places fewer restrictions on shareholders. *(Ferrell, 2002)*

Limited Warranty: A written warranty which fails to meet one or more of the minimum standards for a full warranty.

Line and Staff: An organizational structure having a traditional line relationship between superiors and subordinates and also specialized managers, called staff managers, who are available to assist line managers. *(Ferrell, 2002)*

Line Function: One of the three identified functions of a procurement department. This function includes its own authorized work to issue bids, requests for proposals, and contracts with vendors in order to obtain the necessary materials and services in support of agency operations; the procurement department is the primary point of contact when doing business with the agency under the principles of the law of agency; functions as a specific department within the agency that has its own budget and organizational hierarchy and appears as an individual department on the agency's organizational chart with other departments such as personnel, finance, police, fire, etc. *Also see Staff Function and Service Function.*

Line Item: An item of supply or service, specified in an invitation for bid or request for proposal, for which the bidder must bid a separate price.

Line Item Budget: Fixed budgets with monies appropriated for a particular period, usually one year, which can be tied to a specific project or item. This money is specifically allocated to that project or item and cannot be spent on other uses. They are easy to understand and are designed to maximize control and ensure financial accountability.

Line of Credit: An arrangement by which a bank or lending institution agrees to lend a specified amount of money to an organization upon authorized request. Assures that cash will be available to meet day-to-day business expenses. *(Ferrell, 2002)*

Line Object: CANADIAN A departmental classification of expenditure at the source. It is either coincident with the economic object or represents a subdivision of it.

Liquidated Damages: Damages paid usually in the form of a monetary payment, agreed by the parties to a contract which are due and payable as damages by the party who breaches all or part of the contract. May be applied on a daily basis for as long as the breach is in effect. May not be imposed as an arbitrary penalty. The key to establishing liquidated damages is reasonableness. It is incumbent upon the buyer to demonstrate, through quantifiable means, that damages did exist. *Also see Damages and Penalty Charge.*

Liquidation: A process in which a company ceases to be a legal entity, usually because it is insolvent. The company's assets are then sold by a liquidator to discharge debts. *(Business, 2002)*

Liquidity: The ability of an asset to be converted into cash. *(Schiller, 2000)*

Liquidity Ratios: Ratios that measure the speed with which a company can turn its assets into cash to meet short-term debt. *(Schiller, 2000)*

List Price: The published price of a product or service offered by the seller for sale to potential buyers. Due to competition in the marketplace, the list price may be subject to price discounting. If there is limited competition or strong demand the price may rise. *Also see Administered Price.* *(Business, 2002)*

LISTSERV: An automatic mailing list server targeting a specified group. When email is addressed to a LISTSERV mailing list, it automatically broadcasts to everyone on the list. *(Jansen, 2002)*

Litigation: One party to a contract bringing suit against the other party in a court of law. *Also see alternative dispute resolution.*

Living Wage: A term used by advocates to refer to the minimum hourly wage necessary for a person to achieve some specific standard of living. In the context of developed countries such as the United Kingdom or Switzerland, this standard generally means that a person working forty hours a week, with no additional income, should be able to afford a specified quality or quantity of housing, food, utilities, transport, health care, and recreation. This concept differs from the minimum wage in that the latter is set by law and may fail to meet the requirements of a living wage. *(Wikipedia 1.17.07)*

LLC: *See Limited Liability Company.*

Loan: *CANADIAN* The authorized issue of materiel on condition that it be returned, normally after a specified period of time and subject to agreed upon conditions.

Local Preference: *See Bid Preference, Buy Local and Preference.*

Local Public Procurement Unit: Any county, city, town, school district, special authority, or any other subdivision of the state, or public agency of any such subdivision, or educational, health, or other institution spending public funds for the procurement of services, supplies, or construction.

Local Purchase Authority: *CANADIAN* Delegated authority to initiate and administer a purchase instrument.

Lockbox: A postal address, usually a commercial bank, at which a company receives payments in order to speed collections from customers. *(Ferrell, 2002)*

Lock-out: A management's version of a strike, wherein a work site is closed so that employees cannot go to work. Any form of work stoppage that will impede a contractor's ability to perform the contracted work. *(Business, 2002)*

LOE: *See Level of Effort Contract.*

Logic Model (Systems approach): The purpose of the model is to identify logical relationships between inputs, resources, activities, outputs and short-, intermediate-, and long-term outcomes. Logic models illustrate a sequence of cause-and-effect relationships – a systems approach to communicate the path toward a desired strategic result. *(W.K. Kellogg Foundation, 2004)*

Logistics Management: The discipline responsible for the movement, routing, distribution, transportation, as well as interrelated activities that apply to goods and commodities. It may include procurement and supply activities in a very broad context.

LOI: *See Letter of Intent. Also see Letter of Interest.*

Long Term Contract: A decision to contract with a specified vendor over an extended period of time.

Long-Term Liabilities: Debts that will be repaid over a number of years, such as long-term loans and bond issues. *(Business, 2002)*

Loss: A business situation in which the total cost of production exceeds total revenue; negative profit. *(Schiller, 2000)*

Lot Tolerance Percent Defective (LTPD): The percent of defective items that a customer is willing to accept.

Lowball: To begin a sales negotiation or sales transaction by quoting low prices and then attempting to raise the prices once the buyer shows interest. *Also see Buying In.* *(Miller, 2006)*

Lowest Responsive and Responsible Bidder: The bidder who fully complied with all of the bid requirements and whose past performance, reputation and financial capability is deemed acceptable and has offered the most advantageous pricing or cost benefit, based on the criteria stipulated in the bid documents.

LTC: *See Less-than-Carload.*

LTL: *See Less-than-Truckload.*

LTPD: *See Lot Tolerance Percent Defective.*

Lump Sum: An aggregate or lot price which may represent the total price for a group of items in place of or in addition to unit prices for each individual item. The total price of a group of items which is priced as a whole for bidding purposes.

M

Macroeconomics: The study of aggregate economic behavior. The study of the economy in a larger context- to view it as a whole. *Also see Microeconomics.* *(Schiller, 2000)*

Mailbox Rule: A common-law rule providing that an acceptance of an offer becomes effective and creates a binding contract when it is transmitted rather than when it is received. *(Nash, Schooner, O'Brien, 1998)*

Maintenance: The upkeep of property that neither adds to its permanent value nor prolongs its intended life appreciably, but instead keeps it in an efficient operating condition.

Maintenance Bond: A surety guarantee which protects the purchaser against defects or inferior materials or workmanship for a specified period of time following the expiration of the initial warranty or guarantee period. An extended warranty guaranteed by a surety. *(Business, 2002)*

Maintenance, Repair, Operating (MRO): A supply management term that refers to various commodities that are generally of low value, purchased frequently and available from multiple sources. These items are often assigned to a buying team who specializes in these commodity areas. Typical examples include oil, rags, grease, tools, and hardware fasteners.

Make or Buy: A procurement decision that examines the cost/benefit of producing an item in-house or from an outside source. Two factors that stand out at the tactical level are: total cost of ownership and the availability of production capacity.

Managed Competition: *See Public-Private Competition.*

Management: A process designed to achieve an organization's objectives by using its resources effectively and efficiently in a changing environment. The management process consists of five functions: planning, organizing, directing, controlling and staffing. *(Ferrel, 2002)*

Management Audit: An audit conducted to determine the degree of management efficiency and effectiveness.

Management Buy-Out: The purchase of an existing business by an individual manager or management group from within the business. *(Business, 2002)*

Management Reports: A technique used to measure progress or to control procurement activities from collected data. These reports enable both procurement officials and managers to assess progress and readjust activities to accomplish the goals and objectives of the organization.

Mandatory: Obligatory, required by order, a provision that may not be waived.

Mandatory Requirements (Conditions): May apply to RFP's and IFB's and are conditions set out in the specifications/statement of work that must be met without alteration. Mandatory requirements should be clearly identified. Not meeting mandatory requirements may be grounds for disqualification.

Manifest: An itemization usually provided by the carrier which details the items included in a particular shipment. A bill of lading or an itemized listing of cargo. *(ISM, 2000)*

Manufacturer: A person or business entity that creates, makes, processes, or fabricates a product or something of value, which changes a raw material or commodity from one form to another or creates a new product or commodity. *(Business, 2002)*

M

Manufacturer Code: *CANADIAN* A numeric code assigned by respective government agencies to organizations which are sources of supply for items produced. The code numbers are also assigned to government manufacturing equipment or to certain special non-manufacturing organizations.

Manufacturer's Price List: A price list published in some form by the manufacturer and available to and recognized by the trade. The term does not include a price list prepared especially for a given bid.

Marginal Propensity to Consume (MPC): The fraction of each additional dollar of disposable income spent on consumption; the change in consumption divided by the change in disposable income. *(Schiller, 2000)*

Marginal Propensity to Save (MPS): The fraction of each additional dollar of disposable income not spent on consumption. *(Schiller, 2000)*

Marine Insurance: Insurance covering loss or damage of goods at sea. *(Ferrell, 2002)*

Market:
1. A group of individuals who have a collective need, purchasing power, and the desire and authority to spend money on goods, services, and ideas.
2. A setting where buyers and sellers establish prices for identical or very similar products, and exchange goods and/or services.
3. The aggregate forces (including economics) at work in trade and commerce in a specific service or commodity.

Market Analysis: The process of analyzing prices and trends in the competitive marketplace to compare product availability and offered prices with market alternatives and establish the reasonableness of offered prices. *Also see Demand Analysis, Procurement Profile, Spend Analysis and Supply Positioning.* *(Business, 2002)*

Market-Based Pricing: A pricing strategy that sets the value of a product from the market prospective and is based on supply and demand.

Market Demand: The total quantities of a good or service people are willing and able to buy at alternative prices in a given time period; the sum of individual demands. *(Schiller, 2000)*

Market Economy: An economy that relies on markets for basic decisions about WHAT to produce, HOW to produce it, and FOR WHOM to produce. Contrast to socialism or communism where political decisions determine market direction. *(Schiller, 2000)*

Market Grades: Used when procuring commodities that are traded regularly on the commodity exchange such as lumber, steel, food products, fuel, etc. Grading determines the quality level of the commodities. Trade associations, commodity exchanges and government agencies are sources of market grade information.

Market-Oriented Pricing: Price setting that occurs when prices are defined according to the range of the quality of the product or service provided by the supplier. Example: the good, better, best models of products with extra features such as are found in automobiles and electronics.

Market Research: Collecting and analyzing information about capabilities within the market to satisfy agency needs. The results of market research are used to arrive at the most suitable approach to acquiring, distributing and supporting supplies and services.

Market Segmentation: A strategy whereby a business divides the total market into groups of people who have relatively similar product needs. *(Ferrell, 2002)*

Market Share:
1. The percentage of total market output produced by a single firm.
2. The ability of a business entity to capture a large segment of a particular market.
3. A company's percentage of the total market in which it is a dominant player. *(Ferrell, 2002)*

Market Supply: The total quantities of a good that sellers are willing and able to sell at alternative prices in a given time period. *(Schiller, 2000)*

Market Survey: An attempt to determine whether there are qualified sources capable of satisfying the specific requirements for supplies, services or construction: may range from written or telephone contacts with knowledgeable experts regarding similar requirements, to consultation of technical or scientific journals, to solicitations for information or planning purposes only.

Market Testing: A service contracting technique which refers to the use of public-private competitions to compare or benchmark in-house service delivery approaches and costs against the private sector. *(Ferrell, 2002)*

Market Value: *CANADIAN* The price which a product, service or property might be expected to bring if offered for sale in a fair market, i.e. a market that is not prone to fluctuations.

Marketable Securities: Temporary investment of "extra" cash by organizations for up to one year in U.S. Treasury bills, certificates of deposit, commercial paper, or Eurodollar loans. *(Ferrell, 2002)*

Marketing: A group of activities designed to expedite transactions by creating, distributing, pricing, and promoting goods, services and ideas. *(Ferrell, 2002)*

Marketing Channel: A group of organizations that moves products from their producer to customers; also called channel distribution. *(Ferrell, 2002)*

Marketing Mix: The four marketing activities—Product, Price, Promotion and Distribution—that the business can control to achieve specific goals within a dynamic marketing environment. *(Ferrell, 2002)*

Maslow's Hierarchy (of Need): A theory developed by Abraham Maslow, that arranges the five basic needs of people: Physiological, Security, Social, Esteem and Self-Actualization—into the order in which people strive to satisfy them. Once a need is satisfied, it is no longer a motivator. *(Ferrell, 2002)*

Mass Production: Large scale manufacturing, often designed to meet the demand of a particular product. *(Business, the Ultimate Resource, 2002)*

Material:
1. A substance from which something is made or can be made such as building materials, paper, plastic, or other materials.
2. A substance that has a particular quality such as a sticky material, explosive materials, genetic material. *(Merriam Webster)*

Material Credit: A credit issued by the warehouse upon the return of requisitioned supplies found to be in excess of requirements.

Material Defects: Defects that are a matter of substance that affect price or quality and do not conform to the solicitation requirements.

Material Life Cycle: The phases through which material assets pass including, assess and plan material requirements; acquisition; operation, use and maintenance; disposal.

Material/Materiel Forecasting: Estimating future needs to avoid stock outs or oversupply.

Material/Materiel Requirements Planning (MRP) System: A technique used to determine the quantity of dependent demand materials used in a planning period. May be used to schedule and control production inventory levels, and deliveries from outside suppliers.

Material Safety Data Sheets (MSDS): Documentation concerning a hazardous chemical that identifies the chemical, the common names

M

of the ingredients, the physical and chemical characteristics, the hazards of the chemicals and the emergency and first aid procedures to be considered when working with the chemical.

Material Substitutions: An example of "second level cost savings" achieved by identifying and qualifying acceptable material alternatives that meet specification requirements but cost less than existing materials. *(Crimi, Kauffman, Inside Supply Management Magazine, March 2003)*

Material Variance/Material Deviation: A major variance, change, deviation or substitution taken to specifications by a bidder/offeror that gives the responder a substantial advantage or benefit not enjoyed by all other responders or that gives the purchaser something significantly different from what was specified. *(Nash, Schooner, O'Brien, 1998)*

M

Matériel: Term commonly used by warehouse environments and the military to refer to equipment, apparatus and supplies used by an organization or institution. *(Merriam Webster)*

Matériel Management: A comprehensive integration of the various supply management functions within a particular organization. May include functions such as purchasing, storage, inventory control, material/materiel forecasting, receiving, transportation, inspection and quality control. Also see Supply Chain Management. *(ISM, 2000)*

Materiel Management Institute: A Canadian non-profit organization offering professional development in the field of public sector materiel and supply management. *(www.mmi-igm.ca)*

Maverick Spending: Used to describe purchases or expenditures not processed through a procurement organization. Direct spending by operational units outside of procurements control. *(Burt, Dobler, Starling, 2003)*

Maximum Stock Level: The level which represents the maximum amount of stock of an item that may be held.

May: Denotes the permissive in a contract clause or specification. *Also see Shall.*

MBE: Minority Business Enterprises. *Also see Economically Disadvantaged Individuals, Small Disadvantaged Business, Historically Underutilized Business (HUB), and Women-Owned Business (WBE).*

McGregor, Douglas: A social scientist who authored "The Human Side of Enterprise" published in 1960 which examines management theories on behavior of individuals at work. He formulated two models which he called Theory X and Theory Y. *Also see Theory X and Theory Y.*

Mean: The arithmetic average. The average value of a set of numbers. *(Business, 2002)*

Mechanic's Lien: A lien in favor of those who have performed work or furnished materials for the construction of a building; is attached to the land as well as the building in order to secure payment.

Median: The mid-point in a list of numbers or occurrences. *(Business, 2002)*

Mediated Arbitration: An ADR process frequently referred to as "med-arb". It begins as mediation until an impasse is reached. When an impasse is reached, the neutral party is authorized by the parties to issue a binding opinion on the cause of the impasse or the remaining issues in dispute.

Mediation: A voluntary, flexible technique for resolving disputes. The contracting parties present their positions to a mediator who then works with them in negotiating a settlement. Generally each party appoints a principal with the authority to settle the dispute. *(Nash, Schooner, O'Brien, 1998)*

Memorandum of Understanding (MOU): A quasi-contract generally entered into between government agencies and private sector contractors who may be providing services to the government. It may also be entered into between inter/intra government agencies and details the essence of the agreement between the parties but lacks the enforceability of a contract.

Merchantable: Of commercially acceptable quality: the quality and condition of the item to be sold to fulfill the requirements of the purchaser.

Merchantable Quality: A requirement of the Sale of Goods Act that goods must be fit for at least one ordinary purpose; adequate for ordinary use.

Merger Clause: The purpose of a merger and integration clause is to prevent the parties to a contract from later claiming that the contract does not reflect their entire understanding. A party entering into a contract which includes this type of language should make sure that all promises and agreements are actually included in the written contract, as otherwise it may be impossible to enforce those unwritten promises. *(www.expertlaw.com/library/business/contract_clauses.html)*

MERX: CANADIAN A Canadian online service that advertises government contracting opportunities to potential bidders. *(Summit Magazine, On-Line)*

Metric: The term given to the measurement of performance. An analytical application of measurements that allows comparison of performance standards.

Metric Conversion Act of 1975: An act designating the metric system as the preferred system of weights and measures for United States trade and commerce requiring all agencies to use the metric system in their acquisitions, unless it is impracticable to do so or is likely to cause significant inefficiencies or loss of market to United States firms. *(FAR 11.002)*

Metric System: A decimal system of weights and measures, based on the meter as the unit of length, the gram as the unit of mass or weight, and the liter as unit of volume.

Microeconomics: The study of individual behavior in the economy, of the components of the larger economy such as consumers or individual households. *Also see Macroeconomics.* *(Schiller, 2000)*

Milestone Code: CANADIAN A generic code which indicates where the goods and/or services are in the materiel life cycle process.

Milestone Payment: A more sophisticated form of progress payment that shifts the risk by tying payments to the successful completion of predetermined work that are deemed significant indicators of progress toward contract completion.

Milestones: Designated steps of the planned acquisition which usually signify a completion of a requirement or delivery of materials. Payments may be targeted to the completion of milestones. *Also see deliverable.* *(Harney, 1992)*

Minimum Cost Differential: *See Hurdle Rate.*

Minimum-Maximum Inventory Levels: A simplistic inventory system in which a minimum quantity and maximum quantity are set for an item and when the quantity drops below the minimum you order up to the maximum. This will guard against stock outs as well as prevent the buildup of stock, either of which can be costly to the organization.

Minimum Order Quantity: Minimum quantity that may be ordered on any one purchase order/ contract.

Minimum Stock Level: The planned lowest level of stock, below which stock is normally flagged for management attention and orders expedited.

Mini-trial: An alternate dispute resolution technique, that is flexible, voluntary and nonjudicial. Principals (top management) hear a short presentation of the factual and legal positions of the parties in dispute and engage in nonbinding negotiations to resolve a claim. The procedure permits either party to withdraw at any time without prejudicing the litigation process.

Minor Irregularity: A variation from the solicitation that does not affect the price of the contract or does not give a respondent an advantage or benefit not enjoyed by other respondents, or does not adversely impact the interests of the contracting party.

Minority-Owned Business Enterprise (MBE): A business which is owned or controlled by a member of a recognized minority group, as defined by the public entity. *Also see Economically Disadvantaged Individuals, Small Disadvantaged Business, Women-Owned Business (WBE) and Historically Underutilized Business (HUB).*

Misrepresentations: In the context of conditions that may lead to a voidable contract, misrepresentation is when one of the parties to the contract made a wrong statement about some material element of the contract and, in reliance on this statement, the other party entered into the contract.

Mission Statement: A short memorable statement of the reasons for the existence of an organization which may encompass its core values. *(Business, 2002)*

Mistake (in Bids): Minor errors made in the form of bidding; for example, failure to insert a decimal point. Clerical mistakes, apparent on the face of the bid, may be corrected. Once a mistake is suspected, the purchasing official is required to request verification of the bid.

M

Mistake of Fact: A misunderstanding of the facts or flawed perception of the real state of affairs, which may be remedied by the Court.

Mistake of Law: An error, not in the actual facts but in their legal significance, relevance or consequence, for which there is no relief from the Courts.

Misuse: Improper or incorrect use of something of value that was intended for another purpose.

Mitigation: The alleviation, reduction, abatement or diminution of a penalty or punishment imposed by law. *(Black's Law Dictionary, 1002, 1990)*

Mixed Economy: An economy that uses both market signals and government directives to allocate goods and resources. *(Schiller, 2000)*

Mobilization: The initial effort to perform a construction contract by hiring necessary personnel and moving the required equipment and facilities on to the site of the work. Contracting agencies frequently include a separate bid line item for this effort on certain construction projects in order to permit the contractor to be paid promptly for this effort. *Also see Demobilization.* *(Nash, Schooner, O'Brien, 1998)*

Mock-Up: The model of a device or item of equipment, either full sized or built to scale, used for analysis, display, testing or to study the details or features of design.

Mode: The type of average that indicates the most frequent instance of a number or happening. The number in a distribution that occurs the most frequently. *(Business, 2002)*

Model Number: An identification number assigned to describe a style or class of item, such as a particular design, composition or function, by the manufacturer or distributor of that item.

Model Procurement Code: *See ABA Model Procurement Code for State and Local Governments.*

Modification: Any written alteration to a provision of any contract accomplished by mutual agreement of the parties to the contract. *Also see Change Order.*

Monetary Policy: The use of money and credit controls to influence macroeconomic outcomes. The Federal Reserve is the chief monetary policy setter in the United States. *(Business, 2002)*

Monetary System: The set of government regulations concerning a country's monetary reserves and its holdings of notes and coins. *(Business, 2002)*

Money: Anything generally accepted as a medium of exchange. *See Functions of Money.* *(Schiller, 2000)*

Monitoring: A contract administration tool, whereby certain procedures are developed to assure the public entity that contracted services are being delivered in accordance to the terms and specifications of the contract. *See Quality Assurance.*

Monopolistic Competition: The market structure that exists when there are fewer businesses than in a pure-competition environment and the differences among the goods they sell are small. *(Schiller, 2000)*

Monopoly: A market situation where there is one seller and many buyers of a product or service that has no close substitution and where the seller has considerable control over price because of the lack of competition. *(NIGP, 2004)* A company or group having exclusive control and ownership. *(American Heritage, 2001)*

Monopsony: A market in which there is only one buyer. *(Schiller, 2000)*

Morale: An employee's attitude toward their job, employer, and colleagues. *(Ferrell, 2002)*

Motivation: An inner drive that directs a person's behavior toward goals and the accomplishment of those goals. *(Ferrell, 2002)*

MOU: *See Memorandum of Understanding.*

Moving Average: A continuous average method used to gather the most current usage information about an item by taking current trends into account and always using the most recent data. For example, a 12-month period would be the average monthly usage for the immediately preceding 12 months; as the year progresses, the forecast is updated by dropping the oldest month's data (13 months ago) and adding the most recent month's data.

MPC: *See Marginal Propensity to Consume.*

MPS: *See Marginal Propensity to Save.*

MRO: *See Maintenance, Repair, Operating.*

MRP: *See Material Requirements Planning.*

MSDS: *See Material Safety Data Sheets.*

Multinational Corporation: A corporation that operates on a world-wide or global scale, without significant ties to any one nation or region. *(Business, 2002)*

Multiple Award: Contracts awarded to more than one supplier for comparable supplies and services. Awards are made for the same generic types of items at various prices. Usually the result of aggregated line item bids of similar product categories.

Multi-Step Bidding: A method of source selection involving two competitive steps, combining the elements of both competitive sealed bids and competitive sealed proposals. The first step may require the submission of technical and price proposals with only the technical proposals being evaluated and scored. The second step involves the opening of price proposals of those firms who have achieved the highest technical scores.

Multi-Year Contract: A procurement contract that extends for longer than one year.

Mutual Assent: In contracts, the agreement of each party to all the terms and conditions in the same context and with the same meaning.

Mutuality of Obligation: One of the elements of a contract. Both parties to an agreement are obligated, or none of the parties is obligated. Both parties must supply consideration to the other party. It is a sub-element of consideration. There may be more than two parties obligated in an agreement.

MWBE: Minority and Women's Business Enterprises. *Also see Economically Disadvantaged Individuals, Small Disadvantaged Business, Historically Underutilized Business (HUB), Minority-Owned and Women-Owned Business Enterprises (MBE and WBE).*

N

NAEP: *See National Association of Educational Procurement.* Previously known as NAEB.

NAFTA: *See North American Free Trade Agreement.*

NAPM (National Association of Purchasing Management): *See Institute for Supply Management (ISM).*

Narrative Evaluations: A form of performance measurement and feedback that can be used as an alternative or supplement to other evaluation criteria. Narrative evaluations generally consist of several paragraphs of written text about the individual's performance. This type of evaluation can be very subjective based on the use of words, phrases, and tone of writing style.

NASPO: *See National Association of State Procurement Officials.*

National Association of Educational Procurement (NAEP): Formerly known as the National Association of Educational Buyers (NAEB), its stated mission is to facilitate the development, exchange and practice of effective and ethical procurement principles and techniques within higher education and associated communities, through continuing education, networking, public information and advocacy.

National Association of Purchasing Management (NAPM): *See Institute for Supply Management (ISM).*

National Association of State Procurement Officials (NASPO): A non-profit association dedicated to strengthening the procurement community through education, research, and communication. It is made up of the directors of the central purchasing offices in each of the 50 states, the District of Columbia and the territories of the United States. NASPO is an organization through which the member purchasing officials provide leadership in professional public purchasing, improve the quality of purchasing and procurement, exchange information and cooperate to attain greater efficiency and economy. *(www.naspo.com, 12.29.06)*

National Contract Management Association (NCMA): An organization composed of individuals who are engaged in public and commercial contracting through government agencies and companies or are in related fields of endeavor.

National Debt: The accumulated debt of the Federal Government. *(Schiller, 2000)*

National Income: The amount of aggregate income earned by suppliers of resources employed to produce GNP; net national product plus government subsidies minus indirect business taxes. *(Schiller, 2000)*

National Institute of Governmental Purchasing (NIGP): A national, membership-based, non-profit organization providing support to professionals in the public sector purchasing profession. NIGP provides its members with education, professional networking, research, and technical assistance. Their mission is to develop, support and promote the public procurement profession through premier educational and research programs, professional support, and advocacy initiatives that benefit members and constituents.

National Institute of Governmental Purchasing Commodity/Service Code: A numbering system developed by NIGP to identify goods and services purchased by public purchasing entities; serves as the cornerstone of an automated purchasing function, helps vendors identify the goods and services to bid, and enables different jurisdictions to share purchasing information.

National Institute of Municipal Law Officers (NIMLO) Model Code: A document prepared by the National Institute of Municipal Law Officers which includes standards against which a jurisdiction can compare its procurement laws.

National Institute of Standards and Technology (NIST): A non-regulatory federal agency (formerly known as the Bureau of Standards) within the U.S. Commerce Department's Technology Administration. NIST's mission is to promote U.S. innovation and industrial competitiveness by advancing measurement science, standards, and technology in ways that enhance economic security and improve our quality of life. *(www.nist.gov, 12.29.06)*

National Item Identification Number: Digits 7 to 13 of a NATO stock number that are non-significant but sequentially assigned by each National Codification Bureau to a unique item of supply.

National Motor Freight Classification (NMFC) Guide: A list of all items, in theory, that could possibly be transported by a common carrier. The list of items then has a class associated with each item. The class is determined by storability, density, handling characteristics and value of the item being shipped. Class (along with distance and weight) is used by the common carrier of the goods to determine the rate of the shipment. *Also see Class Rate.*

National Purchasing Institute (NPI): A non-profit organization designed to establish cooperative relationships among its members and to develop efficient purchasing methods and practices in the areas of governmental, educational, and institutional procurement. The mission of NPI is to facilitate the educational and professional development of its members. NPI is an affiliate of the Institute of Supply Management, (ISM). *(www.npiconnection.org/home/index.htm, July 2007)*

NATO: *See North Atlantic Treaty Organization.*

NATO Codification System: A uniform system used as a common method to classify, identify and designate all items of supply by means of a stock number.

NATO Standard Item: An item selected by an officially constituted NATO standardization group, which would, when manufactured in any NATO country, always meet the same performance, application, and quality standards.

NATO Stock Number: A 13 digit number used to identify items of supply consisting of the NATO Supply Classification, the NATO Nation Code Number, National Item Identification Number, and the NATO Item Identification Number.

NATO Supply Classification: Digits 1 through 4 in the NATO Stock Number, includes the group and the class within the group, the whole being known as the supply class.

Natural Resources:
1. Land, forests, minerals, water, and other things that occur naturally without human intervention.
2. "Gifts of nature" that are used to produce goods and services. *(Schiller, 2000)*

NCMA: *See National Contract Management Association.*

Near Money: Assets that can be quickly turned into cash but that cannot be used directly as a medium of exchange like paper money or checks. *(Business, 2002)*

Negotiate: To communicate or confer with another party to reach an agreement or compromise to settle some matter.

Negotiated Fee: CANADIAN The monetary fee negotiated by Supply and Services Canada with customer departments for cost recovery revenue on services provided.

Negotiation: Conferring, discussing, or bargaining to reach agreement in business transactions. A bargaining process between two or more parties, each with its own agenda and objectives, seeking to reach a mutually satisfactory agreement on, or settlement of, a matter of common concern. A process of planning, reviewing, and analyzing used by a buyer and a seller to reach acceptable agreements or compromises.

Negotiation Team: A group of people, typically including a procurement official, project manager, technical staff, financial analyst, and legal expert who have the essential skills or knowledge necessary to reach a sound agreement. This team can determine: the most appropriate type of contract; terms of the contract; special warranty or delivery provisions; technical and engineering specifications; subcontractors needed, as well as other negotiable goals. The complexity of the negotiation will determine the size of the team. A negotiation team is usually selected for a major acquisition and may include some or all members of the Evaluation Committee. *Also see Evaluation Committee/Team.*

Net Cash: Payment for goods sold, to be made within a rather short period with no deduction allowed from the invoice price.

Net Income: The total profit (or loss) after all expenses including taxes have been deducted from revenue; also called net earnings. *(Schiller, 2000)*

Net Investment: Gross investment less depreciation. *(Schiller, 2000)*

Net Lease: A lease that requires the lessee to pay for things that the owner usually pays for. *(Business, 2002)*

Net Present Value (NPV): The total present value (PV) of a time series of cash flows. It is a standard method for using the time value of money to appraise long-term projects. Used for capital budgeting, and widely throughout economics, it measures the excess or shortfall of cash flows, in present value terms, once financing charges are met. In short, it is today's value of future cost and benefits

Net Price: Price after all discounts, rebates, etc. have been allowed.

Net Proceeds: CANADIAN The amount received for the disposal of a material asset after subtracting the costs associated with completing the disposal action.

Net Stock Position: CANADIAN The current on-hand balance of inventory.

Net Weight: The actual weight of the contents of a container or the cargo of a vehicle.

Net Worth: The amount stated on a company's balance sheet when liabilities are subtracted from assets. This amount provides a rough appraisal of the amount of money a company has retained in its business and thus gives an indication of the financial capability of the company. It is used in making the determination of whether the company is a responsible contractor. *(Nash, Schooner, O'Brien, 1998)*

Neutral Advisor: An individual who functions specifically to aid parties in resolving controversies through Alternative Dispute Resolution procedures.

New York Mercantile Exchange (NYMEX): A stock exchange resident in New York City, that is self-regulated but must comply with the regulations of the U.S. Securities and Exchange Commission. *(Ferrell, 2002)*

Niche Market: A very specific market segment within a larger market. It may involve very specialized goods or services with very few if any competitors. The niche market may be characterized by exclusiveness or a particular differentiating feature that makes it unusual or unique. *(Business, 2002)*

NIGP: *See National Institute of Governmental Purchasing, Inc.*

NIGP Commodity/Service Code: *See National Institute of Governmental Purchasing Commodity/Service Code.*

NIMLO Model Code: *See National Institute of Municipal Law Officers Model Code.*

NIST: *See National Institute of Standards and Technology.*

NMFC: *See National Motor Freight Classification.*

No Bid: A response to an IFB (Invitation for Bid) stating that the respondent does not wish to submit a bid; functions to prevent suspensions from the bidders list for failure to show active interest or submit bids.

NOI: *See Notice of Intent.*

Nolo Contendere: A Latin phrase meaning "I will not contest it." As a plea in criminal proceeding, it has an effect similar to pleading guilty; however, the defendant neither admits nor denies the charges, and the plea cannot be used against the defendant in a civil action based on the same acts. *(Black's Law Dictionary, 1048, 1990)*

Nominal Group Technique: A group decision-making technique that focuses on generating alternatives and selecting among them by asking group members to independently write down ideas, present them in turn, clarify them for the group, and rank them by voting privately. A brainstorming technique used by cross-functional purchasing teams. *(Business, the Ultimate Resource, 2002)*

Non-Branded Goods: Goods that are not linked to a particular brand name, manufacturer, or producer, and may be perceived to be of low quality. *(Business, 2002)*

Non-Competitive Negotiation: The process of arriving at an agreement through discussion and compromise when only one source is available to meet the requirement.

Non-Conformance: The failure of material or services to meet specified requirements for any characteristic or requirement.

Non-Durables: Consumer goods only expected to last less than three years. *(Schiller, 2000)*

Non Excusable Delay: A foreseeable delay caused by either party to the contract which often occurs as a result of financial difficulties, lack of equipment and facilities, lack of materials or lack of knowledge.

Non-Expendable (Items or Supplies): Supplies that are not consumed during use or that do not loose their identity during use.

Nonperforming Asset: An accounting term that refers to an asset that is not producing income. *(Business, 2002)*

Nonrecurring Costs: Costs that are incurred by a contractor/vendor at the beginning of the contract and are not expected to recur on future work. Certain nonrecurring costs may be recoverable upon cancellation of a multi-year contract provided they have been addressed in the contract documents. Examples of nonrecurring costs include special tooling, plant relocation and workforce training. *(Nash, Schooner, O'Brien, 1998)*

Non-Responsible (Bid): A response to a bid or offer from a contractor, business entity or individual that does not have the ability or capability to fully perform the requirements of the bid or offer. A business entity or individual who does not possess the integrity and reliability to assure contractual performance.

Non-Responsive (Bid): A response to a bid or offer that does not conform to the mandatory or essential requirements contained in the Invitation for Bids (IFB).

Non-Stocked Item: CANADIAN An item which is not held in a supply system inventory for issue to customers when ordered, but which may be obtained on demand.

Non-Waiver Agreement: A written agreement signed by the parties to the agreement that they understand the agreement in its entirety and nothing shall be deemed to constitute a waiver of the agreement.

Norm: Informal, unstated rules that govern and regulate group behavior. *Also see Ethics.* *(Ferrell, 2002)*

Normal Inspection: Type of examination used when there is no statistically significant evidence that the quality of the product being submitted is better or poorer than the specified quality level.

Normative Economics: Considers "what ought to be"—value judgments, or goals of public policy. *(Schiller, 2000)*

Norming: A term used in group development where interaction changes as members agree on a common goal, assign individual tasks, and define a set of rules and roles to ensure effective and productive team interaction.

North American Free Trade Agreement (NAFTA): Passed by Congress in 1993, it is an agreement between Canada, Mexico and the United States, designed to create a Free Trade Area (FTA) consistent with World Trade Organization's (WTO) rules, whereby all tariffs will be eliminated within the FTA over a transition period.

North Atlantic Treaty Organization (NATO): An International organization made up of 26 countries that each retains their full sovereignty. NATO provides a forum in which the United States, Canada and European countries can consult together on security issues of common concern and take joint action in addressing them. *(www.nato.itn, July 2007)*

Notary Public: A public officer authorized to attest and certify, by signature and official seal, certain types of documents, to give them credit and authenticity so they may be used as evidence and qualified for recording and to take affidavits and deposition.

Notice of Award: A written notification from the public entity to the successful bidder, or offeror stating that there is an award of a contract in accordance with a bid or proposal previously submitted, and that effective with receipt the vendor or contractor shall proceed with performance; allows work to start while contract is printed and readied for distribution.

Notice of Intent (NOI): Public notice issued to announce the intended award of an agreement to a certain supplier or service provider without formal competitive sourcing. Any bidder that wishes to participate in this work may object to the award. These types of solicitations are often used if a satisfactory relationship exists with a supplier or service provider and it is not in the organization's best interest to change providers. Organizations should consider the value attached to an alternate firm, stage in the project life cycle, proprietary product, parts or components compatibility, etc. before ending a supplier relationship.

Notice of Intent to Award: As a result of a competitive process, a public notice is issued and in some instances, where local laws allow, a Notice of Intent to Award is issued and award will occur only upon receipt of the specified items. For example: performance securities.

Notice of Letting: The public advertising of a sealed bid solicitation to advise the suppliers of a potential business opportunity to do business with the agency.

Notice of Proposed Procurement: A general opportunity available to suppliers to provide specified products or services. Also referred to as a Notice of Bidding Request.

Notice to Proceed (NTP): A notice issued to the successful bidder advising them that it is the government's intent to award a contract. In construction contracting, it is common practice to require completion of performance in a specified number of days after issuance of the notice to proceed. *(Harney, 1992)*

Novation: Under common law, an agreement where a contracting party accepts a new party in place of the prior party (relieving the prior party of any further obligations). *(Garner, 2004)*

Novation Agreement: A legal document executed by the original parties to a contract and a successor to whom interest in the contract has been transferred by one of the parties, which transfers all obligations and rights under the contract to the successor.

NPI: *See National Purchasing Institute.*

NTP: *See Notice to Proceed.*

NYMEX: *See New York Mercantile Exchange.*

O

Object Classification: CANADIAN Financial classification used on expenditure, revenue and other transactions which classify the type of goods and services acquired (for expenditures), transfer payments, source of receipts (for revenues), or the method of acquiring/disposing of a financial claim or obligation.

Objective: A specific, measurable and observable result of an organization's activity which advances the organization towards its goal.

Obligation: A legal requirement for the disbursement of funds as a result of orders placed, contracts awarded, supplies, services, or construction received, or other contractual activity.

OBS: *See Open Bidding Service Canadian.*

Obsolescence: The decline of products in a market due to the introduction of better competitor products or rapid technology developments. Is a critical part of a product's life cycle, and if a product cannot be turned around, it may lead to product abandonment. *(Business, 2002)*

Obsolete Supplies/Equipment: Items that are out of date, no longer in use or are effectively unusable; examples: 8 track audio tapes, 5-1/4 floppy computer disks. Obsolete supplies/equipment become outdated because of new technology, new regulations or new procedures instituted by the agency. For example: In accordance with the new ANSI guidelines, the agency decides to change the color of their highway worker's safety vests from orange to lime green for greater worker visibility. Therefore, the orange safety vests are now considered "obsolete" in favor of the lime green safety vests. *Also see Surplus.*

Occupational Safety and Health Administration (OSHA): A division within the U.S. Department of Labor that was created by the OSHA Act of 1970. OSHA's mission is to assure the safety and health of America's workers by setting and enforcing standards; providing training, outreach, and improvement in workplace safety and health. *(www.osha.gov)*

Ocean Bill of Lading: A bill of lading used by ocean carriers for marine transportation of goods.

OCR: *See Optical Character Recognition.*

OEM: *See Original Equipment Manufacturer.*

Offer: A response to a solicitation that, if accepted, would bind the offeror to perform the resulting contract.

Offeree: The person/entity to whom an offer is made usually in response to a Request for Proposal (RFP).

Offeror: The person/entity who submits a proposal in response to a Request for Proposals (RFP). One who makes an offer in response to a solicitation. *Also see Bidder.*

Office of Management and Budget (OMB): A government agency, in the Executive Office of the President of the United States, that serves as the President's principal arm for exercising the managerial functions of the Presidency. OMB strives to improve government organization, information, and management systems and devises programs for career executive talent throughout the government. OMB assists the President in preparing the annual budget and in overseeing its execution. *(Nash, Schooner, O'Brien, 1998)*

Official Responsibility: Direct administrative or operating authority, whether intermediate or final, either exercised alone or with others, either personally or through subordinates, to approve, disapprove, or otherwise direct governmental action.

Offshoring: A form of corporate downsizing and outsourcing, where manufacturing and other business processes are moved abroad in order to improve profit by taking advantage of lower labor costs and other expenses which may be more favorable in the host country. *(Business, 2002)*

Off-the-Shelf: Common use items that are readily available in the marketplace and do not have to be specially ordered. Generally they are not affected by supply and demand issues and are price stable. May also refer to systems or services readily available to commercial users that are not produced in accordance with rigid specifications. Typical examples include basic electrical and basic plumbing items. *(Schiller, 2000)*

Oligarchy: A market situation in which a few companies control or dominate the market for a product or service.

Oligopoly: A market in which few firms produce all or most of the market supply of a particular good or service. For example: oil cartel, steel, computers, de-regulated electric. *Also see Imperfect Competition.* *(Schiller, 2000)*

OMB: *See Office of Management and Budget.*

OMB Circular A-102: "Grants and Cooperative Agreements with state and local governments", establishes consistency and uniformity among federal agencies in the management of all federal cooperative agreements and grants with state and local governments. The 1988 version revised the 1981 version and rescinded Attachments A through P of the Circular. *Also see Uniform Administrative Requirements for Grants in Aid to States and Local Governments.*

OMB Circular A-110: "Uniform Administrative Requirements for Grants and Agreements with Institutions of Higher Education, Hospitals, and other Non-Profit Organizations." Issued by the Office of Management and Budget (OMB); governs the administration of purchases made by institutions of higher education, hospitals, and other non-profit organizations with federal funds.

One Hundred Percent (100%) Inspection: Inspection of every unit of product, each of which is accepted or rejected individually for the characteristics inspected.

Online Transaction Processing: Web based transaction processing systems operating together as opposed to a strict client-server model where the server could handle the transaction processing. Examples are on-line banking, bill payments and web based ERP systems. *(Jansen, 2002)*

On Order: CANADIAN The quantity of stock represented by the total of all outstanding replenishment orders that have been requested from stock but not yet delivered or received.

Open Account Purchase: A purchase by a buyer who has established credit with the vendor, payment for which is to be made at some future date, in accordance with terms agreed to when the account was established.

Open Bidding Service (OBS): *CANADIAN* An on-line electronic bulletin board and bid document request system that gives suppliers flexible and open access to government procurement opportunities.

Open-End Contract: A contract which sets forth the general provisions of supplies and services that may be delivered or performed within a given period of time, but in which quantity and/or duration is not specified. The quantity and delivery are specified with the placement of orders. *Also see Blanket Order, Price Agreement and Requirements Contract.*

O

Open-End Pricing: The amount paid will be based on price in effect at the time of delivery. *Also see Price at Time of Delivery and Price Prevailing at Date of Shipment.*

Open Insurance Policy: A form of insurance covering shipments for a specified time, or a stated value, and not limited to a single shipment; the premium is determined based on values reported.

Open Market Operations: Federal Reserve purchases and sales of government bonds for the purpose of altering bank reserves. *(Schiller, 2000)*

Open Market Purchase: A purchase, usually of a limited monetary amount, from any available source.

Open Order: Items of supply not delivered or not accepted by the ordering organization.

Operating Budgets: All of the revenues and expenditures to cover the current fiscal period of the government.

Operating Lease: A service lease, usually short-term, including both financing and servicing of the item leased; payments made under the lease are generally not sufficient to recover the full cost of the equipment. *Also see Financial Lease.*

Operational Audit: A structured review of the systems and procedures of an organization in order to evaluate whether they are being carried out efficiently and effectively. The audit involves establishing performance objectives, agreeing to the standards and criteria for assessment, and evaluating actual performance against targeted performance. *(Business, 2002)*

Operational Research: The application of scientific methods to the solution of managerial and administrative problems, involving complex systems or processes. *(Business, 2002)*

Opportunity Cost: The most desired goods or services that are forgone in order to obtain something else. The next best alternative that must be given up when a choice is made. *(Schiller, 2002)*

Optical Character Recognition (OCR) (Optical Scanning): Computer systems designed to translate images of text (usually captured by a scanner) into machine-editable text - to translate pictures of characters into a standard encoding scheme representing them. First used by the U.S. Postal Service in 1965 to sort mail. Also used in the Warehousing and Inventory Control arena of public procurement. *(Jansen, 2002)*

Optimized Production Technology: A production planning and control system, based on finite loading procedures, that concentrates on reducing bottlenecks in a production system in order to improve efficiency. Its key task is to increase total system throughput by realizing existing capacity in other parts of the system. *(Business, 2002)*

Option: A unilateral right in a contract which the jurisdiction may choose to exercise to purchase additional supplies or services called for in the contract, or to extend the period of performance. *Also see Buyer's Option.*

Option to Extend: In accordance with contract terms, an option that allows a continuance of the contract for an additional period of time. *Also see option to renew.*

Option to Renew: A contract provision that allows a party to reinstate the contract for an additional term, beyond that stated in the original contract, in accordance with contract terms. *Also see option to extend.*

Oral Presentations: In most solicitations, there will be a requirement for oral presentations from the top-ranked offerors. Oral presentations are conducted to allow the offerors to bring to the attention of the Evaluation Committee any aspects of their offer that may contribute to the selection of their response. It is an opportunity for the offerors to sell the merits of their submission, often using slide shows and illustrative presentations.

Order: An instruction issued to a vendor for goods to be delivered to a given place at a given price.

Order: *CANADIAN* A written requirement; direction or prescription made or issued to obtain a good or service.

Order Bill of Lading: A negotiable bill of lading between carrier and consignor by which legal possession of the shipment may be ordered by endorsement from person to person. It enables a shipper to collect for a shipment before it reaches its destination. Sometimes used by shippers to consign shipments to themselves so that delivery is made only upon the shipper's order.

Order Level: The level of stock of any item at which an order is initiated for more supplies of that item.

Order Picking: Selecting and withdrawing goods or components from a store or warehouse of inventory system to meet production requirements or to satisfy customer orders. *Also see Picking.* *(Business, 2002)*

Order Point: *CANADIAN* That point in time or level of the net stock at which an order is placed.

Order Quantity: The predetermined standard order size that will be placed with the vendor to replenish inventory.

Order Record: A central record of orders issued.

Ordered Suspension: An action in which an agency orders work to be suspended in accordance with a contract suspension of work clause. The contractor may be compensated only if the delay is unreasonable. Contractors are not entitled to compensation if the Suspension of Work is the contractor's fault. Suspension of work due to faulty performance is an example. *Also see Suspension of Work Clause.*

Ordering Costs: The costs associated with issuing a purchase order or placing an order.

Ordering Office: *CANADIAN* A client or customer location from which goods or services are ordered.

Ordinances: Generally refers to laws that county and municipal legislative bodies, such as boards of supervisors and city councils, pass applicable to those jurisdictions. May include requirements specific to the procurement of supplies and services. *Also see By-Law.* *(Harney, 1992)*

Organization: An arrangement of people and resources working in a planned manner toward specified strategic goals. May include any structured body such as a business, company, or firm in the public or private sector, or not-for-profit association. *(Business, 2002)*

Organization Chart (Org chart): A graphic illustration of an organization's structure, showing hierarchical authority and relationships between departments and functions. *(Business, 2002)*

Organizational (Corporate) Culture: The companies shared values, beliefs, traditions, philosophies, rules and heroes. *(Business, 2002)*

Organizing: The structuring of resources and activities to accomplish objectives in an efficient and effective manner. One of the primary management functions. *(Ferrell, 2002)*

Original Equipment Manufacturer (OEM): A supply management term for the purchase of parts and material directly from the manufacturer of the equipment or from an authorized reseller. For example, Ford automotive replacement parts would be purchased from an authorized Ford reseller. *(ISM, 2000)*

Originator: CANADIAN One who initiates a procurement, issue, or disposal transaction.

OSHA: *See the Occupational Safety and Health Administration.*

Outcome: A measure of the results that occur because a service is provided. Used in performance contracting to measure contractor compliance.

Outputs: The goods, services, and ideas that result from the conversion of inputs. Outsourcing:
1. Occurs when an organization makes an informed decision to contract out a product, service or business process that was previously provided by internal (in-house) resources.
2. The transferring of manufacturing or other tasks and business processes to other companies and countries where labor and supplies are less expensive.
3. A form of privatization. *Also see Contracting Out and Insourcing.*

Outsourcing of Non-Core Activities: Evaluating purchasing and supply activities in order to place non-core activities with outside contractors or suppliers. A form of "second-level" cost savings. *(Crimi, Kauffman, Inside Supply Management Magazine, March 2003)*

Overage: CANADIAN The quantity disclosed by count as being in excess of the quantity indicated on associated records; surplus.

Overhead Cost: The indirect recurring costs of running a business. *(Business, 2002)*

Overrun: An amount by which the actual cost of performance exceeds the amount budgeted for the work or the amount contracted for.

P

P3: *See Public Private Partnership.*

Packaging: The use of wrappings, cushioning materials, containers, markings, and related techniques to protect items from deterioration, prevent loss or damage, facilitate handling and identify the item packaged.

Packing List (Slip): A document that itemizes in detail the contents of a particular package or shipment. It is provided to the carrier by the shipper and accompanies the shipment.

Pallet: A portable platform upon which goods are placed in unit loads to facilitate stacking and handling by mechanical equipment such as a forklift truck or pallet jack. *(ISM, 2002)*

PAP: *See Performance Assessment Plan.*

Paper Trail: All of the documentation of a procurement which is required for future reference and for audit purposes. *(Business, 2002)*

Par Value: The face value of a bond; the amount to be repaid when the bond is due. *(Ferrell, 2002)*

Pareto Award: An award issued by the National Institute of Governmental Purchasing Inc. (NIGP) to recognize outstanding achievement by public purchasing entities based on a rigorous self-assessment and SWOT analysis. It is the pinnacle award of excellence in public procurement.

Pareto Charts: A subset of the 80/20 Pareto Law. The charts are used to distinguish between the critical and trivial problems. A commonly used quality control tool. *(Business, 2002)*

Pareto, Vilfredo (Pareto Principle): Italian economist and sociologist born in 1848. He created the 80/20 theory of income distribution which suggested that 80% of the wealth is created by only 20% of the income producers in an economy. This theory was adapted to a modernistic interpretation of the critical few and the trivial many. It has been further adapted to many supply management situations such as, " 80%

of the purchasing volume is created by 20% of the purchase orders issued". In the supply management area this is known as the 80-20 Rule or the Pareto Principal in its application to inventory control methodology. *(Business, 2006)*

Parol Evidence Rule: To ascertain, in an orderly fashion, the specific terms of an agreement between two parties. The ability of either party to produce evidence of orally agreed upon additional terms to a written contract is governed by the Parol Evidence Rule. In the absence of fraud, duress, mutual mistake, or something of the kind, the Parol Evidence Rule will preclude a party from presenting prior written or oral agreements to prove that the words of a contract have a meaning contrary to their clear meaning. *(Nash, Schooner, O'Brien, 1998)*

Part Category A: *CANADIAN* Accessory and miscellaneous parts and pieces which are attached to a master or host piece of equipment.

Partial Payment: Payments that permit the contractor to invoice at intervals to coincide with the delivery and acceptance of incremental supplies and/or services. *Also see Advance Payments and Progress Payments.*

Partial Shipment/Delivery: A delivery made against a purchase order or contract which is less than the quantity ordered. May be indicative of a back-order situation, or a temporary material shortage. *Also see Backorder.* *(Miller, 2006)*

Participant Code: *CANADIAN* A two character international standard organization code which represents the name of the participant as to whether it is a federal or provincial government.

Partnering: Creating a mutually beneficial relationship with a supplier or contractor for the specific performance of work where the relationship is trusting and supportive rather than adversarial.

Partnership: A form of business organization defined by the Uniform Partnership Act as "an association of two or more persons who carry on as co-owners of a business for profit." Each partner is liable for losses to the extent of his or her personal assets. *(Ferrell, 2002)*

Part Number: An identification number assigned to an individual part by the manufacturer or distributor of that part; usually includes a combination of alpha and/or numeric characters.

Parts-Per-Million (PPM): A measure of quantity that may be used as a quality reference, whereby defective parts must not exceed a specified number of parts per million parts supplied; a ratio of number of failures to number of parts supplied. *(ISM, 2000)*

Password: A series of characters that enable a user to access a private file, website, computer or software application. *(Business, 2002)*

Patent: A set of exclusive rights granted by a government to an inventor or applicant for a fixed period of time usually 20 years in the U.S. It gives the grantee the right to exclude others from making, using, selling, offering for sale, or importing the patented invention. There are a number of international treaties governing patent law. The most global is the WTO TRIP's Agreement, to which almost all countries are a party. The United States, European Union and Japan are parties to all of the existing treaties governing patents. The authority for patent statutes in different countries varies. In the U.S., the Patent and Trademark Office gets its authority from Article One, Section 8 of the U.S. Constitution. *(Miller, 2006)*

Payback Period: The time required to recover an investment through net cash flow.

Payment Authority: *CANADIAN* The authority granted to an individual to requisition payments and authorize the charge to appropriations, after reviewing the legality of payments and the exercise of all appropriate financial controls.

Payment Bond: A financial or contractual instrument, issued by a surety that guarantees that subcontractors will be paid for labor and materials expended on the contract. Acceptable forms of payment bonds may include: cashier's check, certified check, or irrevocable letter of credit issued by a financial institution; a surety or blanket bond; United States Treasury bond; or certificate of deposit. *Also known as Labor and Materials Bond.*

Payment Method: CANADIAN An identifier of the means of payment whether it be advanced, normal or progress payments to vendors as applicable to the contract.

Payment Terms: The terms applicable to the payment including any discount. *Also see Cash Discount, Discount, and Prompt Payment Discount.*

Pay-Per-Click (PPC): An online advertising payment model in which payment is based only on the number of click-throughs that are generated. The model is also adaptable to eProcurement methods. (Jansen, 2002)

pCard: *See Procurement Card.*

PDF: *See Portable Document Format.*

Pecuniary: Of or pertaining to money.

Peer/360 Evaluations: With the increased focus on teamwork, employee development, and customer service, the emphasis has shifted to employee feedback from the full circle of sources such as superior, subordinates, peers, internal customers, external customers. This multiple-input approach to performance feedback is sometimes called "360 degree assessment" to connote the full circle of feedback resources. The process provides a full circle view of input.

Penalty Charge: A clause in a contract specifying the sum of money to be paid if the contractor defaults on the terms of the contract, particularly with respect to time. *Also see Damages and Liquidated Damages.*

Penalty Clause: Punitive language inserted in a competitive solicitation which details what action will be taken if the contractor does not perform in a satisfactory manner. *Also see Liquidated Damages.* (ISM, 2002)

PE Ratio: *See Price/Earnings Ratio.*

Percentage Preference: A policy of adding a fixed percentage to the bid price of a non-preferred business unit.

Per Diem:
1. Paid by the day; based on use or service by the day.
2. A daily allowance for travel, meals, hotel, car rental, etc.

Perfect (Pure) Competition: A market in which no buyer or seller has market power. The market contains a large number of buyers and sellers of approximately equal importance.

Performance: The technical, operational, and quality characteristics of the end item.

Performance Assessment Plan (PAP): A key element of successful contract administration. It provides specific information on how the Contract Administration Team will observe and evaluate performance according to the standard required in the contract. The PAP includes information on how the "evaluators" will observe, survey, sample, test, evaluate and document supplier performance.

Performance Based Budgeting: Budgeting that attempts to link resource allocation decisions to performance criteria that include both output and outcome measures. Also referred to as Results oriented budgeting, these forms of budgeting add performance measures that look at outcomes of activities rather than at individual process steps. In order to be effective, these budget methods must be linked to the overall strategic plan of the organization, and each decision unit must support a particular goal and objective (similar to decision units in Zero Based Budgeting). *Also see Results Oriented Budgeting.*

Performance Based Contract: A results-oriented contracting method that focuses on the outputs, quality, or outcomes that may tie at least a portion of a contractor's payment, contract extensions, or contract renewals to the achievement of specific, measurable performance standards and requirements. These contracts may include monetary and non-monetary incentives as well as specific remedies.

Performance Bond: An instrument executed, subsequent to award, by a successful bidder that protects the public entity from loss due to the bidder's inability to complete the contract as agreed. A risk mechanism that secures the fulfillment of all contract requirements. May be referred to as a Completion Bond.

Performance Budget: A budget that links the consumption of resources (inputs) to outputs/outcomes of services for each unit of an organization. This type of budget is commonly used by the government to show the link between the funds provided by the public and the outcome of these services. Decisions made on these types of budgets focus more on outputs or outcomes of services than on decisions made based on inputs.

Performance Measures: Tools used to measure performance and quantitatively evaluate progress toward planned targets.

Performance Rating: CANADIAN The assignment of a rating to a supplier based on effective performance.

Performance Record: Documentation of a vendor's past history regarding reliability, on-time delivery, quality issues, and other data that allows the buyer to evaluate overall performance.

Performance Requirement: CANADIAN Requirements that define what the product or service is to do.

Performance Specifications: A description of a product or service that provides a general functional recital of performance characteristics required to achieve an end result or outcome desired. It does not require the bidder/offeror to comply with specific design requirements. *Also see Design Specifications.*

Performance Work Statement (PWS): Similar to a statement of work and is used in performance based request for proposals. It describes the requirements in terms of outcomes rather than prescriptive specifications.

Periodic Inventory Control System: A time-based inventory control system involving scheduled reviews of the stock level of each inventory item.

Periodic Ordering: Orders placed at intervals for quantities needed to bring stocks up to the desired levels.

Period of Assignment: CANADIAN The starting and finishing dates for the services being called up. *Also see Call Up.*

Perishable Goods: Material subject to spoilage or deterioration within a relatively short time if proper conditions, such as temperature, are not maintained.

Perpetual Inventory Control System: An ongoing record of all stock items, showing stock levels, withdrawals, replenishment, placement of purchase orders, receipt, issues, balances, quantities available and stock adjustments.

Personal Liability: A contracting risk whereby an individual (an agent) may be held personally liable if they have committed an unlawful, negligent or criminal act in the performance of their duties. *(Ferrell, 2002)*

Personal Property:
1. Tangible or intangible property, other than real property.
2. Movable property subject to ownership, with exchangeable value.

PERT: *See Program Evaluation and Review Technique.*

Petites et Moyennes Entreprises: CANADIAN A French phrase meaning small and medium-sized businesses. *(www.summitconnects.com)*

Physical Distribution: All of the activities necessary to move products from producers to customers—inventory control, transportation, warehousing, and materials handling. *(ISM, 2002)*

Picking: The process of pulling or selecting items from inventory and staging them for delivery or distribution; assembling the items required to fill

P

an order, usually performed with the assistance of a "picking list". *Also see Order Picking.* (Business, 2002)

Piggyback (Piggyback Cooperatives): A form of intergovernmental cooperative purchasing in which an entity will be extended the pricing and terms of a contract entered into by a larger entity. Generally a larger entity will competitively award a contract that will include language allowing for other entities to utilize the contract which may be to their advantage in terms of pricing, thereby gaining economies of scale that they normally would not receive if they competed on their own. Example: A smaller government agency has the ability to use its state issued contract to obtain goods and services which is also known as Riding a Contract.

Piracy: Illegal copying of a product such as software or music. *(Jansen, 2002)*

P

Planned Obsolescence: A manufacturing or assembly policy whereby products are deliberately designed to have a limited or premature life cycle which will require customers to purchase replacements. *(Business, 2002)*

Planned Order Release (POR): A planned authorization for a supplier to ship material against an existing contract. An essential element of a material requirements planning (MRP) system. *(ISM, 2002)*

Planning: CANADIAN Analysis and evaluation of the ways in which material requirements can be met using a life cycle management approach.

Plant-Matter Based or Bio Based Product: A product derived from renewable resources, including fiber crops, such as kenaf; chemical extracts from oilseeds, nuts, fruits and vegetables such as corn and soybeans; agricultural residues, such as wheat straw and corn stover; and wood wastes generated from processing and manufacturing operation. These products stand in contrast to those made from fossil fuels and other less renewable resources such as virgin timber. An important component of Green Purchasing. *(Miller, 2006)*

PM: *See Preventive Maintenance.*

PMAC: *See Purchasing Management Association of Canada.*

Point-Click-Buy-Ship: A reference to eProcurement and eBusiness protocol that allows buyers to access an Internet shopping site, make an authorized purchase from a pre-determined contract supplier and charge the purchase to a credit card. Frequently used for just-in-time, next day procurements. *Also see Click-and-Ship.* *(Miller, 2006)*

Point of Origin: The location where shipment is received by a transportation line from the shipper. The shipping point.

Point of Shipment (POS): One of many designated F.O.B. terms which means that title passes from seller to buyer at seller's loading dock. Same as F.O.B. Factory, F.O.B. Point of Origin.

Point Rating: An evaluation procedure in which a list of criteria, to which values have been assigned, is used to ascertain the individual merits of proposals that have met the mandatory factors specified in a Request for Proposal (RFP).

Policy: A governing principle or plan which establishes the general parameters for the organization to follow in carrying out its responsibilities.

Policy of Insurance: The formal document delivered by the insurance company to the insured which evidences the rights and duties between the parties.

Political Subdivision: A political entity within a state, which has been delegated certain functions of local government. May include counties, cities, towns, villages, hamlets, boroughs, or parishes.

POR: *See Planned Order Release.*

Portable Document Format (PDF): A file format developed by Adobe Systems for representing documents in a manner that is independent of the original application software, hardware and operating system used to create the document. A PDF file can describe documents containing any combination of text, graphics, and images in a device independent and resolution independent format. *(Jansen, 2002)*

POS: *See Point of Shipment.*

Post-Award Activities: Activities that ensue after the contract has been awarded which ensures that the buyer receives what was ordered on time and at the price and quality specified. These activities may include supplier development, technical assistance, trouble shooting, and the management of the contract and the resulting relationship.

Post-Award Start-Up Conference: A meeting held with the contractor awarded the contract prior to the beginning of contract performance. It ensures that the contractor fully understands the expectations, performs accordingly and can provide the foundation for an effective contract effort. Objectives of the post-award are to: ensure the contractor understands the technical requirements of the contract; to clarify the rights and responsibilities of both parties; and to determine the need for follow-up meetings.

Postconsumer Material: A material or finished product that has served its intended use and has been diverted or recovered from waste destined for disposal, having completed its life as a consumer item. Postconsumer materials are part of the broader category of recovered materials. *(www.epa.gov/cpg/glossary)*

PPI: *See Producer's Price Index.*

PPM: *See Parts per Million.*

PPP: *See Purchasing Power Parity.*

PPU: *See Public Procurement Unit.*

PR: *See Purchase Requisition.*

Practicable: Possible, a situation where it is deemed that a given factual result can occur.

Pre-Award Contract Review: An audit or survey performed before a contract is awarded to determine the vendor's or contractor's technical, managerial and financial ability to perform under the proposed contract, as well as the establishment of and compliance with appropriate procurement system procedures.

Pre-Bid/ Pre-Proposal Conference(Meeting): A meeting held by the buyer with potential bidders/offerors, prior to the opening of the solicitation for the purpose of answering questions, clarifying any ambiguities and responding to general issues in order to establish a common basis for understanding all of the requirements of the solicitation. May result in the issuance of an addendum to all potential providers. In certain situations, a mandatory conference may be advisable. *Also see Bidder's Conference and Pre-solicitation Conference.*

Preconsumer Material: Materials generated in manufacturing and converting processes, such as manufacturing scrap and trimmings/cuttings. *(www.epa.gov/cpg/glossary)*

Predatory Pricing: Temporary price reductions designed to alter market shares or drive out competition. *(Business, 2002)*

Preference: An advantage given to bidders/offerors in a competition for contract award which may be granted based on pre-established criteria such as ethnicity, residence, business location, origination of the product or service, business classification (e.g., small business) or other reasons. A governmental bias. *Also see Buy Local, Disadvantaged Business Preference, and Local Preference.*

Preferred Stock: A special type of stock whose owners, though not generally having a say in the running of the company, have a claim to profits before other stockholders do. *(Ferrell, 2002)*

Prepaid: A term denoting that transportation charges have been or are to be paid at the point of shipment.

Prepay and Add: A transportation term indicating that the seller pays the carrier and adds the freight charges onto the invoice for goods purchased. *Also see Free on Board (F.O.B.) terms.* *(ISM, 2000)*

Pre-Qualification (of bidder/offeror): The screening of potential vendors/contractors in which such factors as financial capability, reputation, and management are considered in order to develop a list of qualified businesses who may then be allowed to submit bids/offers.

Present Value: The value in current dollars of work, goods and services to be performed or supplied in the future. Used frequently in long term lease and rental transactions. *(Business, 2002)*

Pre-solicitation Conference: An informal, typically non-mandatory, meeting inviting comments and suggestions from a representative group of vendors on the draft of a proposed solicitation; This conference provides useful market analysis information to the Buyer; Usually used for solicitations involving high technology or complex services. *Also see Bidders Conference, Pre-bid/ Pre-Proposal conference, Request for Comments (RFC) and Request for Information (RFI).*

Prevailing Wage Rate: The rate of wages, including fringe benefits, paid to a majority of the workers in a geographic area for the same type of work on similar projects. *(Nash, Schooner, O'Brien, 1998)*

P

Preventive Maintenance (PM): Planned activities undertaken to retain equipment or material in a serviceable condition; includes scheduled inspection, testing, servicing, classification as to serviceability, repairs, rebuilding and reclamation.

Price:
1. A value placed on an object or service provided by a seller to a buyer.
2. The money value of a unit of a good, service, or resource.
3. The total amount, in money or other consideration, to be paid or charged for a commodity or service; normally includes all costs (direct labor, overhead, materials) and profit or fee.

Price Adjustment Clause: A clause in a contract allowing for adjustment in price in accordance with circumstances arising during the term of the contract. A provision that must be included in contracts requiring contractor certification of cost and pricing data stating that price, including profit or fee, shall be adjusted to exclude any significant sums by which the jurisdiction finds the price was increased because the contractor-furnished cost or pricing data was inaccurate, incomplete, or not current.

Price Agreement: A contractual agreement in which a purchaser contracts with a vendor to provide the purchaser's requirements at a predetermined price. *Also see Blanket order, Open end contract, and Requirements contract.*

Price Analysis: The process of examining and evaluating a prospective price without performing cost analysis; that is, without evaluating the separate cost elements and profit of the offeror included in that price. The end result of price analysis is to ensure fair and reasonable pricing of a product or service. Price analysis may include a variety of techniques such as comparing proposed prices with prices of same or similar items obtained through market research. *(Nash, Schooner, O'Brien, 1998)*.

Price At Time of Delivery: A term used in sales contracts when market prices are so volatile that the vendor will not give a firm price or use an escalator clause, but will only agree to charge the same price to all customers for similar purchases on the day of shipment or delivery of goods. *Also see Open-End Pricing and Price Prevailing at Date of Shipment.*

Price Ceiling: Upper limit imposed on the price of a good. The highest price that a buyer is willing to pay. *(Business, 2002)*

Price Competition: Selection of a contractor, from two or more vendors, based either solely on prices submitted, or on the final prices resulting from a negotiation with all contractors within a competitive range.

Price Control: The fixing or restricting of prices, especially by a government agency. *(Business, 2002)*

Price Differentiation: A pricing strategy in which a company sells the same product at different prices in different markets. *(Business, 2002)*

Price Discrimination: The sale of an identical good at different prices to different consumers by a single seller. *(Business, 2002)*

Price/Earnings (PE) Ratio: The price of a stock share divided by earnings per share. *(Business, 2002)*

Price Elasticity: The responsiveness of demand to price changes. An elastic situation is one in which small changes in prices charged result in large differences in the quantity demanded. *(ISM, 2000)*

Price Fixing: Explicit agreements among producers regarding the prices at which goods are to be sold. *See Sherman Antitrust Act and the Clayton Act.*

Price Index: A ratio expressing the relationship between the price of a commodity at a given point in time to its price during a specified base period. *(ISM, 2002)*

Price Leadership: An oligopolistic pricing pattern that allows one firm to establish the market price for all firms in the industry. *(Business, 2002)*

Price prevailing at the Date of Shipment: Sales agreement that states the selling price may be modified by the vendor/seller between the order and the shipment dates. *Also see Open End Pricing and Price at Time of Delivery.*

Price Protection: Sales agreement granting purchaser any reduction in price the vendor may establish prior to shipment of the goods; sometimes extended for a period beyond the date of shipment.

Price Range: The variety of prices at which competitive products or services are available in the market. *(Business, 2002)*

Price Rebate: A reduction in price, usually given after the completion of the contract and based on the quantity or value of goods purchased.

Price Reduction: A decrease in the assigned value for a commodity or service exchanged relative to its worth determined in some previous time period. The act of reducing the agreed upon value of selling price where the incurred price paid is lower based upon what was previously paid; usually refers to a lower price paid by the buyer. *Also see Cost Savings, Cost Reduction.*

Price Skimming: Charging the highest possible price that buyers who want the product will pay. *(Ferrell, 2002)*

Price Stability: The absence of significant changes in the average price level - officially defined as a rate of inflation of less than 3%. *(Schiller, 2000)*

Pricing: The process of establishing a reasonable amount to be paid for goods and services. Generally includes labor, material, ancillary costs and profit.

Pricing Data: Factual information about prices for goods and services substantially similar to those being procured; can include offered or proposed selling prices, historical selling prices and current selling prices.

Pricing Method: CANADIAN The method by which the contract price is determined, such as fixed, lot, cost plus, or target.

Prime Contract: A contract entered into by a public entity with a business entity for the purpose of obtaining supplies, services or construction items of any kind.

Prime Contractor: The business entity that has entered into a contract with a jurisdiction.

Principal: One who employs an agent. A person who has authorized another to act for him/her. *Also see Agent, Buyer and Law of Agency.*

Principle: A basic truth, law or assumption; a rule or standard of behavior; a rule of conduct that derives from ethical values.

Priority: The degree of precedence given to a particular item or task over other items or tasks.

Private Carrier: A transportation line not engaged in business with the general public. *Also see Common Carrier and Contract Carrier.*

Private Goods: A commodity that benefits the individual. An example is a pen I own is a private good; a bridge built with governmental funds and usable by all is a public good. *(Guess, 2002)*

Private Label: A product or range of products offered by a retailer under their own name or under a brand that they own. They compete with branded goods.

Private Sector: That part of an economy in which goods and services are produced by individuals and companies as opposed to the government and the non-profit sector. The ultimate aim of the private sector is to secure a profit as opposed to government and the non-profit sector which aims to achieve other objectives.

Privatization: The divestiture of both management and assets of a public function to the private sector in order to change the status of a function formerly performed by the public entity to one that is privately controlled and owned including the transfer of real and personal property.

Privilege Clause: CANADIAN A clause traditionally used in Canadian tenders which says "the lowest or any tender will not necessarily be accepted". A "privilege clause" provides the tendering authority with broad discretion in relation to the acceptance or rejection of tenders. It usually reserves to the owner the discretion to accept or reject the lowest, or any, tender. It does not displace the overarching duty of procedural good faith that the Courts have found is an implied term of the bid contract (contract A).

P

Privity of Contract: The direct contractual relationship existing between parties that allows either party to enforce contractual rights against the other and seek remedy directly from the other party with whom the relationship exists.

Probity: CANADIAN Integrity and uprightness. Uncompromising adherence to the laws, regulations and policy imperatives concerning government contracting. An ethical course of action. *(Summit Magazine, On-Line)*

PROC (Product-Resource-Operating-Contingent): CANADIAN *See Product-Resource-Operating-Contingent.*

Procedure: The detailed series of related activities that must be completed, and the order in which they must be done, to accomplish a given task.

Process Control: The inspection of work-in-progress to provide feedback on, and correct a production process. A quality control technique used in manufacturing. *(Business, 2002)*

Process Improvement: The increase in value (or decrease in applicable costs) resulting from a modification in any phase of the purchasing and/or supply process. *(ISM, Inside Supply Management Magazine, March 2003)*

Process Knowledge: A knowledge sharing trend in organizations that proactively fosters collaboration, sharing of knowledge and organizes around customer-centric processes by encouraging workers to form collaborative teams responsible for the completion of an entire process from end to end. This system organizes work flow to support cross-functional business processes that emphasize the importance of sharing product-related and process-related knowledge across functional boundaries.

Process Mapping: An examination of the steps, activities, and interrelationships associated with performing a specific task. This tool is used in business process reengineering to determine where processes can be enhanced or minimized in order to improve efficiencies. *(ISM, 2002)*

Procurement: Purchasing, renting, leasing, or otherwise acquiring any supplies, services, or construction; includes all functions that pertain to the acquisition, including description of requirements, selection and solicitation of sources, preparation and award of contract, and all phases of contract administration. The combined functions of purchasing, inventory control, traffic and transportation, receiving, inspection, storekeeping, salvage and disposal operations.

Procurement Card (pCard): A payment method whereby internal customers (requisitioners) are empowered to deal directly with suppliers for purchases using a credit card issued by a bank or major credit card provider. Generally a pre-established credit limit is established for each card issued. The cards enable eProcurement and facilitate on-line ordering, frequently from pre-approved suppliers under blanket contracts. *(Miller, 2006)*

Procurement Code Exceptions: Public sector procurement codes (legislation) provide for the direct purchase of specific products or services without following the competitive requirements. Example: Authorized or mandated preferred source (prisoners, blind, and disabled), emergency procurements as well as others provided by local laws and regulations.

Procurement Lead Time: The total lead time required to obtain a purchased item. Includes purchasing lead time, vendor lead time, transportation time, receiving and inspection.

Procurement Methods: Methods by which goods, services, or material may be acquired by public purchasers. The methods may include blanket orders, emergency purchases, standing offers, purchase orders, transfers, competitive bidding, competitive negotiation, intergovernmental cooperative agreements, small purchase contracts, purchases via a credit card, etc.

Procurement Officer: Any person duly authorized to enter into and administer a contract and make written determinations and findings thereto. Also includes an authorized representative of the procurement officer acting within the limits of his or her authority.

Procurement Outsourcing: The contracting out of the procurement function to a third-party or private contractor. *(Miller, 2006)*

Procurement Profile: The result produced after conducting a series of various analyses on the procurement expenditures of an organization, the range of commodities and services acquired through purchasing (Spend Analysis), the markets that provide them (Market Analysis), the level of influence of the suppliers and the entity in the marketplace, and the risks inherent in the market that could affect the entity's operations (Supply Positioning). *Also see Spend Analysis, Market Analysis and Supply Positioning.*

Procurement Records: Accounts maintained by a procurement organization sufficient to detail the significant history of a procurement and which may be needed for future audit purposes. Typically defined in a retention schedule description.

Procurement System Review: An audit of the procedures of the procurement system of the governmental entity. For federal agencies, OMB Circular A-102 provides guidance.

Producers: People who use resources to make goods and services. *(Ferrell, 2002)*

Producers Price Index (PPI): A measurement tool compiled by the U.S. Bureau of Labor Statistics reflecting the average change in prices charged by producers during a given time period, compared to those charged in a base year. The PPI measures inflation at earlier stages of the production and marketing process than does the Consumer Price Index. *(ISM, 2000)*

Product Differentiation: Features that make one product appear different from competing products in the same market. Automobiles and breakfast cereal are examples of markets that have products that are greatly differentiated for consumer choice. *(Business, 2002)*

Product Identification: *CANADIAN* An identifier which is unique for a given product. It may be any combination of the following: A NATO stock number, a supplier's part number, a supplier's catalog number and GSIN code.

Product Launch: The introduction of a new product into a market. The beginning stages of the product life cycle. *(Ferrell, 2002)*

Product Life Cycle: A product generally has the following life cycle stages: introduction, growth, maturity and decline. *(Ferrell, 2002)*

Product-Resource-Operating-Contingent (PROC): *CANADIAN* Identifies four types of costs (product, resource, operating and contingent) used to identify all costs associated with a requirement over its useful life to determine the best value.

Production: The making of goods available for use; total output especially of a commodity or industry. *(Schiller, 2000)*

Productivity: Output per unit of input, e.g. output per labor hour. *(Business, 2002)*

Professional Services: Services rendered by members of a recognized profession or possessing a special skill. Such services are generally acquired to obtain information, advice, training, or direct assistance.

Profit:
1. The difference between total revenue and total cost. (P=TR-TC). The difference between total revenues and the full costs involved in producing or selling a good or service; it is a return for risk taking.
2. The difference between what it cost to make and sell a product and its final selling price.
3. The difference between the costs incurred by the contractor to provide the supplies, services, or construction and the amount received from the purchaser in payment.

Profit Margin: An item that appears on an income statement and is calculated by dividing the gross profit by sales. *(Business, 2002)*

Profit Sharing: A form of compensation whereby a percentage of company profits is distributed to the employees based on a variety of factors such as longevity, company status, etc. *(Business, 2002)*

P

Pro-Forma: A document issued before all relevant details are known, usually followed by a final version. *(Business, 2002)*

Pro-Forma Invoice: An invoice received before the purchase informing the buyer of the terms of sale. Often applicable to foreign purchases as the buyer's proof of a future purchase to support the buyer's request to governmental authorities for import permits and foreign exchange.

Program Budgeting: Program budgets relate expenditures and revenues to public goals.

Program Evaluation and Review Technique (PERT): Similar to the critical path method of project scheduling, PERT was developed in 1955 by the Du Pont and Remington Rand companies for use in coping with complex plant maintenance problems. Now available in software applications that show time and dependency relationships between the activities that make up the total project. *(Ferrell, 2002)*

Program Identification Code: CANADIAN A two-digit code identifying the program to which a contract may apply.

Progress Payments: A timed sequence of payments made during the performance of a contract; periodic payments made over the life of a contract; allow the contractor to submit invoices for payment as progress is made in performing the contract. Progress payments shift risk to the public agency since payment for progress made does not guarantee that the work will be completed. *Also see Advance Payment and Partial Payment.*

Progress Report: A report prepared by a contractor during the performance of a contract. A useful means of assessing the routine progress of the contractor in selected areas of the contract.

Progressive Award: The award of a definite quantity contract under the same solicitation to two or more vendors or contractors to furnish the same or similar supplies or services, where more than one vendor is needed to meet the contract requirements for quantity, delivery, or service.

Progressive Tax System: A tax system in which taxes get higher for wealthier residents; it's the opposite of a regressive tax system. Sometimes referred to as a "graduated" tax system. *(Business, 2002)*

Prohibited Articles: Articles which will not be handled, as listed in transportation carrier's tariffs.

Project Approval-Class Estimate: CANADIAN Four types, A,B,C,D, defined as follows:
Class Estimate A - based on working drawings and specifications and other significant conditions of production/construction.
Class Estimate B - based on the design of major systems and sub-systems as well as all site/installation investigations.
Class Estimate C - based on the general description of the end item, production/construction experience, and market conditions.
Class Estimate D - based on a comprehensive statement of requirements in mission terms and an outline of potential solutions.

Project Approval Effective: *CANADIAN* Approval based on reliable and up-to-date cost estimates which provides authority to proceed with a project or complete it in those instances where there is already a preliminary approval, and spend all project funds, based on a specific budget in constant and current (budget-year) dollars.

Project Approval-Preliminary: *CANADIAN* Approval based on Class C Estimates which provides authority to initiate a project as the preferred option for fulfilling a justified need, and spends only those funds necessary to cover such activities as concept and preliminary design and to develop at least a Class B Estimate.

Project Duration: *CANADIAN* Duration of time from project announcement to completion.

Project Manager: Designated individual within the agency to administer a specific task or contract.

Promissory Estoppel: A legal doctrine binding a person to a promise when another party has relied on the promise to its detriment and the person making the promise could have reasonably foreseen the reliance. *(Nash, Schooner, O'Brien, 1998)*

Promissory Note: An unconditional written promise to pay a certain sum in money, on demand or at a fixed or determinable future date, either to the bearer or to the order of a designated person.

Prompt Payment Act: This law provides requirements to government procurement offices that ensure that federal contractors supplying goods and services are paid on time and within agreed upon payment terms. Many states and local governments have enacted similar laws. *(ISM, 2000)*

Prompt Payment Discount: An incentive for early payment on a "Net Days" basis. For example, if company policy is to pay contractors on a "Net 90" basis, the company will pay within 30 days in return for a percentage discount, such as 2% of the total amount due. *Also see Cash Discount, Discount and Payment Terms.* *(Juricidical Dictionary, 2007)*

Proposal: A proposal is a document submitted by a vendor in response to some type of bid solicitation to be used as the basis for negotiations or for entering into a contract.

Proprietary (Article): An item produced and marketed by a person or company having the exclusive right to manufacturer and sell it. May result from a trade secret or patent.

Proprietary Funds: Funds used to account for a government's business-type activities. There are two types of proprietary funds – enterprise funds and internal service funds. Both enterprise and internal service funds recover the full cost of providing services (including capital costs) through fees and charges on those who use their services. *Also see Enterprise Fund and Internal Service Fund.* *(cityofnorthlasvegas.com/Departments/Finance/PDFs/Budgets/2004_2005/4-OtherFunds/113-126-ProprietaryFunds.pdf)*

P

Proprietary (Information): Owned by a private individual or corporation under a patent, copyright, trademark or other exclusive right. Usually protected from release to the general public. Not subject to public disclosure. *Also see Trade Secret and Confidential Information.* *(Business, 2002)*

Prospectus: A document that sets out corporate and financial information for prospective investors. May be submitted by a company in response to a due diligence search by purchasing in an attempt to determine financial responsibility. *(Business, 2002)*

Protectionism: The economic policy of promoting favored domestic industries through the use of high tariffs and other regulations to discourage imports. Historical variants of this policy have included mercantilism, a trade policy aimed at maximizing currency reserves by running large trade surpluses; and import substitution, a trade policy in which targeted imports are replaced by local manufactures in order to stimulate local production. *(Explanation-guide.info/meaning)*

Protest: An oral or written objection by a potential interested party to a solicitation or award of a contract, with the intention of receiving a remedial result. May be filed in accordance with agency policy and procedure within predetermined time lines. *Also see Bid Protest (pre-award), Award Protest (post-award) and Dispute.* *(Harney, 1992 - modified)*

Protocol:
1. The forms of ceremony and etiquette observed by diplomats and heads of state.
2. A code of correct conduct: safety protocols; academic protocol.
3. The first copy of a treaty or other such document before its ratification.
4. A preliminary draft or record of a transaction.
5. The plan for a course of medical treatment or for a scientific experiment.
6. Computer Science: A standard procedure for regulating data transmission between computers. *(Heritage Dictionary, 2007)*

Prototype: An initial version or working model of a new product or invention. Usually constructed and tested in order to evaluate the feasibility of a design and to identify problems that need to be corrected. Purchasing may request a prototype to evaluate prior to purchase. *(Miller, 2006)*

Provisioning and Supply: *CANADIAN* The process of determining requirements, initiating procurement and providing a stock of supplies for future needs.

Public Agency: A public entity subject to or created by a governmental jurisdiction.

Public Bid Opening: The process of opening and reading bids at the time and place specified in the solicitation and in the presence of anyone who wishes to attend.

Public Finance Law: Legislative laws governing the financial activities of government or public sector organizations. *(Business, 2002 - modified)*

Public Good: A product or service that is provided to an individual or a group of individuals for the benefit of many For example, a public-health measure that eradicates a disease protects the general public, not just those paying for the vaccinations. *(Schiller, 2000 - modified)*

Public Law:
1. The body of law, such as criminal, administrative and constitutional law, that is not civil law. It also is the name given to a law that Congress or a state legislature has passed, and that the President or a governor of a state has signed. Public laws become statutes when they are integrated into existing statutes.
2. Public law is the law governing the relationship between individuals and the state. Constitutional law, administrative law and criminal law are subdivisions of public law. *(Wikepedia, 2006)*

Public Management: The process of planning, organizing, staffing and executing the use of people, time and fiscal resources for the purpose of providing goods, services and protection valued by the citizens of the entity in response to the laws and regulations of the governing body.

Public Notice: An announcement made by a public agency concerning a solicitation or other information of general public interest. Usually placed in a newspaper of general circulation, a web-site, circular, magazine or other vehicle of general publication. Must comply with legal requirements of the jurisdiction.

Public Policy: The fundamental policy on which laws rest, especially policy not yet enunciated in specific rules. *(www.factmonster.com)*

Public-Private Competition: In-house governmental departments and private companies who compete to provide government services; occurs when a government agency targets a service for possible outsourcing and allows the in-house operation currently providing the service to compete against the private sector and submit a proposal to provide the government service. May be referred to as Managed Competition.

Public-Private Partnership (P3): An arrangement for service delivery, whereby government and private enterprise pool their skills and resources to meet a particular objective. *Also see Concession Model.*

Public Procurement: The designated legal authority to advise, plan, obtain, deliver, and evaluate a government's expenditures on goods and services that are used to fulfill stated objectives, obligations, and activities in pursuit of desired policy outcomes.

Public Procurement Process Model: An integrated public procurement planning model that consists of four stages: Planning-Formalization-Implementation-Evaluation.

Public Procurement Unit (PPU): Local public procurement unit; External procurement activity (any buying organization not located in the state, which, if located in this state, would qualify as a public procurement unit); state public procurement unit; Federal Government; and any not-for-profit entity comprised of more than one of the above. *(ABA Model Procurement Code)*

Public Property: CANADIAN All property, other than money, belonging to the Crown.

Public Purchasing: The processes utilized by public entities for the procurement of construction, supplies, materials and services at the most favorable overall total cost through the utilization of accepted practices that encourage competition, including best value and quality considerations, thus ensuring that the public good is best served.

Public Sector: That section of the economy that is financed and controlled by a central government, local authorities, and publicly funded corporations. *(Business, 2002)*

Pull Strategy: The use of promotion to create consumer demand for a product so that consumers exert pressure on marketing channel members to make the product available. *(Ferrell, 2002)*

Punitive Damages: Damages that are awarded in a civil action, in addition to compensatory damages, to punish a defendant for gross or willful misconduct. Generally are not recoverable in breach of contract actions. *(Garner, 2004)*

Purchase Description: The words used in a solicitation document to describe the requirements to be purchased; includes specifications that are attached to or made part of the solicitation.

Purchase Document: CANADIAN A written or electronic document which sets out all terms and conditions of a purchase transaction with a supplier.

Purchase Log: A register of all requisitions received and all purchase orders issued, containing information such as requisition number, purchase order number, bid number, the vendor, commodity code or description of the material or service, and the value of the order. Generally contained in a legacy data base.

Purchase Order: A purchaser's written document to a vendor formalizing all the terms and conditions of a proposed transaction, such as a description of the requested items, delivery schedule, terms of payment, and transportation.

Purchase Order Change Notice: A form documenting a change made to a purchase order.

Purchase Price: CANADIAN The price quoted by a supplier for a materiel item; may include delivery and installation costs.

Purchaser:

1. One who acquires goods, construction and services on behalf of an organization.
2. A buyer agent who purchases on behalf of an organization.
3. A procurer of goods, commodities, services, and construction.

Purchase Requisition (PR): A document created by a requestor authorizing the commencement of a purchasing transaction. Typically will include a description of the need and other information that is relative to the transaction. May be submitted in hard copy or via eProcurement software.

Purchase Requisition: CANADIAN A request to obtain materiel or services and authority to commit funds to cover the purchase.

Purchase Requisition Status: CANADIAN A status report on a purchase requisition. Also called milestone status.

Purchasing Agency: Any governmental body which is authorized to enter into contracts.

Purchasing Audit: A comprehensive, systematic, independent, and periodic examination of an organization's purchasing environment, objectives, strategies, and activities with a view toward identifying strengths and weaknesses, including a plan of action to improve purchasing performance. *(ISM, 2000)*

Purchasing Cycle: The sequence of activities carried out by a purchasing department in the acquisition of supplies and services. *Also see Cradle-to-Grave.*

Purchasing Ethics: *See Ethics.*

Purchasing Management Association of Canada (PMAC): CANADIAN An educational and technical organization of purchasing and materiel management personnel and buying organizations, both public and private sector. *(Summit Magazine, On-Line)*

Purchasing Manager: Public purchasing employee with responsibility and authority to act for the public agency in certain areas.

Purchasing Manual: A document that describes rules, regulations, policies and procedures to be followed by the purchasing organization and the agencies/departments it serves.

Purchasing Methods: CANADIAN Canadian public procurement methods to procure goods and services include: Invitation to Tender (ITT), Request for Proposal (RFP), Request for Quotation (RFQ), Request for Standing Offer (RFSO) and Telephone Buy (T-buy). *(www.summitconnects.com)*

Purchasing Officer: An official in charge of the procurement operation, from the determination of needs to follow-up, ensures timely delivery.

Purchasing Organization: Employees responsible for purchasing needed supplies, services, and construction; the purchasing department.

Purchasing Policy: A course of action adopted by the public agency that provides guidance relative to procurement actions.

Purchasing Power Parity (PPP): A method for calculating the correct value of a currency, which may differ from its current market value. PPP is helpful when comparing living standards in different countries, as it indicates the appropriate exchange rate to use when expressing incomes and prices in different countries in a common currency. As public purchasing moves to global procurement, it is essential to understand the basics of international currency standards. *(Bishop, 2004)*

Purchasing Procedure: A mode of conducting purchasing activities.

Push Strategy: An attempt by manufacturers, wholesalers and other distribution channels to motivate intermediaries to push the product down to their customers. *(Business, 2002)*

PWS: *See Performance Work Statement.*

QA: *See Quality Assurance.*

QC: *See Quality Control.*

QOH: *See Quantity on Hand.*

QPL: *See Qualified Products List.*

Qualified Bidder: A bidder determined by the purchasing organization to meet the minimum standards of business competence, reputation, financial ability, and product quality for placement on the bidders list. *Also see Responsible Bidder.*

Qualified Products List (QPL): A list of items (products) that have been examined and tested and have satisfied all applicable qualification requirements. These lists are used on procurements to restrict bidders/offerors to those products on the lists. May also be referred to as an Approved Brands List (ABL) or an Approved Products List (APL). *(Nash, Schooner, O'Brien, 1998)*

Qualified Products List (QPL) Specifications: QPL Specifications are based on a list of products identified by manufacturers' names and model numbers, which are the only items which will be acceptable. These are used when quality is such a critical factor and testing so lengthy or expensive that the agency wants to stay with proven products. The list is prepared by testing products, either in the lab or in daily use. Items may be added to the list by the supplier demonstrating their quality by meeting specifications that have been defined by the using entity.

Qualitative Measurement: Pertaining to or concerning quality aspects; tends to be more subjective in nature; decides suitability or effectiveness. Example: The navy blue color of this week's shipment of motors is slightly lighter in color, however, it will not affect its performance and therefore this shipment is still acceptable from a qualitative point of view.

Quality:
1. In absolute terms, quality is a function of excellence, intrinsic value, or grade, as determined over time by society generally or by designated bodies in specialized fields.
2. The composite of all attributes or characteristics, including performance, that satisfy a user's needs.
3. Conformance with the stated requirements.

Quality Assurance (QA):
1. Assuring that quality performance criteria contained within the contract is provided during contract delivery. A contract administration process that assures technical performance that conforms to the quality performance criteria.

2. Specific to technology, a planned and systematic pattern of all actions necessary to provide adequate confidence that the product optimally fulfills customers' expectations. When a new technology product is introduced it may involve an alpha and beta testing. Faults are identified and fixed before the product is released commercially. *Also see Monitoring.*

Quality Assurance Code: CANADIAN The code specifying DND (Canadian Department of National Defence) quality assurance requirements.

Quality Assurance Teams (Quality Circles): Small groups of workers brought together from throughout the organization to solve specific quality issues in order to improve a process, procedure, or production method. *(Burt, Dobler, Starling, 2003)*

Quality Control (QC):
1. A manufacturing or service delivery process that incorporates tools and methodologies to provide assurance that the standards criteria specified will be delivered to the customer.
2. The processes an organization uses to maintain its established standards.

Quality Standard: A framework for achieving a recognized level of quality within an organization. Achievement of a quality standard demonstrates that an organization has met the requirements laid out by a certifying body. Quality standards recognized on an international basis include ISO 9000 and ISO 14000. *(Business, 2002)*

Quantitative Measurements: A measurement capable of being expressed as a quantity or a number of things. Example: The terms and conditions of this contract require the awardees to deliver three complete compressor units per day.

Quantitative Research: The gathering and analysis of data that can be expressed in numerical form. Involves data that is measurable and can include statistical results, financial or demographic data. *(Business, 2002)*

Quantity Demanded: The amount of a product consumers will purchase at a specific price. An economic impact on pricing that is relational to supply and demand. *(Schiller, 2000)*

Quantity Discount: A reduction in the unit price offered for a large volume contract. Economies of scale would dictate that the larger the volume/quantity the lower the unit price or total cost. *Also see Economies of Scale, Volume Discount, and Volume Leveraging.*

Quantity on Hand (QOH): Material owned by the agency that is immediately and physically available for use by the agency that has not otherwise been specifically allocated or reserved for others.

Quantity Supplied: The amount of a product that producers will produce and sell at a specific price. Consumer demand influences producer production and pricing. *(Schiller, 2002)*

Quasi-Contract: *See Implied Contract.*

Quasi-Judicial: A quasi-judicial body is an individual or organization which has powers resembling those of a court of law or judge and is able to remedy a situation or impose legal penalties on a person or organization. Such bodies usually have powers of adjudication in such matters as: breach of discipline; conduct rules; trust in the matters of money or otherwise. Their powers are usually limited to a particular area of expertise, such as financial markets, employment, public standards, immigration, or regulation. *(Wikipedia, 1.22.07)*

Quasi-Legislative:
1. Having a partly legislative character by possession of the right to make rules and regulations having the force of law.
2. Essentially legislative in character but not within the legislative power or function especially as constitutionally defined. *(Merriam-Webster online, 1.22.07)*

Quasi-Public Corporation: Corporations owned and operated by federal, state, or local governments. A revenue authority or water authority are examples. *(Business, 2002)*

Quick Ratio (Acid Test): A stringent measure of liquidity that eliminates inventory. A good tool to utilize when assessing the financial health of a business. *(Business, 2002)*

Quid Pro Quo: A Latin phrase meaning, what for what or something for something. An equal exchange or substitution. Used to describe a negotiation technique where two or more parties agree to give something in order to receive something in return. *(Harney, 1992)*

Quota: A limit on the quantity of a good that may be imported in a given time period. Example: Steel import quota. *(Ferrell, 2002)*

Quote: An informal purchasing process which solicits pricing information from several sources.

Quotation: A statement of price, terms of sale, and description of goods or services offered by a vendor to a prospective purchaser; may be non-binding if solicited to obtain market information for planning purposes.

R

R&D: *See Research and Development.*

Radio Frequency Identification (RFID): An emerging technology, which consists of identification tags composed of silicon chips and an antenna that can transmit data to a wireless receiver. RFID tags are used to track assets, manage inventory, authorize payments as well as other supply management applications. There are three types of RFID: high frequency (850-950 MHz and 2.4-5 GHz), intermediate frequency (10-15 MHz) and low frequency (100-500kHz). *(Jansen, 2002)*

Random sampling: A technique that results in a representative subset of the population where each element has the same chance of being selected as every other element in the population; such as to select items from the inspection lot so each item in the lot has an equal chance of being included in the sample. A form of quality assurance often used in modern polling, market research and manufacturing.

Rate: As applied to the transportation or movement of goods and material, the cost of, or charge that applies to the service rendered by the carrier.

Rate of Exchange: *See Exchange Rate.*

Ratio Analysis: Calculations that measure an organization's financial health. Often mentioned in financial information provided by a public company to determine if they are a responsible bidder/offeror. *(Business, 2002)*

Raw Materials: Items bought for use in the manufacturing process of a business. May include components, subassemblies, and complete products. Generally includes virgin materials such as wood, steel, petroleum products, etc. *(Business, 2002)*

RCA: *See Root Cause Analysis.*

REA: *See Request for Equitable Adjustment.*

Reactive Maintenance: Maintenance for equipment and facilities provided only in response to a breakdown which results in a loss of production. It may create emergency requests to the purchasing organization. *(Business, 2002)*

Real Property:
1. Land and its permanently affixed buildings or structures.
2. Any property which is not personal property.

Reasonable Cost: A cost that by its nature or amount does not exceed what would normally be incurred by an ordinarily prudent person in the conduct of competitive business. Often used in the context of "fair and reasonable" cost/price.

Reason for Call-Up: *CANADIAN* A brief explanation of reasons for calling-up temporary help services.

Rebate: A sum of money returned by the vendor to the buyer in consideration for the purchase of an agreed upon amount, quantity or value of goods and services, generally within a limited period of time.

Rebilling: In freight handling, issuing a new waybill at a junction point to which shipment has been billed by a connecting line.

Receipt: Written acknowledgement that one party has obtained money or something of value from the other, without any affirmative obligation upon either party.

Receivables Turnover: Sales divided by accounts receivable. May be used to determine the financial health of a company and to determine if they are a responsible bidder/offeror. *(Business, 2002)*

Receiving: The function of accepting from all sources all items of supply used in the organization.

Receiving Inspection: Comparing material and services received to the specifications.

Receiving Report: A document used in the receiving and inspection process that identifies the item, quantity, and date of delivery. It may also note any discrepancies or problems.

Receiving Voucher: *CANADIAN* A document used to record the receipt of material.

Recession: A decline in total output for two or more consecutive quarters. An economic downturn that may impact price, terms and conditions of purchasing transactions and usually reflective of a buyers market. *(Bishop, 2004)*

Reciprocity:
1. The act of buying from or selling to another business in return for sales or purchases from the first organization.
2. Illegal under the antitrust provisions of the Sherman Act.
3. A reciprocal condition or relationship.
4. A mutual or cooperative interchange of favors. *(ISM, 2000)*

Recommended By: *CANADIAN* An authorized officer's signature (within the department).

Re-consignment:
1. A privilege extended to shippers allowing goods to be forwarded to a point other than the original destination without removal from the carrier and at the through rate from initial point to that of final delivery.
2. A change, as in consignee, destination, or route, in the original billing of goods in transit.

Recycled Material Content: The portion of a product made with recycled materials consisting of pre-consumer materials (waste), post-consumer materials (waste), or both.

Recycled Materials: Materials, goods, or products that contain recyclable items that are used in manufacturing a new product.

Redistribution: The transfer of control, utilization, or location of material between organizations or activities.

Reduced Inspection: Inspection under a sampling plan using the same quality levels for normal inspection, but requiring a smaller sample.

Reference: A component of due diligence to determine the capability of performing contractual requirements whereby previous businesses are contacted concerning the potential contractors skills, qualifications and capabilities.

Reference Groups: Groups with whom buyers identify and whose values or attitudes they adopt. May be applicable to purchasing cooperatives. *(Business, 2002)*

Refused Shipment: A delivery of freight or goods and materials that the consignee refuses to accept. Any delivery from a carrier that is not accepted.

Regressive Tax System: One in which effective tax rates fall as income rises. The burden tends to be overly high on the state's less-affluent residents. A public policy issue that may impact governmental procurement decisions. *Also see Sales Tax.* *(Schiller, 2000)*

Regulation: A statement by a governmental body to implement, interpret, or prescribe law or policy, or to describe organization, procedure, or practice, often promulgated in accordance with an administrative procedures act.

Regulatory Body: An independent organization, usually set up by government, that regulates the activities of companies in an industry.

Reinsurance: A contract in which an insurance company agrees to indemnify another insurance company in whole or in part against risks the first company has assumed.

Rejection: Refusal of a delivered supply or service that does not meet contract specifications or requirements.

Relationships (between Buyer and Seller): *See Buyer-Seller Relationships.*

Relative Price: The price of one good in comparison with the price of other goods. A key component of benchmarking. *(Bishop, 2004)*

Remanufactured Product: Any product diverted from the supply of discarded materials by refurbishing and marketing said product without substantial change to its original form. *(Burt Dobler, Starling, 2002)*

Remedial Training: A technique utilized to improve or upgrade an individual's knowledge and skills when job performance is not meeting predetermined expectations.

Remedy: The means by which a contractual right or obligation is enforced or the violation of such a right is prevented, reduced or compensated. Remedies may be defined in the contract, by agreement between the parties such as by accord and satisfaction, by arbitration, by operation of law or judicial remedy such as by action or suit.

Renegotiation: Deliberation, discussion, or conference to change or amend the terms of an existing agreement.

Rent: A contract giving the right to use real estate or property for a specified time in return for monetary compensation. *(Business, 2002)*

Re-Order Cycle Quantity: The quantity of goods required to sustain operations for a specified period of time, after which time, orders will be placed for more goods.

Re-Order Level: CANADIAN A pre-determined stock level such that, if the net stock falls to or below it, action is taken to replenish stock.

Re-Order Point: The level of stock or inventory, above the safety stock level, at which orders are placed to obtain more goods.

Re-Order Quantity: CANADIAN The fixed quantity which should be ordered each time the available stock (on hand plus on order) falls below the re-order level.

Repair and Overhaul: CANADIAN The repair of an item of equipment to return it to serviceable condition, overhaul may or may not coincide with repair.

Repair Work Order: CANADIAN A document describing the repair activities required for one or more materiel items.

Replacement Materiel: CANADIAN Materiel assets which are required to replace disposed items.

Replenishment Inventory Control System: An inventory control system that relies on accurate estimates of usage rates and delivery lead times to allow orders to be completed and to ensure stock does not run out. *(Business, 2002)*

Replevin: A legal term meaning the action for the recovery of property. A writ of replevin allows for the repossession of property. *(Garner, 2002)*

Report of Partial Shipment: Report showing the items received from a vendor when an order is incomplete, or has items backordered.

Repositioning: A marketing strategy that changes aspects of a product or brand in order to change market position and alter consumer perceptions. A strategy used to increase product sales in certain markets. *(Business, 2002)*

Repudiation: Rejection, disclaimer, or renunciation. Refusal to perform a duty or obligation owed to the other party. *(Garner, 2002)*

Request for Comments (RFC): A document generated prior to an authorized procurement in order to request feedback from the contracting community or potential proposers/bidders, to seek information about a product or service in order to assist in the finalization of technical specifications, design specifications, or a statement of work. *Also see Pre-Solicitation Conference and Request for Information (RFI).* *(ISM, 2000)*

Request for Equitable Adjustment (REA): Changes to a contract may require additional work and expense on the contractor. Change work, either directed by formal contract modification or through constructive change, entitles the contractor to seek an equitable adjustment. The contractor must prove that they are entitled to an equitable adjustment. The contract must contain language specifying the conditions under which an REA will be considered.

Request for Information (RFI): A non-binding method whereby a jurisdiction publishes via newspaper, internet, or direct mail its need for input from interested parties for an upcoming solicitation. A procurement practice used to obtain comments, feedback or reactions from potential suppliers (contractors) prior to the issuing of a solicitation. Generally price or cost is not required. Feedback may include best practices, industry standards, technology issues, etc. *Also see Pre-Solicitation Conference and Request for Comments (RFC).*

Request for Proposal (RFP): The document used to solicit proposals from potential providers for goods and services (Offerors). Price is usually not a primary evaluation factor. Provides for the negotiation of all terms, including price prior to contract award. May include a provision for the negotiation of Best and Final Offers. May be a single step or multi-step process. Introduced in the Armed Services Procurement Act of 1962 as well as by the Competition in Contracting Act of 1984.

Request for Qualifications (RFQu): A document which is issued by a procurement entity to obtain statements of the qualifications of potential development teams or individuals (i.e. consultants) to gauge potential competition in the marketplace, prior to issuing the solicitation.

Request for Quotation (RFQ): A small order amount purchasing method. Generally used for small orders under a certain dollar threshold, such as $1000.00. A request is sent to suppliers along with a description of the commodity or services needed and the supplier is asked to respond with price and other information by a pre-determined date. Evaluation and recommendation for award should be based on the quotation that best meets price, quality, delivery, service, past performance and reliability.

Request for Standing Offer (RFSO): CANADIAN A method of supply used by Public Works and Government Services Canada (PWGSC) to satisfy the requirements of departments and agencies by arranging with suppliers to submit a standing offer to provide goods, services or both during a specified period. An RFSO is an invitation to suppliers to provide PWGSC with a standing offer. The quantity of goods, level of services and estimated expenditure specified in the RFSO are only an approximation of requirements given in good faith. Standing offers are not contracts. If and when the government issues a call-up against a standing offer, a contract is created. *(http://sacc.pwgsc.gc, 1.19.07)*

Requirement Delivery: *See Delivery/Indefinite.*

Requirements Analysis: Value analysis applied to the writing of specifications to eliminate products or services that are not cost effective.

Requirements Contract: A contract used to order only the material or services actually required during a contract term. An indefinite quantity contract for frequently used commodities or products. *Also see Blanket Order, Price Agreement and Open-end Contract.*

Requirements Determination: A method used to determine what is needed, when it is needed and how much is needed. Such methods may include reviewing past usage of an item, future need, program objectives, trends, performance of a demand analysis, market analysis, the use of software or other forecasting tools, with the objective of satisfying the need.

Requisition: An internal document by which a using agency sends details of supplies, services, or materials required to the purchasing department.

R

Requisition Certified By: *CANADIAN* Signature of the financial officer who has authority to certify funds availability.

Requisitioner: Anyone who initiates a purchase requisition or request for goods or services.

Requisition Item Quantity: *CANADIAN* The quantity required based on the correct unit of issue.

Requisition Number: *CANADIAN* An alphanumeric code applied to a requisition for control purposes.

Requisition Originator: *CANADIAN* A person who initiates a procurement, issue or disposal transaction.

Requisition Serial Number: *CANADIAN* A four-character serial number, which the department uses for requisitioning control purposes.

Rescission of Contract: The relieving of a party from all obligations under a contract. A remedy for mutual mistake when reformation is not possible, and for other defects in contract formation such a duress, fraud, misrepresentation and unconscionability. *(Nash, Schooner, O'Brien, 1998)*

Research and Development (R&D): A process of scientific discovery and application of knowledge in which new products are created and uses are found for them.

Residency Preference: *See Preference.*

Residual Value: The proceeds, less removal and disposal costs, if any, realized upon disposition of a tangible capital asset (FAR 31.001).

Resources: All natural, human, and man-made aids to production of goods and services. *(Schiller, 2000)*

Responder: One who submits a response to a solicitation document. *(Harney, 1992)*

Responsibility Centre: *CANADIAN* The organizational unit which has been delegated responsibility for the control and monitoring of a financial budget.

Responsible Bidder/Offeror: A contractor, business entity or individual who is fully capable to meet all of the requirements of the solicitation and subsequent contract. Must possess the full capability, including financial and technical, to perform as contractually required. Must be able to fully document the ability to provide good faith performance. *Also see Qualified Bidder.*

Responsive Bidder/Offeror: A contractor, business entity or individual who has submitted a bid or request for proposal that fully conforms in all material respects to the IFB/RFP and all of its requirements, including all form and substance.

Restocking Charges: On occasion, a public entity may inadvertently order more product or equipment than is required or, in error, order the wrong material. This is the charge incurred when returning the oversupply to the seller. It is good practice to include a restocking charge clause allowing the public entity to return the product for a negotiated restocking fee.

Restraint of Trade: The effect of an act, contract, conspiracy, or combination which eliminates or stifles competition, effects a monopoly, artificially maintains prices, or otherwise hampers or obstructs the course of trade and commerce as it would be carried on if left to the control of natural and economic forces.

Restrictive Specifications: Specifications that unnecessarily exclude a potential bidder from competing for a procurement. Precludes full and open competition. Specifications that are written around a specific product or service.

Results Oriented Budgeting: Budgeting that attempts to link resource allocation decisions to performance criteria that include both output and outcome measures. Also referred to as performance based budgeting, these forms of budgeting add performance measures that look at outcomes of activities rather than at individual process steps. In order to be effective, these budget methods must be linked to the overall strategic plan of the organization, and each decision unit must support a particular goal and objective (similar to decision units in ZBB). *Also see Performance based budgeting.*

Retailer: Intermediaries who buy products from manufacturers (or other intermediaries) and sell them to buyers rather than for resale or for use in producing other products. *Also see Wholesaler.* *(Business, 2002)*

Retainage: A specified amount or percentage of the progress payment due usually under a construction contract. Upon completion of all contract requirements, retained amounts must be paid promptly. *Also see Holdback.* *(Harney, 1992)*

Retained Earnings: Earnings after expenses and taxes that are reinvested in the assets of the firm and belong to the owners in the form of equity. *(Business, 2002)*

Retained Profits: The amount of profit remaining after tax and distribution to shareholders that is retained in a business and used as a reserve or to finance expansion and investment. *(Business, 2002)*

Retention: To withhold a certain percentage of the payment due to the contractor until the work is completed and accepted. The contractual terms (contained within the IFB/RFP) will stipulate the amount to be retained as well as the time period of the retention.

Retention Schedule Records: A jurisdiction's established timetable for maintenance and destruction of purchasing records, based on administrative, historical, and legal requirements.

Retraining: Techniques used to prepare the employee for revisions in current processes and procedures or to reinforce existing skills and abilities.

Return On Investment (ROI): A calculation used in business to determine whether a proposed investment is a wise business decision and how well it will repay the investor. It is calculated as the ratio of the amount gained or lost relative to the basis. The analysis takes the form of a dynamic model or a statistical model. *(Business, 2002)*

Revenue Bond: A bond that a government issues, to be repaid from the money made from the project financed with it. *(Business, 2002)*

Revenue Generating Contract: A contract whose primary purpose is to generate revenue or to create a business opportunity for the organization. This type of contract may also serve a need such as operating an organization-owned golf course or tennis center.

Reverse Auction: An online auction in which sellers bid against each other to win a buyers business. Typically used to purchase commodities from multiple pre-qualified providers. Also referred to as eAuction.

Reverse Trade Show: An event that offers businesses, suppliers and contractors an opportunity to maximize connections with purchasing professionals who source goods and services. The governmental agencies are the exhibitors and the suppliers and contractors may visit and meet to determine needs and procedures when dealing with governmental entities.

RFC: *See Request for Comments.*

RFI: *See Request for Information.*

RFID: *See Radio Frequency Identification.*

RFP: *See Request for Proposal.*

RFQ: *See Request for Quotation.*

RFQu: *See Request for Qualifications.*

RFSO: CANADIAN *See Request for Standing Offer.*

Riding a Contract: *See Piggyback.*

Rightsizing: To re-structure an organization, with the aim of reducing costs, and improving efficiency and effectiveness.

Risk: The chance of injury, damage or loss; the probability of some occurrence (e.g., a failure) and the consequences and impact of the occurrence.

Risk Analysis: The stated findings of a factor, element or cause involving uncertain harm or loss.

Risk Management: The process of identification and analysis of risk; and the decision to either accept or mitigate the exposure to such risk when compared to the potential impact on the achievement of the organization's objectives.

Risk Matrix: *See Risk Register.*

Risk Register: A list of risks associated with a specific procurement and the responses to those risks. Responsibility for acting on the risk is assigned to a specific person to manage. The list is applicable only to the particular procurement and the principle is to identify risk and allocate this to the party best suited to manage, mitigate or eliminate it. The register is a live document throughout the project and should be reviewed on an ongoing basis. *Also referred to as Risk Matrix.* *(Carmarthenshire County Council – Wales, n.d.)*

Robinson-Patman Price Discrimination Act (U.S. Law): Amended the Clayton Antitrust Act in 1936. It is intended to eliminate discriminatory and predatory pricing practices. Private individuals as well as government prosecutors may initiate lawsuits under this Act. *Also see Clayton Antitrust Act, Sherman Antitrust Act and Federal Trade Commission Act.*

ROI: *See Return on Investment.*

Roll On/Roll Off (RO/RO): A method of ocean cargo service using vessels with ramps which allow wheeled vehicles to be loaded and discharged without the use of cranes. *(ISM, 2000)*

Root Cause Analysis (RCA): A technique that enables the manager to determine what happened, why and methods of preventing the occurrence in the future by examining all factors that could contribute to a problem, including but not limited to factors such as environmental, human and procedural matters.

Routing: A determination of how a shipment will move from the point of origin to the destination, including the selection of carriers and geographic routes.

Royalty (Royalties): Compensation for the use of property.

Rubbish: Refuse that does not have any market value but must be disposed of. *Also see Scrap and Waste.*

Rules of Interpretation: Refers to a set of well-established principles in common law that courts use to interpret the meaning of contracts. *(Garner, 2004)*

S

SA: *See Strategic Alliance.*

Safety Stock: The quantity of material exceeding immediate needs held for the purpose of ensuring continuity of supply and guarding against unforeseen shortages. *(ISM, 2000)*

Sales: The activity of selling a company's products or services, the income generated by this, or the department that deals with selling. *(Business, 2002)*

Sales Promotion: Marketing activities, usually short-term, designed to attract attention to a particular product and to increase its sales using advertising and publicity. *(Business, 2002)*

Sales Representative: A person acting on behalf of a vendor who visits purchasers to discuss requirements. One who sells products and services to buyers. *(Business, 2002)*

Sales Tax: A levy on a vendor's sale by an authorized level of government. Governmental entities are generally tax exempt. Sales taxes are regressive because they impose higher taxes on lower incomes. *Also see Regressive Tax System.* *(Schiller, 2000)*

Sales Territory: A defined area within which a designated salesperson is responsible for selling a product or service. *(Business, 2002)*

Salvage: Property having some value in excess of its basic material content or scrap value, but is in such condition as to be no longer usable, and its repair or rehabilitation for use is clearly impractical.

Sample: One or more units selected from the material or process lot and represented as a specimen of quality.

Sampling: A technique used to avoid examination of each item in a population, yet will still be able to determine whether the entire population shall be accepted as complying with the acceptable quality level or stated requirements.

Sanction:
1. Authoritative permission or approval that makes a course of action valid.
2. An action by a government body, such as restriction on trade. *(Schiller, 2000)*

Sarbanes-Oxley Act: Passed by Congress in 2002, also know as SarbOx or SOX, its intent is to curb financial abuses in large public companies. The act demands that public companies enhance their accounting oversight and adopt stringent internal controls. *(Miller, 2006)*

SAVE: *See Society of American Value Engineers.*

Saving: That part of disposable income not spent on current consumption; disposable income less consumption; any income that is not spent. *(Bishop, 2002)*

Say's Law: Supply creates it own demand. Economic theory developed by French economist Jean-Baptiste Say (1767-1832). *(Bishop, 2002)*

SBA: *See Small Business Administration.*

Scalability: The ease with which the supply of a product or service can be expanded to meet increased demand. Technology now allows new products to enter the market more quickly and win market share at a much more rapid pace. Suppliers often reference "scalability" in market literature and on their internet sites. *(Bishop, 2002)*

Scarcity: The fact that available resources are insufficient to satisfy all desired uses thereof. An economic indicator that drives prices higher. *(Bishop, 2002)*

Scenario Analysis: An important technique in Risk Management, whereby various possible scenarios are developed based on best to worse outcomes. May be applied to procurement situations in order to achieve effective future planning. It is a tool used to anticipate the future and plan accordingly. *(Miller, 2006)*

Schedule Contract: A contract that consolidates agency requirements by pre-establishing a bid opening date and requiring using agencies to submit requirements by a specified time. *Also called schedule purchase.*

Schedule of Events: Also referred to as a "timetable or timeline". It identifies the projected milestones in the procurement process from the beginning of the procurement to its finalization.

SCM: *See Supply Chain Management.*

Scope of Work: A detailed, written description of the conceptual requirements for the project contained within a Request for Proposal. The scope of work should establish a clear understanding of what is required by the entity.

S-Corporation: A corporation taxed as though it were a partnership with restrictions on shareholders. *(Business, 2002)*

SCPA: *See Supply Chain Pollution Avoidance.*

Scrap: Salvageable materials which are damaged, defective, deteriorated or residue from operations with market value. The value exceeds the selling expense and the materials are sold. *Also see Waste and Rubbish.*

Sealed Bid: A formal submission from a bidder/offeror submitted in response to an invitation to bid (ITB). It is submitted in a sealed envelope to prevent its contents from being revealed before the time and date set for the bid opening.

Search Costs: The cost associated with finding the right product or service to meet your needs. The economic cost of procuring an item may be more than just the price you pay. Technology changes, such as the internet, may sharply reduce search costs and thus lead to more efficient procurement decision making. *(Bishop, 2004)*

Seasonally Adjusted: The adjustment of pricing to reflect seasonal patterns. For example, pricing on consumer goods tends to be higher during certain holidays. Road salt and ice melt would be more expensive during the winter rather than the summer. *(Schiller, 2000)*

Seasonal Unemployment: Unemployment due to seasonal changes in employment or labor supply. *(Schiller, 2000)*

S

Secondary Markets: Stock exchanges and over-the-counter markets where investors can trade their securities with others. *(Business, 2002)*

Seconds: Usable products containing imperfections or slight defects that may be marked down below normal list price.

Secured Bonds: Bonds that are backed by specific collateral that must be forfeited in the event that the issuing firm defaults. *(Schiller, 2000)*

Secured Loans: Loans backed by collateral that the bank can claim if the borrowers do not repay them. *(Schiller, 2000)*

Securities: Financial contracts such as bonds that grant the owner a share in an asset. *(Bishop, 2002)*

Selective Distribution: A form of market coverage whereby only a small number of all available outlets are used to expose products. *(Business, 2002)*

Self-Directed Work Teams: A group of employees responsible for the entire work process or segment that delivers the product to an internal or external customer. *(Business, 2002)*

Self Evaluation: A self assessment of the way a person views him/herself and their work performance and accomplishments. A supervisor prepares an evaluation of the subordinate independently and at the same time the subordinate is asked to do a self-evaluation using the same evaluation criteria. Once both evaluations are completed, the supervisor and subordinate meet to discuss their evaluations and to see where there are points of agreement, differences of opinion and where disconnects can be remedied.

Self Insurance: Assumption or retention of the risk of loss by a government or a contractor. To retain a risk of loss up to a certain dollar threshold. *(Business, 2002)*

Seller's Lien: A lien in favor of a vendor granting the vendor the right to withhold goods sold, surrendering them only upon receipt of payment.

Seller's Market: An economic condition within a competitive market place that occurs when the demand of a product or service exceeds the supply. Generally results in higher prices for the buyer. *(Bishop, 2004)*

Seller's Option:

1. A vendor's right to compel a purchaser to buy at a particular price and time.
2. On option granted to the vendor to make delivery within a specified, limited period.

Sensitivity Analysis: A component to take into consideration when conducting a "make or buy" analysis and deciding if a service should be done in-house or outsourced, if the two costs are almost even. A sensitivity analysis can be performed to determine the consideration of the costs relative to the assumptions. This additional information and any intangible factors could influence the final make or buy decision.

Sequential Sampling Plan: A unit-by-unit approach to sampling in which the sample units are selected one at a time. After each unit is inspected, the decision is made to accept, reject, or continue inspection until the acceptance or rejection criteria are met.

Serial Bonds: A sequence of small bond issues of progressively longer maturities. *(Business, 2002)*

Service Function: Procurement Department serves the agency's departments by providing professional and knowledgeable purchasing services thereby relieving the departments of the need to perform those purchasing activities which are common to all. Example: Purchasing Department enters into a contract for office supplies for the entire agency's requirements and thereby individual departments can focus on their core mission and responsibilities, i.e., Police Department can focus on policing issues instead of being distracted with purchasing related issues such as purchasing office supplies. *Also see Line Function and Staff Function.*

Service Level Agreement (SLA):
1. An agreement between the Application Service Provider (ASP) and the user to determine the scope of work to be provided by the ASP.
2. An agreement between a customer and a service provider, that details the level of service and the quality of the service to be provided. May be a legally binding agreement. *(Business, 2002)*

Services: CANADIAN Any professional or general service work performed which does not result in the delivery of goods or materials, e.g. repairs, training, surveys, consulting, etc.

Service/Services Contract:
1. An agreement calling for a contractor's time and effort.
2. The furnishing of labor, time, or effort by a contractor or vendor, which may involve to a lesser degree, the delivery or supply of products. The UCC/state commercial codes only apply to a procurement of a product, while state common law would apply if it is considered a procurement of a service.

Set-Aside: An acquisition or procurement exclusively or partially reserved for the participation of small or minority business concerns or a special class of contractors. *Also see Contract Goals and Goals.*

Set-Off: An agreement between two parties to balance one debt against another or a loss against a gain. May be used in construction contracting to minimize the cost of change orders or other unanticipated costs.

Settlement Conference: Involves a pre-trial conference conducted by a settlement judge or referee and attended by representatives for the opposing parties in order to reach a mutually acceptable settlement of the matter in dispute.

Set-Up Cost: The cost incurred to change machine tooling or to change the production line to produce a different item or product.

Shall: Denotes the imperative in contract clauses or specifications. *Also see May.*

Shared Services: An intergovernmental agreement for the provision of goods or services that is commonly used by two or more entities. The agreements are commonly created to address economic and logistical needs in an effective and efficient manner. Example: municipal town agreement allows multiple towns' residents to an EMS (Emergency Medical Services) station that is shared across organizations. *Also see Intergovernmental contract.*

Shareware: Downloadable Internet software that is available for testing and sampling prior to purchase. It is generally copyrighted and distributed on "a free-will donation basis". Use of the software after a trial period requires payment of a registration fee. *Also see Freeware. (Jansen, 2002)*

Sharp Practices: The term typically is illustrated as evasion and indirect misrepresentation, just short of actual fraud. Unscrupulous practices that focus on short-term gains and ignore the long-term implications for a business relationship. An example, would be lying to a salesperson or grossly misleading them in a negotiation.

Shelf Life: The length of time which an item of supply can be stored under specified environmental conditions and continue to remain suitable for its intended use.

Sherman Antitrust Act (U.S. Law): Passed by Congress in 1890, it prohibits contracts and conspiracies in restraint of trade, conspiracies to monopolize trade, and attempts to monopolize. The act makes price fixing, bid rigging, territorial market allocation, and some types of tying arrangements and boycotts illegal. *Also see Clayton Act, Price Fixing and Tying Arrangement. (Business, 2002)*

Shipper's Load and Count: Where the contents of a conveyance were loaded and counted by the shipper, and not checked or verified by the transportation agency.

Shipping: The activities performed in preparation of the outgoing shipment of products and material, which may include packaging, marking, weighing, and loading for shipment.

Shipping List: A memorandum that includes all items shipped at one time on a given order.

Short List: Names of candidates that have been narrowed considerably from a longer list of top-ranked offerors.

Shortage: The situation resulting when the quantity demanded exceeds the quantity supplied of a good or service, usually because the price is for some reason below the equilibrium price in the market. Shortages generally drive up prices and create a sellers market. *(Schiller, 2000)*

Show Cause Notice: A preliminary written notice given to the contractor by the procurement official when termination for default appears to be appropriate. *(Nash, Schooner, O'Brien, 1998)*

Shrinkage: Refers to inventory that is lost, stolen, misplaced or otherwise unaccounted for.

SIC Code: *See Standard Industrial Classification Code.*

Simplification Program: A process used to screen the agency's inventory in order to determine which items should be consolidated, updated or no longer maintained in inventory.

Single Sampling Plan: The sampling procedure that uses a single sample size with associated acceptance and rejection criteria.

Single Sourcing: A procurement decision whereby purchases are directed to one source because of standardization, warranty, or other factors, even though other competitive sources may be available. *Also see Sole Sourcing.*

Site Inspection: Visit to the actual location where the contract is to be performed by potential bidders or offerors to become familiar with site conditions. May be held in conjunction with a pre-bid or pre-proposal conference.

Six Sigma: A quality management theory that can be traced to the work done by Walter Shewart, Edward Deming, Joseph Juran, and Genichi Taguchi. Motorola combined TQM problem-solving tools and focused on the voice of the customer with advanced statistical tools, such as hypothesis testing, correlation and regression, analysis of variance, experimental design, and statistical process control. As a result, Motorola achieved breakthrough improvements in quality. Six Sigma seeks to reduce the process variation around the target. The term has come to represent the achievement of 3.4 defects per million transactions. *(M. Millstein, ISM, August 2002)*

Skid: A wood or metal platform fitted with two runners, or with legs, upon which material is placed or transported.

Skills Gap: Gap between skills required for emerging jobs and the skills of workers. A stress metric pushing employers to provide additional training opportunities for their employees. A possible factor in labor hour contracts where training is a component of the labor rate. *(Business, 2002)*

SKU: *See Stock-Keeping Unit.*

SLA: *See Service Level Agreement.*

Slap and Ship: A supply management term used to describe the process of applying RFID tags in the distribution center prior to shipment. *(ISM, 2000)*

Small Business: An independently owned firm, corporation, or establishment, having a small number of employees, low volume of sales, small amount of assets, and limited impact on the market.

Small Business Act: 1999 act which establishes the Federal Government's responsibility to aid, counsel, assist, and promote the interests of small businesses (as defined by the Small Business Administration), and to place with such businesses a fair proportion of Federal Government purchases and contracts for goods and services.

Small Business Administration (SBA): An independent agency of the Federal Government that offers managerial and financial assistance to small businesses. The SBA mission is to maintain and strengthen the nation's economy by aiding, counseling, and assisting the interests of small businesses. *(www.sbs.gov)*

Small Disadvantaged Business: A business offered preferential treatment: a small business that qualifies for preferential consideration for government contracts, usually because it is largely owned by a socially and economically disadvantaged person or group. *Also see Economically Disadvantaged Individuals, Historically Underutilized Business (HUB), Minority-Owned Business (MBE) and WBE.* *(Encarta® World English Dictionary © & (P) 1998-2004 Microsoft Corporation. All rights reserved.)*

Small Purchase: Any procurement not exceeding a given upper monetary limit, as established by law, regulation, executive order, etc. Usually applies to purchases of small dollar amounts under a certain monetary threshold.

Smart Card (Smartcard): A plastic card embedded with a microchip that can store programmable data. Available in two types: memory cards and processor cards. Facilitates wireless and paperless transactions. It contains a tiny secure cryptoprocessor embedded within a credit card sized or smaller card. Invented and patented in France by Roland Moreno in the1970's. *(Jansen, 2002)*

SME: *See Subject Matter Expert.*

Smith, Adam: Economist (1723-1790) who stressed the importance of the "invisible hand" of competition in a free market. He wrote that technical progress and capital investment were the main engines of economic growth. *(Bishop, 2004)*

Social Costs: The full resource costs of an economic activity, including externalities. *(Schiller, 2000)*

Social Responsibility: The obligation of an organization to maximize its positive impact on society. *(Schiller, 2000)*

Society of American Value Engineers (SAVE): An International Society devoted to the advancement of value methodology. Value methodology benefits include decreasing costs, increasing profits and improving quality.

Society of Logistics Engineer (SOLE): A non-profit international professional society composed of individuals, organized to enhance the art and science of logistics technology, education and management.

Socioeconomic Benefits: CANADIAN Benefits expected to result from a project such as: Canadian content (percentage of total project funds to be spent directly and indirectly in Canada), person-years of employment, and monetary value of industrial offsets (e.g. technology transfers, non-project contracts, investment). May also refer to any environmental aspects of the project.

Socioeconomic Programs: Using governmental purchasing power to promote public policy. Examples include: encouraging living wage programs in public contracting, establishing small business and minority procurement goals and establishing environmental procurement initiatives. *(Schiller, 2000)*

Soft Currency: A currency that is expected to drop in value relative to other currencies. Global currency fluctuations impact supply and demand and pricing of commodities in the global market place. For example, gas and oil prices may be impacted by a currency devaluation in China. *(Miller, 2006)*

SOLE: *See Society of Logistics Engineers.*

Sole Proprietorship: A business owned and operated by one individual; the most common form of business organization in the United States. *(Schiller, 2000)*

Sole Source Procurement: A situation created due to the inability to obtain competition. May result because only one vendor or supplier possesses the unique ability or capability to meet the particular requirements of the solicitation.

The purchasing authority may require a justification from the requesting agency explaining why this is the only source for the requirement.

Sole Sourcing: CANADIAN Under government policy, this non-competitive method is used, subject to obligations under the trade agreements, only when: the product or service is required immediately due to pressing emergency; there is only one qualified company, that has developed a patented or copyrighted product or service; or it is not in the public's interest to hold a competition, for example, for requirements falling under the national security umbrella.

Sole Sourcing: U.S. Selection of one particular supplier to the exclusion of all others. This decision may be based on lack of competition, proprietary technology, copyright or a supplier's unique capability. In government procurement, a sole source justification may be required from the requestor. *Also see Single Sourcing.*

Solicitation: An invitation for bids, a request for proposals, telephone calls or any document used to obtain bids or proposals for the purpose of entering into a contract. *Also see Bid and Tender.*

Solicitation Protest: *See Protest.*

SOR: *See Statement of Requirement.*

Source List: A record of prequalified, prospective bidders for the purchase or sale of specific goods or services. *Also see Bidders List.*

Source of Goods and Services: CANADIAN Principal location where goods or services are produced or where economic activity is generated.

Sourcing: The identification and selection of the supplier whose costs, qualities, technologies, timeliness, dependability, and service best meet the organization's needs. *(Burt, Dobler, Starling, 2003, 16)*

Sourcing Strategies: Alternative procurement plans that give guidance to assess, evaluate, and manage the supply base in ways that are consistent with overall agency objectives.

Sovereign Immunity: A legal doctrine that precludes a litigant from asserting an otherwise meritorious cause of action against a sovereign or a party with sovereign attributes unless the sovereign consents to suit. Sovereignty is the supreme, absolute, and uncontrollable power to make laws, regulate, collect taxes, wage war or make peace. *(Nash, Schooner, O'Brien, 1998)*

SOW: *See Statement of Work.*

SP2: *See Strategic Procurement Planning.*

SPC: *See Statistical Process Control.*

Special Agent: An agent who has limited authority to perform only special tasks for its principal. Example: Salespeople may or may not have the authority to commit their company to anything other than catalog prices or routing deliveries.

Special Procurement: A type of procurement, as practicable under the circumstances and initiated by the head of the entity, for an unusual or unique situation. The contract is not awarded based on the application of requirements of competitive sealed bidding or competitive sealed proposals that could be contrary to the public interest or the needs of the entity.

Special Revenue Funds: Funds that provide services financed from various specifically designated revenue sources, such as recreation fees used to support a specific recreation activity.

Specification: A precise description of the physical or functional characteristics of a product, good or construction item. A description of goods and/or services. A description of what the purchaser seeks to buy and what a bidder must be responsive to in order to be considered for award of a contract. Specifications generally fall under the following categories: design, performance, combination (design and performance), brand name or approved equal, qualified products list and samples. May also be known as a purchasing description.

Spend Analysis: The process of collecting, cleansing, classifying and analyzing expenditure data from all sources within the organization (i.e. purchasing card, eProcurement systems, etc.). The process analyzes the current, past and forecasted expenditures to allow visibility of data, within the organization at various levels, e.g. by supplier, commodity, service, or by department. Spend analysis can be used to make management decisions by providing answers to such questions as: what was bought; when was it bought; where was it purchased; how many suppliers were used, how much was spent with each supplier; and how much was paid for the item. *Also see Market Analysis, Procurement Profile and Supply Positioning.*

Spending Authority: CANADIAN The authority assigned to incur expenditures, including advance and progress payments, and to confirm satisfactory contract performance and price, as a prerequisite to the requisitioning of payment.

Spiraling Agreement: A negotiation technique that begins by reaching a minimum agreement even though it is not related to the objectives and build, bit by bit, on this first agreement.

Spot Price: The price quoted for a transaction that is to be made on the spot, that is, paid for now for delivery now. *Also see forward contracts and futures markets, where payment and/or delivery will be made at some future date.* *(Bishop, 2004)*

Spot Purchase: A one-time purchase occasioned by a small requirement, an unusual or emergency circumstance, or a favorable market condition. *Also called Spot Buy.*

Staff Function: Procurement Department advises agency management and operating departments about general business market conditions, new ideas and products suggested by vendors, and assists by providing anticipated budgeting prices for materials and their availability. *Also see Line Function and Service Function.*

Staffing Level: The number and type of personnel employed by an organization for the performance of a given work load. May be expressed in terms of full time equivalent (FTE) which typically represents one full time employee working 40 hours per week. *(Miller, 2006)*

Stagflation: An economic meltdown consisting of rampant inflation, high unemployment and general economic stagnation in a country. The simultaneous occurrence of substantial unemployment and inflation. May cause supply shortages that result in sellers being unable to provide commodities and services. *(Schiller, 2000)*

Stakeholder: Any organization group, or individual that can place a claim on the organization's resources or services or is affected by what the organization does or the services it provides.

Standard: Level of quality accepted as norm; a level of quality or excellence that is accepted as the norm or by which actual attainments are judged. An established and fixed measure used in assessing quality or performance. *(Encarta® World English Dictionary © & (P) 1998-2004 Microsoft Corporation. All rights reserved.)*

Standard Contract: A pre-established document containing certain pre-determined terms and conditions. A template contract that may be used for the most basic contractual obligations.

Standard Deviation: A measure of how far a variable moves over time away from its average (mean) value. *(Bishop, 2004)*

Standard Industrial Classification (SIC) Code: A comprehensive code classifying all business by what is produced or sold and for whom it is produced, or to whom it is sold.

Standard Object: CANADIAN The highest level of the object classification used for parliamentary and executive purposes, which is reported to Parliament in the estimates and Public Accounts.

Standard Specification: A specification that is to be used for all or most purchases of an item; describes all required physical and functional characteristics of goods, services or construction.

Standard of Value: One of the functions of money whereby the value of goods and services is expressed in money terms (prices). *(Schiller, 2000)*

S

Standardization: The adoption of a single product or group of products to be used by different organizations or all parts of one organization. *(Nash, Schooner, O'Brien, 1998)*

Standardization of Specifications: The process of establishing a single specification for an item, or range of items.

Standards (Standardization) Committee: Generally an internal committee consisting of cross-functional representation including procurement, users, and other internal stakeholders impacted by the decisions of the committee. Examples of key functions and activities may include:

- Developing standards through a simplification process for designated products and services;
- Establish specifications;
- Review items to determine which items should be incorporated into a standards program;
- Approving products for the Qualified Products List.

S

Standing: The legal right to initiate a lawsuit and/or protest. To do so, a party must be sufficiently affected by the matter at hand and there must be a case or controversy that can be resolved by legal action. *(Taken from the 'Lectric Law Library,' www.lectlaw.com)*

Standing Offer: CANADIAN An arrangement whereby a supplier offers to provide on demand goods and services described in the offer, at the price or on the pricing basis stated, and subject to all the terms and conditions set out therein. A standing offer is not a contract.

Standing Order: Similar to a blanket order except it has specified quantities and specified delivery dates. *Also see Blanket Order.*

Stare Decisis: A basic legal principal whereby once a decision (a precedent) on a certain set of facts has been made, the courts will apply that decision in cases which subsequently come before it embodying the same set of facts. A precedent which is binding; must be followed. *(Garner, 2004)*

Startup: A relatively new, usually small business, particularly one supported by venture capital and within those sectors closely linked to new technologies. *(Business, 2002)*

Statement of Account: A detailed listing, usually prepared by the supplier/vendor, of transactions taking place over a stated period, usually concluding with the open or unpaid balance.

Statement of Requirement (SOR): Describes the procurement deliverables. *Also known as a Statement of Work (SOW). (Harney, 1992)*

Statement of Work: The response from the supplier/contractor outlining very specifically how the supplier proposes to complete the work as outlined in the Scope of Work. It defines what will be done, how, by whom, and cost factors.

State-Use Law (Industries): Laws established by state legislatures, Federal law or executive order which establish preference for purchases from correction/prison industries.

Statistical Process Control (SPC): A method, technique or procedure to analyze or monitor a process. SPC looks to achieve or maintain a state of control, improve a process capability or remove waste. Much of SPC lies in the ability to examine a process and sources to measure output. Used mainly in manufacturing lines, SPC seeks to provide in the governmental environment "continuous product or service improvements" and leads to the reduction of wait time.

Statute of Frauds: refers to the requirement that certain kinds of contracts be memorialized and signed in writing with sufficient content to evidence the contract. The following types of agreements are included:

1. Sale of goods over $500 (not services);
2. A promise to pay a debt of another;
3. Sale of land or interest in land;
4. Agreements that have a duration greater than one year;
5. Agreements in consideration of marriage.

Statutes: The written laws approved by legislatures, parliaments or house of assembly. *Also known as legislation.*

Statutory Information: *CANADIAN* Information specifically called for, collected, distributed, reported in accordance with legislation, e.g., a statement of the financial transactions of the fiscal year as part of the Public Accounts, as required by the Financial Administration Act.

Statutory Law: The written law established by enactments of government, expressing the will of the legislature. A statute is the written law as opposed to common law, which is unwritten law. Statutes are written at all levels of government

Stock: An item maintained on hand in a supply system to meet future needs. May be held in an inventory control system and issued on demand.

Stock Control: Continuously evaluating and arranging for receipts of supplies and issues from stores to ensure that stock balances are adequate to support the current rate of consumption.

Stock-Keeping Unit (SKU): A common term for a unique numeric identifier, typically in a database. A specifically assigned product number for each variation of an item. The SKU number represents variations of the item by size, color, type or by any other specific designation in order to aid in computer ordering and inventory control. Example: The yellow raincoat is only offered in 4 sizes: small, medium, large and extra large which equates to 4 SKUs. If the raincoat came in those 4 sizes in both yellow and orange colors then there would be 8 SKUs for this raincoat. *(ISM, 2000)*

Stockless Purchasing: A contracting method that incorporates just-in-time delivery concepts thus enabling the buyer to avoid carrying inventory to meet demand requirements. Suppliers own the inventory and deliver products directly to the customer with a pre-determined time frame, i.e. 24 hours, 3 working days, etc.

Stock Level: The desired quantity of stock to be carried in inventory for a given item. This quantity is adjusted periodically depending on economic issues such as cost, supply and demand. A minimum stock and maximum stock level is predetermined based on existing requirements.

Stock Location Records: *CANADIAN* The records that indicate the locations of stocks in a storeroom or warehouse.

Stock Number: A standard number that is assigned to identify like items. Examples of standardized stock numbering systems include the NIGP Commodity/Services Code or the NATO Stock Numbering System.

Stock On Order: *CANADIAN* The quantity represented by the total of all outstanding replenishment orders.

Stock Out: A condition in which there is a lack of sufficient inventory on hand to fill an order from a using agency/requisitioner.

Stock Record: Information on the items in stock showing stock level position.

Stocktaking: *CANADIAN* The procedure of counting and reconciling actual holdings against stock records.

Stock Usage/Turnover Rate: The historic rate at which a stocked item is used, based on the number of times the stock is issued to determine the annual (or periodic) turnover rate.

Stop Work Order: Written notice to the contractor to immediately stop all work and work cannot resume until the stop work order is removed.

Storage:
1. The act of storing, or state of being stored in a designated storage place for safekeeping.
2. A function of warehousing which involves the receipt, putting away, and subsequent retrieval of an item.
3. Specific to technology, a computer memory that retains data for some period of time. Storage can be categorized in many ways such as: primary or secondary; read-only, random access and magnetic storage.

Stores Accounting: The act of recording the details of stock movements and balances in value.

Stores Management: To provide for the efficient storage and handling of goods to be redistributed to the using agencies.

Straight Bill of Lading: A Contract document which provides for direct shipment to a consignee.

Straight-Line Depreciation: A form of depreciation in which the cost of a fixed asset is spread equally over each year of its anticipated lifetime. *(Business, 2002)*

Strategic Alliance (SA): An agreement between two or more organizations to cooperate in a specific business activity, so that each benefits from the strengths of the other, and gains competitive advantage. *(Business, 2002)*

Strategic Plans: Documents that establish the long-range objectives and overall strategy or course of action by which an organization fulfills its mission. *Also see tactical planning.* *(Business, 2002)*

Strategic Procurement Planning (SP2): The transformation of the organization's mission, goals, and objectives into measurable activities to be used to plan, budget and manage the procurement function within the organization. The ultimate goal is to effectuate positive change in organizational culture, systems, and operational processes.

Strategic Sourcing: A systematic continuous improvement process that directs supply managers to assess, plan, manage, and develop the supply base in line with the agency's stated objectives. It involves the constant re-evaluation of purchasing activities to ensure alignment with the long-term organizational goals.

Strategies: Methods to achieve specific goals and are used to carry out objectives. All strategies must be sensitive to financial and other resource allocation decisions.

Straw Man: The first offer received in a competitive negotiation to get the negotiations moving forward. It is generally of little merit, but intended to move toward more purposeful negotiation.

Straw Vote: An RFP evaluation technique, whereby the evaluation team takes an informal vote of no consequence to gauge the feeling of the group toward a proposal or group of proposals. Used to informally determine the predisposition of the group.

Structural Deficit: Deficit that remains across the business cycle, because general tax levels are too low for the general level of government spending. *(Wikipedia 2007)*

Structural Unemployment: Unemployment caused by a mismatch between the skills or location of job seekers and the requirements or location of available jobs. For example: Structural Unemployment occurred in West Virginia when the coal mines closed and the unemployed miners lacked the technology skill required by high tech companies. *(Schiller, 2000)*

Subcontract: A contract that assigns some of the obligations of a prior contract to another party.

Subcontractor: Any person or business entity employed to perform part of a contractual obligation under the control of the principal contractor. Any supplier, distributor, vendor, or firm that furnishes supplies or services to a prime contractor or another subcontractor.

Subject-Matter Expert (SME): An individual whose possesses exceptional skill and knowledge in a particular area of expertise. Generally the SME understands technical details and terminology, is current with changing trends and possesses historical knowledge. Procurement may invite SMEs to provide technical assistance or to serve on evaluation committees. *(Business, 2002)*

Subrogation: The substitution of one person in the place of another with reference to a lawful claim, demand, or right, so that the one substituted succeeds to the rights of the other in relation to the debt or claim and its rights, remedies, and securities. *(Black's Law Dictionary, 1427, 1990)*

Subsidy: Money paid, usually by a government, to keep prices below what they would be in a free market, or to keep alive businesses that would otherwise fail. Subsidies can be a form of protectionism by making domestic goods and services artificially competitive against imports. *(Schiller, 2000)*

Substitute Goods: Goods/products for which an increase (or fall) in demand for one leads to a fall (or increase) in demand for another. Examples: Ford vs.GM, Pepsi vs. Coke and Dell vs. Hewlett Packard. *(Schiller, 2000)*

Succession Planning: The process of identifying and developing internal personnel with the potential to fill key or critical organizational positions. Succession planning ensures the availability of experienced and capable employees that are prepared to assume these roles as they become available. *(Source: Wikipedia))*

Sunshine Law: A law that requires public disclosure of a government act. Laws that require state and local agencies to conduct their business in the sunshine. In 1992 Florida voters reaffirmed the right to open government by approving an amendment adoption Article 1, [section] 24(b) of the Florida Constitution which "grant[ed] constitutional status to the public's right of access to all levels of government. Many other states have also adopted similar laws. Public officials have a duty to conduct meetings in the sunshine. They also have a duty to protect the trade secrets of the vendors with whom they do business. *(http://findarticles.com/p/articles/mi go1671/is 200202/ai n6714457, 01.05.07)*

Superfund: *See Comprehensive Environmental Response, Compensation and Liability Act (CERCLA).*

Supplemental Agreement: Any contract, addendum or modification accomplished by the mutual action of both parties.

Supplier:
1. The person or business unit actually performing services, or manufacturing, producing, or shipping supplies required by the contract.
2. The seller of goods.

Supplier Analysis: A review conducted of specific suppliers to assess their qualifications, availability, performance, past performance, and product quality. To look at specific traits and elements of that specific vendor as opposed to the aggregate. *Also see Demand Analysis and Market Analysis.*

Supplier Development: A systematic organizational effort to create and maintain a network of competent and pre-qualified vendors.

Supplier Evaluation: Objective analysis of vendors by evaluating past performance, used with current vendors, or as a preliminary assessment of new vendors; an evaluation of any or all the capabilities of a supplier that pertain to its competence as a source of supply. Vendors/Suppliers are usually evaluated on their technical quality, delivery, service, cost, and managerial capabilities.

Supplier Lead Time: The time that normally elapses between the time an order is received by the vendor and shipment of the material. *Also see Lead Time.*

Supplier Manual: A guide to provide basic instructions necessary to conduct business with the agency. Developed by the agency, it clearly states the general code of ethics and business relationships and, may include but is not limited to:
1. The standards of conduct expected of agency staff and suppliers and;
2. The limitations surrounding their relationship and extent of contacts that suppliers should have with all agency departments and agency staff.

Also referred to as Vendor manual

Supplier Performance Report: A report that evaluates a vendor's performance based on certain criteria, such as, quality, delivery, timeliness, responsiveness, etc.

Supplies: All tangible items purchased or consumed by an organization.

Supply:
1. The ability and willingness to sell (produce) specific quantities of a good at alternative prices in a given time period.
2. The amount of a good or a service available at any particular price.

S

Supply and Demand: The quantity of goods available for sale at a given price, and the level of consumer need for those goods at a given price. The balance of supply and demand fluctuates as external economic factors such as the cost of materials and the level of competition in the marketplace influence the level of demand from consumers and the desire and ability of producers to supply the goods. *(Business, 2002)*

Supply and Provisioning: *CANADIAN* The operation normally involved in furnishing, providing, affording, or distributing items of supply to a user to satisfy stated requirements.

Supply Centre/Depot: *CANADIAN* A specialized facility designed, equipped, and staffed to perform warehousing functions and conduct other supply and distribution activities, particularly those associated with the maintenance of stocks.

Supply Chain: A linear description of an organization's supply function which includes all internal functions plus external suppliers who are connected with one another to identify and satisfy the needs for materials, equipment and services. The "chain" may begin with raw materials extracted from the earth and would include extractors, converters, original equipment manufacturers, distributors and finally the end user (customer). *(Burt, Dobler, Starling, 2003)*

Supply Chain Management (SCM):

1. Those actions and values responsible for continuous improvement of the design, development, and management process of an organization's supply system, with the objective of improving its profitability and survival of its customers and suppliers. It has a major impact on net income and shareholder value. *(Burt, Dobler, Starling, 2003)*
2. The identification, acquisition, access, positioning and management of resources the organization needs in the attainment of its strategic objective. *Also see Materials Management.* *(ISM, 2005)*

Supply Chain Pollution Avoidance (SCPA): The broadest and most logical approach to protecting the environment. SCPA focuses on processes that prevent or minimize pollution from being created throughout the supply chain. An integrated management approach to pollution avoidance which provides a logical framework for environmental objectives. *(www.epa.gov/cpg/glossary)*

Supply Networks: Flexible virtual supply systems linked together by communication systems and alliances. They optimize the flow of materials, services, information and money. They focus on speed, are highly adaptive, innovative and tightly integrated. *(Burt, Dobler, Starling, 2003)*

Supply Positioning: An analysis of the complexity of the supply marketplace and its impact on agency service delivery based on such factors as: dependency of agency service delivery upon particular goods and services; risk to agency service delivery arising from potential disruption, such as discontinuity of supply or significant increase in price; the makeup of the marketplace; lead times and the complexity of the technology involved; and the source of the original manufacture or service supply and any related opportunities. *Also see Market Analysis, Procurement Profile and Spend Analysis.*

Supply-Side Policy: The use of tax incentives, deregulation, and other mechanisms to increase the ability and willingness to produce goods and services. *(Schiller, 2000)*

Supply Voucher: *CANADIAN* A document used to obtain materiel items from stock. Usually used to obtain consumable items.

Surety: A pledge or guarantee by an insurance company, bank, individual or corporation on behalf of the bidder/offeror which protects against default or failure of the principal to satisfy the contractual obligations.

Surplus:

1. Results in an overstock situation when the quantity of goods on hand exceeds the quantity of goods needed. The overstocked goods may be returned to the vendor, sold at auction or disposed of in a method acceptable to the entity.
2. Refers to goods or materials that are obsolete or no longer needed by the agency and are designated for disposal. Surplus becomes available for disposal outside of the entity because of some unforeseen situation that

affects the use of the item. An example would be chairs or desks that have been replaced with new items. *Also see Obsolete Supplies/ Equipment.*

Surveillance: Term often used in Performance-Based Contracting. *Also see Contract Administration and Contract Management.*

Suspension: Prohibiting a supplier from submitting bids and offers for a definite or indefinite period of time. A temporary determination to exclude a supplier from obtaining any contracts for a period of time, usually before initiating debarment. Reasons for this action may include poor performance, late deliveries, violations of previous contract terms, etc. *Also see Debarment.*

Suspension of Work Clause: A contract provision that allows an agency to suspend, interrupt, or delay work for the agency's convenience. A contractor is not entitled to compensation if the delay is the contractor's fault. A contractor may be compensated only if the resultant delay is considered unreasonable. *Also see Ordered Suspension.*

Sustainable Procurement: Purchasing and investment process that takes into account the economic, environmental and social impacts of the entity's spending. *Also see Environmentally Preferable Purchasing (EPP).*

Sustainability The capacity to endure. Sustainability requires a reconciliation of environmental, social and economic demands. It encompasses the concept of stewardship which is the responsible management of resource use. *Also see Environmentally Preferable Product (EPP).*

SWOT Analysis (Strengths, Weaknesses, Opportunities, Threats): Utilized as a strategic planning tool to improve organizational effectiveness. Developed by Alfred Humphrey for business analysis.

System Infrastructure: CANADIAN The fundamental enabling structure upon which a system operates, including the technology platform, software and other standards, shared services, management support and capabilities.

Systems Analysis: The process of analyzing existing systems for the purpose of evaluating possible improvements in methods and procedures. *(Jansen, 2002)*

Systems Contract: A contract that establishes a source of supply for a specified period for a large group or related family of materials; a method of procurement designed to improve reordering of materials used repeatedly. May include a catalog with a list and description of items that can be purchased. *Also see Blanket Order.*

T

T & C: *See Terms and Conditions.*

T & M: *See time and materials contract.*

Tabulation of Bids/Responses: The recording of responses to bids and proposals for the purposes of comparison, analysis and record keeping.

Tactical Planning: Short–range plans, usually less than one year, designed to implement the activities and objectives specified in the strategic plan. *(Ferrell, 2002)*

Taguchi, Genechi: Served as the director of the Japanese Academy of Quality and is a four-time recipient of the Deming Prize. Believed that poor design resulted in poor quality. *See Six Sigma.* *(Business, 2002)*

Taguchi Method: The pioneering techniques of quality control developed by Genichi Taguchi, which focus on improving the quality of a product or process at the design stage rather than after manufacturing or delivery. *(Business, 2002)*

Tare Weight: The weight of the packaging materials used to wrap or protect the item being shipped.

Target Market: A specific group of consumers on whose needs and wants a company focuses its marketing efforts. *(Ferrell, 2002)*

Tariff:
1. A schedule containing the rate, rules and regulations under which transportation carriers handle the shipment of goods.
2. A tax imposed on imported goods. *(Ferrell, 2002)*

Task Order Contract: *See Delivery Order Contract.*

Tax Base: The amount of income or property directly subject to nominal tax rates. *(Schiller, 2000)*

Tax Burden: A measure of the taxes paid relative to another constant factor, such as total personal income. *(Schiller, 2000)*

TCO: *See Total Cost of Ownership.*

Team Development Stages:
•*Forming:* Members decide whether to join the group, learn the traits and strengths of other members and identify a leader.
•*Storming:* The team experience developmental issues due to personality conflict and difficulty to agree on goals and priorities.
•*Norming:* Team defines a set of rules and roles to coordinate group interaction and make the pursuit of goals effective. Team begins to work cohesively.
•*Performing:* Team members work within the team structure agreed upon to achieve its goals and objectives
•Adjourning: The team completes the project/task and disbands. *(Ferrell, 2002 and NIGP, 2005)*

Team Leadership: Professor Robert Trent of Lehigh University has identified ten requirements for effective team leadership:
•Work with the team to establish and commit to performance goals.
•Secure individual member involvement and commitment.
•Manage internal team conflict.
•Help maintain team focus and direction.
•Secure required organizational resources.
•Prevent team domination by a member or faction.
•Deal with internal and external obstacles confronting the team.
•Clarify and help define each member's role.
•Provide performance feedback to team members.
•Coordinate multiple tasks and manage the status of team assignments.

Technical Proposal: A response to a solicitation which describes in detail what an offeror proposes to furnish and the method of delivery. May be part of a two-step response contained within an offer, the second part being the price proposal.

Technical Specifications: Specifications that establish the material and operating requirements of products and services.

Tender: A bidding process for goods, services or construction that is open to all qualified bidders and where the sealed bids are opened in public for scrutiny and are chosen on the basis of compliance with the bid requirements and lowest price. Also referred to as competitive tender or public tender and is a term normally used in Canadian procurement. *Also see Bid and Solicitation.*

Term Contract: A type of contract in which a source of supply is established for a specified period of time for specified services or supplies; usually characterized by an estimated or definite minimum quantity, with the possibility of additional requirements beyond the minimum, all at a predetermined unit price.

Termination for Convenience: A contract clause which may be contained within boilerplate language that allows for contract to be ended at the discretion of the governmental entity. Action by which the purchasing entity, in accordance with contract provisions, unilaterally cancels all or part of the contract work for the best interest of the jurisdiction, and with no reflection on the contractor's performance. *Also see Cancellation of a Contract, Discharge by Mutual Assent, and Termination for Default.*

Termination for Default: A contract clause which may be contained within boilerplate language that allows either contracting party the right to cancel a contract, either in whole or in part, due to failure of the other party to perform satisfactorily. *Also see Cancellation of a Contract, Discharge by Mutual Assent and Termination for Convenience.*

Terms and Conditions (T's and C's): Standard boilerplate language that includes standard clauses and rules which apply to bids and offers formally solicited that may become incorporated into the final contract. *Also see Boilerplate.*

Terms of Contract: Stipulations made in contracts.

Terms of Payment: The methods of payment stipulated in a sales or purchasing contract.

Testing: That element of inspection that determines the physical, chemical, performance properties, and functional operation of items, or components thereof, using established scientific principles and procedures.

Theory of Constraints (TOC): Overall management philosophy introduced by Eliyahu Goldratt that is geared to help organizations continually achieve their goal. The philosophy holds that any manageable system is limited in achieving more of its goal by a very small number of constraints. There is always at least one constraint. The TOC process seeks to identify the constraint and structure the rest of the organization around it.

Theory X: A management theory of Douglas McGregor's which takes a traditional view of management, whereby it is assumed that workers generally dislike work and must be forced by managers and supervisors to do their jobs. *(Business, 2002)*

Theory Y: A management theory of Douglas McGregor's which takes a humanistic view of management whereby it is assumed that workers like to work and that under proper conditions employees will seek out responsibility in an attempt to satisfy their social, esteem, and self-actualization needs. *(Business, 2002)*

Theory Z: A management philosophy that stresses employee participation in all aspects of company decision making. *(Business, 2002)*

Third Party: Generally a contractor or vendor who ultimately receives monetary payment (grant funds) from the grantee as a result of rendering contractual goods or services in satisfaction of a contract that was funded by the grant. *Also see Grantee.*

Tie Bid Preference: A policy adopted by a public agency, which gives preference to a local bidder only if the bid is identical to a bid from a non-resident bidder, all other aspects of the bid being equal. A way to break a tie bid. Other preference may include awarding the tie bid to a minority firm or small business or a bidder that resides within the state in which the bidding occurred.

Tie Bids: Bids submitted by two or more bidders that have identical pricing. May signal collusion.

Time and Materials (T & M) Contract: A contract which provides for contractor payment based on a direct labor, hourly rate that includes benefits, payroll taxes, overhead and contractor profit and for the cost of materials and equipment used in performance of the contract.

Time-Critical-Shipments: A predetermination between buyer and seller that the shipment will be routed non-stop, door-to-door delivery; shipment is not co-mingled with freight of other shippers. *(ISM, 2000)*

Time Series Forecasting: Methods that use historical data as the basis of estimating future outcomes. A prediction based on the assumption that the trend of variations in the value of a variable will continue to recur in the future; that tomorrow will more or less resemble yesterday and today. For example: an organization that replaces a third of its administrative automobile fleet each fiscal year can generally forecast both the anticipated prices and delivery schedules based upon previous years' data and any new information concerning the automotive industry.

Time Utility: Utility that is created by making a product available when customers wish to purchase it. Time utility is an important consideration in most supply management decisions and it has a major impact on cost/price considerations. *(Schiller, 2000)*

Time Value of Money: The idea that a dollar today is worth more than a dollar in the future, because the dollar in the hand today can earn interest during the time until the future dollar is received. *(Bishop, 2004)*

TINA: *See Truth in Negotiations Act.*

Title: The instrument or document whereby ownership of property is established.

TL: *See Truckload.*

TOC: *See Theory of Constraints.*

Token Bid: A perfunctory offer submitted by a bidder with no serious intent of being the lowest bidder, usually submitted when the bidder wishes to maintain eligibility on the bidders list, or as a collusive device.

Tolerance: A specified allowance for variation in weight, size or other designated measurement; the range of allowable deviation within which an item or service is classified as acceptable.

T

Tort: In common law, it is a civil wrong for which the law provides a remedy. The "law of torts" is a body of civil law or private law that covers the legal and equitable remedies which the law provides for civil wrongs arising from certain contractual liability. Under U.S. law, torts are generally divided into two categories: intentional and non-intentional. Among non-intentional torts, negligence is the most common source for litigation. Remedies for torts can be in the form of compensation for damages or injunctive relief. (www.encyclopedia.thefreedictionary.com)

Total Cost of Ownership (TCO): A measure of all of the cost components associated with the procurement of a product or service. The sum of all fixed and variable costs attributed to a product or service. A philosophy for understanding all supply chain related costs of doing business with a particular supplier for a particular good or service. *(Burt, Dobler, Starling, 2003)*

Total Quality Management (TQM): Received recognition in the 1980's in answer to the increasing need for firms to compete on a quality basis. The International Organization for Standardization defined TQM as "a management approach to an organization centered on quality, based on the participation of all of its members, and aiming at long-term success through customer satisfaction and benefits to the members of the organization and to society. Other concepts such as Continuous Improvement, Just-In-Time, Quality Circles, and Six Sigma were part of the TQM approach. *Also see Continuous Improvement.* *(Miller, 2006)*

Total Supply: A concept of purchasing, the objective of which is to plan in advance and provide for the broadest scope of purchasing and purchasing- related activities as possible to minimize costs, increase managerial effectiveness, and improve operational efficiency. It is concerned not only with ordering, but also with requirements planning, logistics, and general procurement management.

TQM: *See Total Quality Management.*

Tracing: Trying to locate a shipment that has been reported undelivered by the consignee; finding the current status of the shipment. Tracing has become more effective through the use of technology, such as radio frequency identification (RFID). *(Miller, 2006)*

Trade Acceptance: A non-interest bearing, negotiable bill of exchange or draft covering the sale of goods, drawn by the contractor and accepted by the purchaser; may include the purchaser's specifications in place of payment.

Trade Deficit: The amount by which the value of imports exceeds the value of exports in a given time period. *Also see Trade Surplus.* *(Schiller, 2000)*

Trade Discount: A discount or reduction from a list price based on the position of the purchaser in the distribution channel, for example as a distributor, retailer, or original equipment manufacturer.

Trade-In Value: The value obtained when trading one piece of equipment for another.

Trademark: A distinctive name, phrase, symbol, design, picture, or style used by an organization to identify itself and its products. Trademarking is a central legal component for corporate branding. The main purpose of trademark law is to protect the public from being confused or deceived about the origin and quality of a product. Trademarks provide an incentive to maintain a good reputation for a predictable quality level. Trademarks protect the source and quality of a product, while copyrights protect literary or artistic works and patents protect useful designs. Trademarks do not expire. Trademarks remain valid as long as the owner actively uses and defends them and maintains their registrations with the appropriate trademark registry. *(www.encyclopedia.thefreedictionary.com)*

Trade-off Analysis: An evaluation technique used to score proposals. This approach requires the Evaluation Team to evaluate the technical differences between proposals in order to determine if these differences justify paying the cost or price differential.

Trade Secret: A confidential practice, method, process, design or other information used by a company to compete with other businesses. It may also be referred to as confidential information. A trade secret generally has the following in common: (a) information that is not shared with the general public, (b) confers some sort of economic benefit on its holder, and (c) is the subject of reasonable efforts to maintain its secrecy. Unless the information is covered by a trademark or patent, trade secrets are not protected by law. *Also see Confidential Information and Proprietary Information.* *(TheFreeDictionary.com, retrieved, 9.21.04)*

Trade Standard: An understanding between buyer and seller as to the meaning of certain words, phrases and characteristics of a given item or service that are established by agreement or general usage. *(Business, 2002)*

Trade Surplus: The amount by which the value of exports exceeds the value of imports in a given time period. *Also see Trade Deficit.* *(Schiller, 2000)*

Trade Terms: The broadest classification applicable to purchase transactions with reference to understandings between buyer and vendor, either as to the meanings of certain abbreviations, words, or phrases, or to customs applicable to transactions as established by agreement between the parties, or as established by general usage.

Trading Company: A firm that buys goods in one country and sells them to buyers in another country. *(Business, 2002)*

Transaction: In computer science, a group of logical operations that must all succeed or fail as a group. Systems dedicated to supporting such operations are known a transaction processing systems. Examples would include bill payment, credit card processing. *(Jansen, 2002)*

Transaction Cost Reduction: Activities or process changes that decrease the cost to process a purchase order or a payment transaction. Procurement credit cards are an example of a transaction cost reduction. *(Cr mi, Kauffman, Inside Supply Management Magazine, March 2003)*

Transactional Leadership: A leadership prospective based on give and take. A transactional leader provides efficiency by securing resources to get the objective completed. A transactional leader links performance to reward. Transactional leaders accept the goals, structure and culture of the existing organization.

Transactional Relationships: A phase in the continuum of Buyer-Seller Relationships, it is the most common and basic relationship. The term describes an arm's length relationship wherein neither party is concerned with the well-being of the other. Each transaction is entered into on its own merits. Little or no basis exists for collaboration and learning. *(Burt, Dobler, Starling, 2003)*.

Transfer: CANADIAN Anything given to another person or organization with no expectation that it will be returned. When a materiel item is transferred custodial control is also transferred to the receiving program manager.

Transformational Leadership: A leadership theory that involves leaders who are charismatic and visionary and can inspire followers to transcend their own self-interest for the good of the organization. These leaders appeal to the follower's ideals and moral values and inspire them to think about problems in new or different ways. The leader exhibits vision which is the ability to bind people together with an idea. Transformational leadership has a lower turnover rate, has higher productivity rates and maintains a higher employee satisfaction.

Transit Charges: Charges made for services rendered while a shipment is in transit.

Transition Plan: A formal, written contract protocol that establishes the approach for planning and managing the interim period between the beginning of a contract and its expiration. A well managed, detailed transition plan will reduce problems that may occur in new contracts, extensions of contracts, and contract renewals. Examples include contracting for uniforms, security guard services, and food services in institutions such as a prison.

Transparency: In an ethical context, the idea that the more information disclosed about a business, financial or economic activity the better. Transparency improves ethical conduct. Maximum disclosure is for the betterment of the public and will help to discourage more regulation. *(Miller, 2006)*

Transponder: A device that transmits and responds to radio waves. May be used in a variety of supply management applications such as smart cards, procurement credit cards, inventory tracking, and Radio Frequency Identification (RFID). *(Jansen, 2002)*

Trendline: The tendency to move in a particular direction shown by data variables over a period of time such as a month. *(Business, 2002)*

Trial Balance: A summary of balances of all general ledger accounts at the end of an accounting period. *(Business, 2002)*

Triple Baseline: Refers to the metrics that operationalize success across economic, environmental and social costs and impacts.

Truckload (TL): A quantity of freight to which truckload rates apply; indicates full truckload as opposed to LT (Less than Truckload) shipment. Motor carriers will charge less per Cwt if a shipper is moving full truckloads (TL).

Truth in Negotiations Act (TINA): Established the requirement for certain federal contracts, contractors to submit cost or pricing data and must certify that, to the best of the contractor's knowledge and belief, the cost or pricing data submitted is current, accurate and complete.

Turnkey: In construction procurement, a requirement whereby the contractor is responsible for the entire project including designing the project, contracting for construction and then furnishing the structure. In technology procurement, one vendor is responsible for the hardware, software and support. May also apply when a contractor is totally responsible for an entire project, from start to finish.

Turnover: Movement (as of goods or people) into, through, and out of a place. A cycle of purchase, sale, and replacement of a stock of goods. *(Wikipedia, 2007)* The number of times that various assets or items of inventory are replaced during a stated period of time.

Two-Bin System: An inventory control system in which identical stock is stored in two separate bins, with the stock in the second bin equal to that calculated for the order point. Withdrawals are made from the first bin and a requisition to replenish the supply is generated when that bin is emptied.

Two-Step Procurement: A combination of competitive procedures designed to obtain benefits of sealed bidding when adequate specifications are not available. May also be applied to a request for proposal negotiated procurement. Step one consists of a request for technical proposals, evaluations and discussion without pricing, and the selection of bidders whose proposals are considered most acceptable; step two consists of the submission of sealed priced bids by those who submitted acceptable technical proposals in step one. *(Harney, 1992)*

Tying Arrangement: A vendor imposed restraint in which the purchaser is forced to buy an unwanted item in order to acquire the desired one. *See Sherman Anti-Trust Act.*

U

UCC: *See Uniform Commercial Code.*

UL: *See Underwriter's Laboratory.*

Ultra Vires Action: An action which is beyond the powers granted by authority or by law.

UMA: *See Uniform Mediation Act.*

Unallowable Cost: Any cost which, in accordance with pertinent laws or regulations, cannot be included in prices or cost-reimbursements under a contract to which the cost is allocable. *(Nash, Schooner, O'Brien, 1998)*

Unbalanced Bid: A bid that contains pricing aberrations, for example, low or nominal prices may be bid for some items and high or enhanced prices may be bid for other work. This may happen in time and material contracts or construction contracts where upfront payment may be made for mobilization. It is wise policy to state in the bid documents that "unbalanced bids may be deemed non-responsive". Unbalanced bids may be deemed to be non-responsive, and may be both mathematically unbalanced and materially unbalanced. Many public entities utilize a bid analysis procedure to help identify unbalanced bids; example: State of Wisconsin DOT Construction and Materials Manual, Section 2.1.2.1.1, revised 10/98. *Also see Front-End Loading.* *(Miller, 2006)*

Unbundling: Dividing a service into smaller portions, in order to encourage competition. Frequently done on the basis of geography, for example, a large service area, such as a city or county is divided into smaller geographical regions.

Unconscionability: Generally implies an absence of meaningful choice on the part of one of the contracting parties. A contract clause that is so one-sided as to oppress or unfairly surprise a party. It is usually grounds for contract avoidance, for example, where it is the result of an obvious mistake on the part of the bidder. *(Garner, 2004)*

Undercapitalization: The lack of funds to successfully operate a business which may lead to business failure. *(Schiller, 2000)*

Underemployment: An economic condition where people seeking full-time paid employment work only part time or are employed at jobs below their capability. *(Schiller, 2000)*

Underwrite: To assume risk, especially for a new issue or an insurance policy. *(Business, 2002)*

Underwriter's Laboratory (UL): A non profit product safety testing organization.

Unemployment: The inability of labor-force participants to find jobs. An economic condition in which a percentage of the population wants to work but is unable to find sustainable employment. *(Bishop, 2004)*

Unemployment Rate: The proportion of the labor force that is unemployed. *(Schiller, 2000)*

Unfair Competitive Advantage: Government action that provides for an advantage of one competitor over other competitors. For example, an unfair competitive advantage may exist when a contractor competing for an award possesses proprietary information that was wrongfully obtained from the government without proper authorization. Occurs when a contractor gains exclusive access to information, not available to other contractor/competitors.

Uniform Administrative Requirements for Grants in Aid to States and Local Governments: Document issued by the Office of Management and Budget (OMB) in 1988 to establish uniform administration rules for federal grants and cooperative agreements. *Also see OMB Circular A-102.*

Uniform Code Council Inc.: *See GS1 US Bar-Codes and eCom.*

Uniform Commercial Code (UCC) (U.S. Law): First published in 1952, it was formulated by the National Conference of Commissioners on Uniform State Laws (NCCUSL) and the American Law Institute. It covers a wide range of commercial activities. The UCC does NOT apply to the purchase of services and is not applicable to Federal Government contracting. The UCC determines rights and obligations on the basis of fairness and reasonableness in the light of accepted business practice. The UCC has been adopted by all of the States. 2003 marked the conclusion of a fifteen-year-long process of re-writing the UCC. In that period every article was either completely revised or substantially amended.

The most important part of the UCC for the public purchasing officials is Article 2, entitled "Sale of Goods." Absent a specific state or federal statute or administrative regulation, Article 2 will govern the public purchasing official's contract for the sale of goods.

Uniform Freight Classification: Governs class rates for rail transportation. *Also see Class Rate.*

Uniform Mediation Act (UMA): Adopted by the National Conference of Commissioners on Uniform State Laws, on February 4, 2002. The UMA was promulgated to harmonize the proliferation of state and local mediation laws in hopes of devising a uniform law that will be adopted by the states.

Unilateral:
1. One-sided.
2. A procurement action initiated by one party.
3. Involving or affecting only one side or one party.

Unilateral Modification (of a contract): The right of one party to a contract to change the contract pursuant to the change clause of a contract. A unilateral modification may occur for two reasons:
1. The right to unilaterally modify the contract has been given to the public agency in the contract itself, or
2. the modification is for a minor purpose. *Also see Bilateral Modification.*

Uninsurable Risk: A risk that insurance firms will not assume. When the risk cannot be transferred to a surety, supply management personnel need to confer with an insurance professional or a risk manager. *(Business, 2002)*

Union Shop: An employment setting in which all workers must join the union usually within 30 days after being employed. *(Business, 2002)*

Unit: A standard or basic quantity into which an item of supply is divided, issued, or used, such as a unit cost or unit of measurement.

Unit Cost: The cost of a unit of product or service, found by dividing the total costs for a given period of operation by the number of units produced in that period of operation.

Unit Labor Cost: Hourly wage rate divided by output per labor-hour. *(Schiller, 2000)*

Unit of Order: *CANADIAN* Order quantity, such as carton, box, bottle.

Unit Price: The cost per unit of a product or service; e.g., price per ton, per labor hour, or per foot.

United Nations' Convention on Contracts for the International Sale of Goods (CISG): The United Nations facilitated the development of a uniform body of law to govern contracts for the international sale of commercial goods. Commonly referred to as CISG, its objective is much like the Uniform Commercial Code, projected to the international level. The CISG does not apply to the purchase of services. *(Burt, Dobler, Starling, 2003)*

United States Code (USC): A consolidated and codification of all the general and permanent laws of the United States. The code provides an organized system for finding federal laws by title headings, primarily alphabetical and section. As officially published, the code is generally updated and reissued every six years. *(Nash, Schooner, O'Brien, 1998)*

Universal Product Code (UPC): Internationally adopted bar code symbology. Its birth is usually set at April 3, 1973, when the grocery industry formally established UPC as the standard bar code symbology for product marking. UPC symbols are fixed in length, can only encode numbers, and are continuous, using four element widths. UPC can be printed on packages and the format allows any package orientation provided the symbol faces the scanner. UPC version A is the basic version of UPC and uses ten digits to describe the item, the eleventh digit indicates the type of product and the twelfth digit is a check digit. UPC version E is the most common version of UPC. The code is smaller because it drops out zeros which would otherwise occur in a symbol. *(Jansen, 2002)*

Universal Public Procurement Certification Council (UPPCC): An independent entity formed to govern and administer the Certified Public Procurement Officer (CPPO) and the Certified Professional Public Buyer (CPPB) certification programs. This non-profit organization was jointly established by the National Institute of Governmental Purchasing, Inc. (NIGP) and the National Association of State Procurement Officials (NASPO) in 1978. The UPPCC is composed of members from the California Association of Public Procurement Officers (CAPPO), Florida Association of Public Procurement Officers (FAPPO), National Association of Educational Procurement (NAEP), and the National Procurement Institute (NPI). The UPPCC is responsible for establishing, monitoring and revising program requirements as well as developing and approving content for the certification examinations.

Unnecessarily restrictive: A term used when specifications or terms and conditions limit competition arbitrarily, without reasonably promoting the fulfillment of the procurement needs of a contracting authority.

Unsecured Loans: Loans backed only by the borrowers' good reputation and previous credit rating. *(Business, 2002)*

Unsolicited Offer/Proposal: A proposal submitted by a contractor/supplier or consultant in the absence of a bid or solicitation from a buyer. May be submitted in response to a perceived need but not in response to a buyer's formal request.

Unstable Markets: Markets that exhibit short-term fluctuations. Oil, minerals, agricultural products, and animal by-products typically dominate these markets The supply of these raw materials is frequently influenced by political forces, weather conditions, speculative financial actions, and other unpredictable reasons not governed by the laws of supply and demand.

Unsuccessful Bidder: A vendor whose bid was not accepted for reasons of price, quantity, or failure to comply with specifications.

UPC: *See Universal Product Code.*

Upgrade: To improve the functionality or to increase the value of equipment or services.

UPPCC: *See Universal Public Procurement Certification Council.*

Usage: The quantity of an inventory item consumed over a period of time expressed in units of quantity or of value in dollars.

USC: *See United States Code.*

U.S. Communities: A national purchasing cooperative known as the U.S. Communities and Government Purchasing Alliance and is co-sponsored by key professional associations serving the public sector: Association of School Business Officers (ASBO), National Association of Counties (NACO), National Institute of Governmental Purchasing (NIGP), the National League of Cities (NLC) and the U.S. Conference of Mayors. In 2004, over 7000 public entities were accessing the U. S. Communities agreements that were hosted by public agencies - generating over $500 million in public spending.

Used Equipment: Pre-owned or rebuilt/remanufactured equipment that may be reconditioned and offered for purchase. Generally sold by brokers and used equipment dealers. Auction sales represent another source of used equipment. Traded on many Web-sites such as eBay. *(Miller, 2006)*

User Charge: Fee paid for the use of a public-sector good or service.

Use Tax: A tax imposed on the user of goods.

Using Agency:

1. A unit of government that requisitions items through a central purchasing organization.

2. A participant in a consortium contract.
3. Any department, commission, board, or public agency requiring supplies, services, or construction procured in accordance with jurisdictional regulations.

Usury: To charge an exorbitant rate of interest. Many countries have some form of usury law imposing limits on how high interest charges can be to protect borrowers from being exploited by unscrupulous loan sharks. *(Bishop, 2004)*

Utility: The ability of a good or service to satisfy a need or want. Utility is the driver behind the basic premise of supply management, i.e. to satisfy a requestors need in the most economical fashion. *(Bishop, 2004)*

V

Valuation Method: ***CANADIAN*** Method by which the replacement cost of a piece of equipment is determined.

Value: A fair return on investment.

Value Added Reseller: A business entity that purchases a product from a manufacturer, adds enhancements and then sells it to another organization. Many large computer manufacturers have agreements with resellers to deliver, install and configure their equipment. *(Business, 2002)*

Value Added:
1. The increase in worth of a product or service as it moves through various stages of production and distribution.
2. What contribution a service function within an organization can make toward return on investment, increased productivity, or improved customer service. *(Business, 2002)*

Value Added Tax (VAT): A tax based on the value added during each stage of a product's production or distribution. Common throughout the European Union. *(Schiller, 2000)*

Value Analysis: An organized effort directed at analyzing the functions of a product or service including specifications, standards, practices and procedures with the intent to satisfy the required function at the lowest possible cost without impacting functional need and suitability. *Also see Value Engineering.* *(Nash, Schooner, O'Brien, 1998)*

Value Based Pricing: A business strategy which sets a product or service price based on the benefit it provides the customer, rather than on the cost of the product, market price, competitor or historical price. Value based pricing includes advertising or surveying to determine or measure the anticipated benefit the customer will receive and align the value delivered. Pricing is based upon the perceived or actual value that the end user will receive. Example: Many times the designer label item is perceived as being better than a department store label.

Value Engineering (VE): A technique by which contractors may (1) voluntarily suggest methods for performing more economically and may share in any resulting savings or (2) be required to establish a program or identify and submit methods for performing more economically. *Also see Value Analysis.* *(Nash, Schooner, O'Brien, 1998)*

Value Incentive Contract: A fixed price contract with a provision for rewarding the vendor for faster delivery or superior performance.

Valued Policy: An insurance policy in which the sum to be paid in case of loss is fixed by the terms of the policy; especially relating to fire insurance.

Value Proposition: A statement by an organization expressing the way in which it can provide value for a prospective customer. A marketing tool that explains why customers can benefit from a company's products or services. *(Miller, 2006)*

Variable Cost: Costs of an organization that vary with the amount of work performed. Variable costs are usually contrasted with fixed costs in analyzing a contractor's indirect costs. If variable costs are a large percentage of a contractors indirect costs, then the contractor's overhead rates can be expected to decrease more sharply with a decrease in volume of work than would be the case if fixed costs were a large percentage of the contractor's indirect costs. *(Nash, Schooner, O'Brien, 1998)*

Variable-Margin Pricing: A pricing policy that permits maximum competition on individual products. Most firms price their products to generate a satisfactory return on the whole line, not on each product in the line. The profits from the most efficiently produced items are often used to offset losses or the lower profit margins of inefficiently produced items. Often is seen in a line item bid of MRO (maintenance, repair, operating) products. *(Business, 2002)*

Variety Reduction: The process of controlling and minimizing the range of new parts, equipment, materials, methods, and procedures that are used to produce goods or services. Its goal is to minimize the variety of all elements in the production or service delivery process. The main techniques of variety reduction are simplification, standardization, and specialization. A methodology used in value analysis. *(Business, 2002)*

VAT: *See Value Added Tax.*

VE: *See Value Engineering.*

Velocity of Money: The number of times per year, on average, that a dollar is used to purchase final goods and services. *(Schiller, 2000)*

Vendor: A supplier/seller of goods and services. A reference to a provider of product or service.

Vendor Code: CANADIAN A code used to identify suppliers.

Vendor Complaint Form: A form completed by the using agency to document unacceptable vendor performance.

Vendor File: The accumulated record maintained by the central purchasing authority on a vendor, including information on the vendor's relationship with the purchasing authority, application for inclusion on the bidder's list, record of performance under contract, and correspondence.

Vendor Managed Inventory (VMI): A form of outsourcing whereby a contract is initiated with a private business to manage and control the inventory of the public entity. The contractor is responsible for all inventory functions which may include re-ordering.

Vendor Rating (Evaluation): A system for recording and ranking the performance of a supplier in terms of a range of issues, including delivery performance, service and quality. *(Business, 2002)*

Vendor's Lien: A seller's right to retain possession of property until payment for the property is recovered.

Vendor Supply Point Code (VSP): CANADIAN Representation of the geographic location at which goods are manufactured or, if not known, from which the goods are shipped by the vendor, or, in the case of services, where the services are mainly performed.

Vendor Supply Point Value: CANADIAN The value in whole Canadian dollars of goods/services for each VSP reported on the document. It is mandatory only if there is more than one VSP on the document.

Verbal Contract: An agreement that is oral and not in writing. Usually enforceable if under $500.00.

Vertical Equity: Economic principle that individuals with higher incomes should pay more taxes. *(Bishop, 2004)*

Vertical Integration: Theory describing a style of business ownership and control. Vertically integrated companies are united through a hierarchy and share a common owner. Usually each member produces a different product, and the products combine to satisfy a common need. An important theory for procurement professionals who become involved in price/cost negotiation to understand. There are three major types of vertical integration: Backward Vertical Integration; Forward Vertical Integration; and Balanced Vertical Integration. *(www.encyclopedia.thefreedictionary.com)*

Vertical Linkage Analysis: A tool that enables analysis of the value chain in order to determine where opportunities for enhancing competitive advantage may lie. Vertical linkage analysis extends the value chain beyond the organization to incorporate the suppliers and users who are at either end of the chain. *(Business, 2002)*

Vertical Training: Specialized, in-depth training on specific topics to prepare the employee for upward mobility and promotional opportunities.

Virgin Product: A product that is made with 100 percent new raw materials and contains no recycled materials. *(Miller, 2006)*

Virtual Store: An eCommerce term that refers to a website that permits a buyer to procure goods and services online. *(Miller, 2006)*

Vision Statement: An organizational statement that clearly and concisely addresses the future nature and purpose of the entity. A short statement that tells who the organization is and where they are going. *(Miller, 2006)*

VMI: *See Vendor Managed Inventory.*

VOC: *See Volatile Organic Compounds.*

V

Void: Of no standing; unenforceable and without legal effect. A contractual reference which implies that the agreement has been terminated or cancelled. *(Garner, 2004)*

Volatile Organic Compounds (VOCs): Compounds that evaporate easily at room temperature. They can come from many products, such as office equipment, adhesives, carpeting, upholstery, paints, solvents, and cleaning products. VOC's can harm the ozone level of the atmosphere and is a harmful outdoor air pollutant. *(Miller, 2006)*

Volatile-Priced Commodities: Commodities so dynamic that prices may dramatically change from day to day or hour by hour. Variables that factor into the pricing of these commodities include hedging strategies, call options and pricing tied to indexes. For example coffee, wheat and oil are examples of commodities subject to extreme volatility. *(Business, 2002)*

Volume Discounts: Discounts offered to a buyer from a supplier based on the quantity purchased, the size of the order, or total annual volume. It is based on the economic theory of economies of scale – the larger the quantity purchased, the lower the unit price. *Also see Economies of Scale, Quantity Discount and Volume Leveraging,*

Volume Leveraging: Activities that attempt to capture as much spend in a materials or service category as possible in order to potentially reduce costs through economies of scale and enable a purchaser to negotiate more competitively with suppliers. A form of "second-level" cost savings. *Also see Economies of Scale, Quantity Discount and Volume Discounts. (Crimi, Kauffman, Inside Supply Management Magazine, March, 2003)*

Voluntary Bankruptcy: A bankruptcy procedure initiated by an individual or business that can no longer meet its financial obligations. *Also see Bankruptcy. (Business, 2002)*

Voluntary Restraint Agreement (VRA): An agreement to reduce the volume of trade in a specific good; a voluntary quota. An example would be an OPIC agreement to curb the production and exportation of crude oil. A critical indices for global supply managers that may have a dramatic effect on cost/price. *(ISM, 2000)*

Voluntary Standards: Standards available for use by any person, organization, or governmental organization, generally established by voluntary participation of interested parties.

Voucher: A document that records a business transaction. A written record of an expenditure or a business transaction.

VRA: *See Voluntary Restraint Agreement.*

VSP: *See Vendor Supply Point Code.*

W

Wage/Salary Survey: A study that tells an organization how much compensation comparable organizations are paying for specific jobs that the organizations have in common. May be helpful for the negotiation of labor classifications on service contracts that are labor intensive. *(Business, 2002)*

Wages: Financial rewards based on the number of hours the employee works or the level of output achieved. *(Schiller, 2004)*

Waiver: The intentional or voluntary relinquishment of a known right, or conduct that warrants an inference that the right has been relinquished. Examples of waivers in supply management may include a waiver of certain contract requirements such as delivery dates, testing requirements, and performance standards.

Waiver of Bids: A process, usually statutory, whereby a government purchasing office may procure items without formal bidding procedures because of unique circumstances related to that particular action. For example, bids are waived for emergency purchases that are needed, due to a threat to the public safety.

Waiver of Mistake or Informality: The act of disregarding minor informalities, errors, or technical nonconformance in the bid which will not adversely affect the competition or prejudice one bidder in favor of another.

Warehouse: A structure used for the storage of material which provides protection against theft, damage, or deterioration.

Warehouse Credits: Used for requisitioned supplies found to be in excess of requirements and which must be returned to the warehouse.

Warehouse Receipt: An instrument showing that the signer has possession of certain described goods for storage, and obligating the signer to deliver the goods to a specified person, or to that person's order, or bearer, upon return of the instrument.

Warehouse Requisition: A document prepared by a government department or agency in order to remove items stocked in inventory from the warehouse.

Warehousing: The performance of those administrative and physical distribution functions incidental to and required in the conduct of the storage activity.

Warranty: A promise made by a seller to a buyer that is legally enforceable. The promise may be expressed or implied and is legally binding.

Warranty of Fitness for a Particular Purpose: *See Implied Warranty of Fitness for a Particular Purpose.*

Warranty of Merchantability: *See Implied Warranty of Merchantability.*

Wastage: CANADIAN The loss in handling, shrinkage, decay, evaporation, etc.

Waste: Salvageable materials which are damaged, defective, deteriorated or residue from operations with little or no market value. The selling expenses exceed the value and the materials are discarded. *Also see Hazardous Material (HAZMAT) and Scrap.*

Waste Disposal: The act of getting rid of unwanted items.

Watch List: A list of critical items that have been identified as high risk areas, which should rank order the identified risk by likelihood and priority. The items contained on the list should be those identified in risk assessment as having the greatest unacceptable impact on the program and/or contract, and the risk reduction tactics that have been identified and will be put into action in the event the risk materializes.

Waybill: A transportation record which shows the origin of the shipment, its destination and may contain other information such as: route, consignor, consignee, description of the shipment and the billing amount.

WBE: *See Women-Owned Business Enterprises.*

Webcast: Broadcast of an audio and/or video presentation over the Web in real time or on-demand. *(Jansen, 2002)*

Weight/Gross: The total combined weight of an article, it's shipping container, and packing material. *(ISM, 2000)*

Weight/Net: The weight of an empty shipping container or the cargo of a transport vehicle. *(ISM, 2000)*

Weight/Tare: The combined weight of an empty shipping container and packing materials. *(ISM, 2000)*

Weighted Average: An average of quantities that have been adjusted by the addition of a statistical value to allow for their relative importance in a data set. *(Business, 2002)*

Weighted-Point Method/Scoring: A methodology used to evaluate a bid/proposal based on subjective criteria each of which is assigned a point value. Evaluators may place different levels of importance on various factors that have been identified. Examples of criteria may include: capacity to perform, past experience, financial strength or references of previous work. Fixed weights and variable weights are the two most common forms of weighting systems.

Welfare Programs: Socio-economic programs which are means-tested income transfer programs, e.g. welfare and food stamps. *(Schiller, 2000)*

Wheel of Retailing: A hypothesis that suggests that new retail operations usually begin at the bottom - in price, profits, prestige - and gradually evolve up the cost/price scale, competing with newer businesses that are evolving the same way. It plays into negotiation strategy whereby a relatively young company may be willing to sell at cost or at minimum profit in order to obtain a prestigious account. *(Business, 2002)*

Whistleblower: An employee who discloses to an outside person or entity an activity by his or her employer that the employee characterizes as illegal, immoral or otherwise improper. *(Nash, Schooner, O'Brien, 1998)*

Whistleblowing: An individual or group of individuals who inform the press or government officials about unethical practices within their own organization. Whistle blowers have uncovered fraud, waste and abuse within businesses and governments. *(Business, 2002)*

Whole Instrument Rule: If the whole instrument [contract], taken together, contains no ambiguities or seeming inconsistencies, there is no room for interpretation; but instruments of that degree of perfection are so rare and the courts are so often called upon to settle questions as to the real intent of the parties expressed in written evidences of contracts... that a large mass of rules of construction have ....been developed ... as forming an integral part of the Law of Contracts.... Rules relating to the construction of a contract as a Whole (1) the intention is to be determined by a reference to the whole instrument, rather than to any particular phrase, clause or sentence. (2) ..... the real intent must be gathered from the whole description, including the general as well as the particular.

Wholesaler: A middleman that sells products to other firms. *Also see Retailer.*

Win-Win Resolution: A win-win situation is one that is reasonably balanced, with each party feeling they obtained something beneficial from the deal.

Women-Owned Business Enterprise (WBE): A business of which a given percentage is owned or controlled by a woman. May also be entitled to minority classification by certain public entities. *Also see Minority-Owned Business, Historically Underutilized Business (HUB), Economically Disadvantaged Individuals, Small Disadvantaged Business and MBE.*

Workaround: A bypass of a recognized problem in a system. A temporary fix that implies that a genuine solution to the problem is needed. Frequently they are as creative as true solutions, involving out-of-the-box thinking in their creation. A workaround is not a permanent solution and may eventually result in system failure. *(Business, 2002)*

Work-In-Process: In the manufacturing, production or construction process, the term given to semi-finished goods, products or equipment. Something that is not completely assembled or manufactured. *(ISM, 2000)*

Work Order: CANADIAN A purchaser's document setting out all terms and conditions of a repair/alteration transaction with a supplier (either sourced from commercial or in-house suppliers).

World Class Manufacturing: The capability of a manufacturer to compete with any other manufacturing organization in a chosen market, with the aspiration of achieving world class excellence in all organizational aspects. It encompasses the practices of total quality management, continuous improvement, international benchmarking, and flexible work schedules. *(Business, 2002)*

World Trade Organization (WTO): An organization established by the General Agreement on Tariffs and Trade (GATT) in 1995 to enforce the provisions of the Uruguay Round and to resolve any disputes arising there from. The WTO consists of 147 member countries and is headquartered in Geneva Switzerland. Its mission is to deal with the rules of trade between nations. *(www.wto.org, 2007)*

World Trade Organization-Agreement on Government Procurement (WTO-AGP): Replaced the General Agreement on Tariffs and Trade (GATT) on January 1, 1996. It is a multilateral agreement to reduce trade barriers between the United States and Canada, the European Union, Japan, Korea, Israel, Norway and Switzerland. *(Business, 2002)*

Write-down: CANADIAN The reduction of the recorded value of materiel as a result of conversion or change of conditions while in inventory.

Write-off: CANADIAN The deletion from records of materiel due to shortage or loss by any cause.

WTO: *See World Trade Organization.*

Yield: The annual income from a security, expressed as a percentage of the current market price of the security. The yield on a share is its dividend divided by its price. *(Bishop, 2004)*

Zero Based Budgeting: A budget process in which budgets are prepared with no predetermined allocation or prior year budget history. Each new budget must be created based on justifiable projected program needs.

Zero Defects Standard: A quality management theory which defines quality from the customer's perspective as conformance to requirements and then improving processes through prevention activities to meet requirements. This quality process was championed by quality guru, Philip Crosby. *(Burt, Dobler, Starling, 2003)*

References

American Heritage Dictionary (4th ed.). (2001). New York: Houghton Mifflin.

American Purchasing Society. Glossary of Purchasing. Available from www.americanpurchasing.com/glossarybusinessterms.htm

Bishop, M. (2004). Essential Economics. London: Profile Books LTD.

Black's Law Dictionary (7th ed). (2004). Eagan, MN: West Publishing Company.

Buffington, J., & Flynn, M. (2010). Legal Aspects of Public Procurement (2nd ed.). Herndon, VA: (NIGP).

Burt, D. N., Dobler, D. W., & Starling, S. L. (2003). World Class Supply Management (7th ed). New York: McGraw-Hill Companies, Inc.

Business—The Ultimate Resource. (2002). New York: Perseus Books Group.

Carmarthenshire county council Wales. (n.d.). Discussion paper on procurement risk and the integration of procurement risk into the procurement cycle. Retrieved from www.tenderwise.com/docs/MitigatingProcurementRisk091205.doc

Crimi, T., & Kaufman, R. (2003, March). Inside Supply Management. New York: Institute for Supply Management.

Davison, W. D., & Wright, E. (2009). Contract Administration (2nd ed.). Herndon, VA: (NIGP).

Ferrell O. C., Hirt, G. (2002). Business—A Changing World (4th ed). New York: McGraw-Hill Companies, Inc.

Garner, Bryan A. (2004). Black's Law Dictionary (8th ed). St. Paul, MN: Thomson West.

Governing Magazine (2003). A Tax Wonk's Dictionary – A Guide to the Buzzwords and Catch Phrases You Won't Be Able to Escape. Florida: Congressional Quarterly, Inc.

Harney, D. (1992). Service Contracting: A Local Government Guide. Washington, DC: International City/County Management Association.

Heinritz, S., Farrell, P., Giunipero, L., & Kolchin, M. (1991). Purchasing Principles and Applications (8th ed.). Englewood Cliffs, NJ: Prentice Hall.

ICG Commerce. (2003). Procurement Terms. Available from http:eu.icgcommerce.com/corporate/doc/html/resource/procurement_terms

Institute for Supply Management (ISM). (2000). ISM's Glossary of Key Purchasing and Supply Terms (3rd ed.). New York: Author.

Jansen, E. (2002). NetLingo—The Internet Dictionary. Available from www.netlingo.com.

Janson, R. L. (1987). Handbook of Inventory Management. Englewood Cliffs, NJ: Prentice-Hall.

W.K. Kellogg Foundation. (Revised Jan. 2004). Using logic models to bring together planning, evaluation, and action – Logic Model Development guide. Battle Creek, MI. Retrieved from www.wkkf.org April, 2010.

Lawther, W. C., & Adler, J. O. (2006). Capital Acquisitions: An Advanced Text. Herndon, VA: (NIGP).

Martin, L. L., & Miller, J. R. (2005). Alternative Dispute Resolution. Herndon, VA: (NIGP).

Martin, L. L., & Miller, J. R. (2006). Contracting for Public Sector Services. Herndon, VA: (NIGP).

McCue, C., & Hinson, C. (2004). Planning, Scheduling and Requirement Analysis. Herndon, VA: (NIGP).

McCue, C. & Johnson, B. (2010). Strategic Procurement Planning in the Public Sector. Herndon, VA: (NIGP).

McCue, C., & Pitzer, J. T. (2005). Fundamentals of Leadership and Management in Public Procurement. Herndon, VA: (NIGP).

Millstein, M. (2002, August). Inside Supply Management. New York: Institute for Supply Management.

Nash, R. C., Jr., Schooner, S. L., O'Brien, K. R. (1998). The Government Contracts Reference Book (2nd ed.). Washington, DC: The George Washington University Press.

National Association of State Purchasing Officials (NASPO). (1994). State and Local Government Purchasing (4th ed.). Lexington, KY: NASPO.

National Association of State Procurement Officials (NASPO). (2001). State and Local Government Purchasing Principles and Practices. Lexington, KY: NASPO.

National Institute of Governmental Purchasing, Inc. (NIGP). (1996). Dictionary of Purchasing Terms (5th ed.). Herndon, VA: NIGP.

Pettijohn, C., & Babich, K. S. (2008). Sourcing in the Public Sector (2nd ed.). Herndon, VA: (NIGP).

Pitzer, J. T. and Thai, J. V. (2009). Introduction to public procurement (3rd. ed.). Herndon, VA: (NIGP).

Rehfuss, J. A. (1989). Contracting out in government: A Guide to Working With Outside Contractors to Supply Public Services. San Francisco: Jossey Bass.

Schiller, B. (2000). The Economy Today (8th Ed.). New York: McGraw-Hill.

Spikes Cavell. (2011). Observatory User Guide – Measure 4. How do I pick a "How Achieved" and "sub-category"?

Stanley, L., & Matthews, D. (2007). Logistics and Transportation. Herndon, VA: (NIGP).

Summit Magazine (Ottawa, ON). Online Glossary of Canadian Public Purchasing Terms. Available from www.summitconnects.com

Thai, K. V. (2007). Developing and Managing RFPs in the Public Sector (2nd ed.). Herndon, VA: (NIGP).

Thai, K. V. (2004). Introduction to Public Procurement. Herndon, VA: (NIGP).

Wikipedia (The Free Dictionary). Available from http://encyclopedia.thefreedictionary.com

Other Books Published by NIGP

Contract Administration

This text places a focus on the achievement of stated goals and objectives through contract performance. The field embraces a longstanding recognition of three broad goals: a quality product, delivered on time and within budget. Quality contract administration must take a two-pronged approach: process and product focus. With emphasis on process and dependent on the specifics of any contractual relationship, this book is a valuable tool for public procurement professionals to develop a strong understanding of the complexities of contract administration and recognize the importance of planning, monitoring, and proactive oversight of contract performance.

Developing and Managing Requests for Proposals in the Public Sector

The text takes an extensive look at the basic knowledge and skills needed by those who select competitive sealed procurements and negotiations as a viable method of procurement. Through the RFP process, public agencies acquire innovative solutions recommended by the supplier community. As governments recognize that the best propositions for problem resolution come from field experts, this method is becoming more important to public procurement professionals who are committed to making a difference in an agency.

Introduction to Public Procurement

This "Introduction to Public Procurement" text is designed to provide both an overview and an overture into the field of public procurement. Public procurement professionals support operations with an uninterrupted flow of goods and services, purchase competitively by keeping ahead of the marketplace and all the while balance the dynamic tradeoffs among efficiency, equity and fairness, in addition to and competing with socio-economic objectives.

Sourcing in the Public Sector

Purchasing, or sourcing, by government organizations is a different and complex process, filled with rules, regulations, procedures, court decision, conflict of interest prohibitions, and a wealth of issues that can complicate and confound the lives of government officials charges with procurement responsibilities. Once considered and administrative support function, the role of the public procurement officer has evolved into an important strategic position as public organizations plan and conduct business. The role of public procurement has been expanded upon as public organizations are faced with the demands of outsourcing our privatizing services.

The Legal Aspects of Public Purchasing

The Legal Aspects of Public Purchasing provides a glimpse of the legal framework that governs public contracting. The procurement professional must know and understand the law of contracts within the context of public purchasing. Every purchasing agent should have a sense of the principles surrounding contract law and the legal consequences of an action. Complete with a glossary of common legal terms that are relevant to the public procurement profession, this book focuses on the most critical and most used portions of the law of contracts.

Strategic Procurement Planning in the Public Sector

Strategic Procurement Planning in the Public Sector provides a comprehensive and definitive resource for understanding how the procurement function's inherent value is maximized when it has a primary contributory role in organizational strategic planning and in the budgeting processes. Clifford McCue, Ph.D. and Barbara Johnson, MPC, CPPO, CPPB reveal effective strategic planning processes and how the strategic plan is reflected in agency budgets to support strategic procurement planning. The authors reflect their deep understanding of operational realities to emphasize the importance of defining client needs, educating and working with suppliers, assessing customer satisfaction, and properly staffing, developing and managing human resources to ensure long term organizational success.

Alternative Dispute Resolution

This book is a practical reference for public contracting professionals seeking better understanding of the alternative dispute resolution vehicles available to them and the environments in which these protocols are most viable. Recognizing that litigation or contract termination may not be in the best interest of either contracting party, Lawrence Martin, Ph.D. and John Miller, CPPO, address the growing need for contracting officials to approach rifts in contractual relationships from a perspective emphasizing mutuality over self- interest and reconciliation over termination.

Capital Acquisitions

In this book, Wendell C. Lawther, Ph.D. and John O. Adler, CPPO, provide a strategic enterprise view of the capital procurement process, the organizational environment in which it occurs, and detail the critical evaluation tools and contracting methodologies public procurement professionals must employ to derive best value for the government services and communities they support.

Contracting for Construction Services

In this text, Wendell C. Lawther, Ph.D., and John O. Adler, CPPO, effectively unveil the many processes and techniques that contribute to successful public works projects. Understanding how construction projects are initially defined and budgeted, the responsibilities of the Project Manager, major methods of construction, and how to select contractors is critical to every capital development program. By defining terms that may be unique to infrastructure development and clarifying the many elements of the pre-, mid- and post-construction phases, Contracting for Construction Services is a comprehensive reference useful to both beginning and experienced construction contract managers.

Contracting for Public Sector Services

This text is a comprehensive examination of this government procurement practice that has truly come of age in the past twenty years. Lawrence Martin, Ph.D. and John Miller, CPPO, provide a historical context for this widely accepted service model, and define the decision-making process and best practices to be followed from development of the initial RFP through completion of the service contract.

Fundamentals of Leadership and Management in Public Procurement

This book offers insights as to how to negotiate the professional hurdles facing public procurement officers through ongoing personal development and consistent modeling of exemplary leadership and management practices. In this collaboration, Clifford McCue, Ph.D. and Jack Pitzer, Ph.D., CPPO, CBM share both theoretical and practical models for understanding organizational behaviors and relationships; differentiate between leadership and management functions; and apply this newly gained knowledge in the context of the public procurement workplace and the profession overall.

Logistics and Transportation

Linda Stanley, Ph.D. and Darin Matthews, CPPO, C.P.M., reveal the benefits of contracting product transport services independent of the product itself. Beginning with an overview of delivery transportation modalities and transport law, the text reveals how public procurement professionals can negotiate greater savings for their communities by understanding the nature of logistics contracting, processes, and the competitive market environment of transportation carriers.

Risk Management in Public Contracting

In this text, Elisabeth Wright, Ph.D., CPCM, offers a concise yet thorough overview of risk and risk management in public sector contracting. Emphasizing the fluid environment of contracting and contract management, Ms. Wright underscores how planning, monitoring, anticipating change, and proactive oversight immediately impact the success of a contract's stated outcomes. Risk Management in Public Contracting not only defines risk in the procurement cycle, provides a theoretical background for understanding the nature of risk, but also identifies a framework and methodology for managing risk successfully to ensure the success of both the public agency and the government supplier.

Warehousing and Inventory Control

This text examines the reality of public warehousing systems in an environment often beset by conflicting operating philosophies and departmental needs. By examining the nature of supply operations from multiple perspectives, Jerry Gianakis, Ph.D., and Darin Matthews, CPPO, C.P.M., provide procurement professionals the insight needed to better understand their operating environment and improve their management of inventory processes.